A CHIP SHOP
IN POZNAŃ

A CHIP SHOP IN POZNAŃ

MY UNLIKELY YEAR IN POLAND

BEN AITKEN

ICON

Published in the UK in 2019
by Icon Books Ltd, Omnibus Business Centre,
39–41 North Road, London N7 9DP
email: info@iconbooks.com
www.iconbooks.com

Sold in the UK, Europe and Asia
by Faber & Faber Ltd, Bloomsbury House,
74–77 Great Russell Street,
London WC1B 3DA or their agents

Distributed in the UK, Europe and Asia
by Grantham Book Services,
Trent Road, Grantham NG31 7XQ

Distributed in the USA
by Publishers Group West,
1700 Fourth Street, Berkeley, CA 94710

Distributed in Australia and New Zealand
by Allen & Unwin Pty Ltd,
PO Box 8500, 83 Alexander Street,
Crows Nest, NSW 2065

Distributed in South Africa
by Jonathan Ball, Office B4, The District,
41 Sir Lowry Road, Woodstock 7925

Distributed in India
by Penguin Books India,
7th Floor, Infinity Tower – C, DLF Cyber City,
Gurgaon 122002, Haryana

ISBN: 978-178578-558-0

Typeset in Baskerville MT by Marie Doherty

Printed and bound in Great Britain
by Clays Ltd, Elcograf S.p.A.

For my parents, who got me going.

Contents

1

We are here to go somewhere else

8 March 2016. I decided to move to Poland in the sauna. It seemed sensible. I had seen Poles in Peterborough and Portsmouth and the Cotswolds and I had followed the conversation about whether there were too many in the UK or too few, whether they were doing all the work or none at all. I wanted to know why the Poles – a notoriously patriotic people – were leaving home in their millions. I am also contrary by nature and design, so the idea of going the other way, of being a British immigrant in Poland, was appealing. Also appealing was the idea of being elsewhere. I had grown tired of Great Britain. Its comforts were a pain. Its nice routines were doing nothing for me. I wanted to be alone and abroad and innocent and curious, to have my character reset, my faults unknown, to find stories in buildings, stories in people, to be childish once more, to be again at the beginning. Moving to Poland is not the only way to deal with a case of itchy feet. I might have moved to the Falkland Islands. But if Britain chooses to leave the European Union in three months' time (a referendum is in the diary) my freedom to move and work and love and learn in twenty-odd countries will be irrevocably lost. Make hay while the sun shines.

Four days after the sauna I flew to Poznań. I chose Poznań because I had never heard of the place and it was the cheapest flight. I didn't want to move to Warsaw or Krakow, where there would be plenty of English speakers. I'd had enough of those. A friend had been on a stag do in Krakow. He was able to consume things that were pronounceable, to take trams and taxis in the right direction, to convince a pair of police officers he had no idea throwing kebab meat at the statue of a Nobel Prize winner wasn't *de rigueur*. (Despite all their practice, the British don't travel well.) He did all these things in English, of course. Polish wasn't necessary to get by. I didn't want that cushion. If I was caught throwing fast food at a national treasure, I would like to defend myself in the local tongue. It would show respect. In short, I wanted to feel that I was fully elsewhere. I wanted to be an alien. 'We are here to go somewhere else,' said the writer Geoff Dyer.

Eastern Energy, Western Style it says in baggage reclaim. What does that even mean? Is Poland on the fence? Is it caught in two minds? Poland was a communist country for 50 years until the early 90s, under the thumb of Russia. It was forced to look east. But now what? I don't have anything to reclaim – or claim for that matter – so spend time in front of touchscreen info-points that issue warnings and invitations. The city is its brands, says the screen, before showing a list of popular retailers. West, indeed.

On the 59 bus I see international brands like old foes, with their inevitable flags and packaging, then a World Trade Centre, squat and beige and laughably low-key, a mile shorter than the one that famously fell. Then endless residential blocks in lime and butter, mint and pink, colour an apology for form, stubbornly stretching along Bukowska Street. The bus's upholstery and layout and adverts beg questions. Simple things, suddenly odd. There is nothing remarkable about the bus or the journey, and yet I am transfixed. A slideshow of paintings by Delacroix and Hockney, of peasants and swimming pools, couldn't hold my attention more tightly. And so it starts, I think, the endless enquiries of the uprooted, the keen eyes of the replaced. I am delighted to feel the questions come on, after months of stale thinking at home, that well-loved place that I often long for, but more often long to betray. Oikophobia is a chronic inclination to leave home. I'm a first-class oik. Home is Clive Road, Portsmouth, England, Britain. Portsmouth was built to build ships that no longer need building. Charles Dickens was born there but moved to London when he was five, already tired of the place. The football club and the sea give people something to look at. That's all you need to know about home.

If ignorance is bliss then I'm in for a good time. I know absolutely nobody in Poland and know nothing of the language. Is it the Roman alphabet? Is there even an alphabet? Perhaps the alphabet was destroyed in the war, along with the rest of the country. In any case, moving to Poland will be rejuvenating. If I work hard over the next year, I'll be able to speak Polish as well as a three year old. The idea appeals to me. Three year olds are some of the happiest people I know. My niece is three. She's ecstatic. She gets a thrill out of the simplest of things, like waking up or tying her laces. Maybe being effectively three won't be such a bad thing. Maybe it will teach me a few things. There is much said or written about travel improving or stretching a person.

'Didn't she grow!' they say. Less is said of travel reducing a person, infantilising them, making a child of them, and how it does them a service thereby.

Even an innocent needs to break the ice. I had bought a phrase book at the airport in London, had committed a few phrases to heart over Germany. By the time I landed I knew how to say 'I love you', that I am 'happy' or 'sad', that something is 'beautiful' or 'ugly'. I would live a binary existence, a yes-or-no lifestyle (not unfashionable these days), surely preferable to a life on the fence, to considering all things alright. It would be liberating to leave such a linguistic centre-ground, such a diplomatic no man's land. I look forward to tapping a stranger on the shoulder and pointing to a child riding a bike for the first time and saying, 'That is not ugly, I love you.'

The bus terminates outside Planet Alcohol and Mr Kebab. Scanning around for bearings, it is apparent that Polish words are longer than average. Most look like Wi-Fi passwords, anagrams to be unscrambled, encryptions to be cracked. No wonder that a lot of the groundwork for the Enigma codebreaking machine was done by Poles. Untangling is in the genes. One of the reasons that Poland's economy is notoriously sluggish, I would like to think, is because everyone is staring at memos and instructions and agendas and emails wondering what on God's earth is meant by them.[1] There is

---

[1] Poland's economy is not notoriously sluggish. If anything it is the opposite. It was the only European country to avoid recession after the

no two ways about it, it will be a hard language to learn. Not only must I learn new letters – e and a and o and s and c have alternatives that are accessorised with tails and fringes – but I must also contend with familiar letters arranged in new ways, with the result that when one finds oneself in front of a door, and is invited to *pchać*, one doesn't know whether to push or pull. Moreover, faced with such an impassable door, such a language barrier, one is unable to ask a passer-by to clarify the situation, for their instruction – 'Push it and see, you immigrant!' – is bound to be equally senseless. An alien in Poland, therefore, can reliably be found stranded before some portal or another, wishing (in English) that it were automated.

I check in at a hotel on Freedom Square then go to a nearby information point. The women at the information point can't answer my questions about registration, health insurance, benefits. They don't seem able to deal with some-one long-term. 'But when are you going home?' they ask. 'When does your holiday *end*?' What they can tell me is where a bank is. I go there for a short interview, during which I'm offered coffee and a translator. If this is the face of Polish bureaucracy, it's a face I could get used to. It wasn't always thus. Michael Moran was not offered coffee. By his account – *A Country in the Moon*, which remembers the author's time

---

2008 financial crisis. A rule of thumb: if you like things reliable, only read the footnotes. The main text is a naive, real-time account, drawn from diaries I kept during my year in Poland. Of course the diaries have been edited, but I was careful to keep their tone and atmosphere, their misconceptions, their errors of judgement.

helping Poland convert to capitalism in the early 90s – it took Michael seven months to post a letter. 'A country in the moon' refers to a remark made by Edmund Burke at the end of the 18th century, when Poland was taken off the map by Austria and Russia and Prussia, and then put on the moon, where it remained until 1919. It was an extraordinary historical circumstance, an exceptional vanishing act, a momentous dislocation. I bet the Polish people remember the moon days keenly.

9 March. I eat dumplings in a park near the hotel. They are either ugly or beautiful, I can't decide. The park is named after Chopin. There is a bust of the composer on a flint pedestal. An ear is missing. A team of high-brow pigeons have had it for lunch. I think of that poem by Shelley or Byron about Ozymandias, about legacy and mortality, and wonder if Chopin wrote music in order to be remembered, to be set in stone and planted in a park where students come to snack and slumber. I can be glib about motives. I can say I came to Poland because the flight was cheap and I fancied a change. My fundamental motives are less glib. To write a book, to write anything, is an attempt to be less dead. I move and write because those things are essential to me. I could go without many things in life – toast, sex, Canada – but I don't think I could go without travel and words.

Being of working-class stock, I am drawn to a bar called Proletariat. I shan't tell you the street name because if I did you'd accuse me of using difficult words for the sake of it. The barman must have seen me outside looking at

WE ARE HERE TO GO SOMEWHERE ELSE

the door and wondering what to do with it, for he issues an English menu before I've chance to say anything. The bar is decorated with busts of Lenin and Chairman Mao, portraits of Marx and Engels and Russell Brand, whose recent book *Revolution* has inspired a million people to stop reading books. I would like to think that the talk at neighbouring tables is of revolting peasants and meaningful social change, but I suspect it isn't. It is a young crowd, affluent looking. They don't seem the revolting type. What they do seem is eager to be branded – New Balance trainers are part of the youthful uniform. They cost the same as they would in the UK, 350 zloty a pair, about £70. To earn that sum here one must work a low-wage job for a week, the minimum wage being roughly 8 zloty. I am starting to understand what was meant by *Western Style, Eastern Energy*. Poles must work thrice the hours to wear the same trainers. The iron curtain was drawn back and onto the stage came a company of trademarks, each ready to impress, to make their mark.

I find the old market square, faithfully repaired after being squashed in the war. I don't try to put my finger on the buildings – to label the gables, spot the styles. The buildings may bear signs of stucco or rococo or art nouveau but what of it? The beauty of this old square is too obvious to invite further analysis. The detail is beside the point. *How is it beautiful?* is not a question we often ask or answer. At any rate, I am invited by a girl with a red umbrella to watch 22 beautiful girls at Euphoria. But it is only the afternoon, I point out. That is not a problem, she says. The girls don't mind. Desire doesn't rest. I can drink a coffee or tea if I wish.

Twenty-two, she repeats, as if one either side would make all the difference.

I resist Euphoria, enter a pub called The Londoner, already attracted to the idea of return. I sit with an imported ale, beneath images of Big Ben and Tower Bridge, mounted encouragements to try Kilkenny, to give London Pride a go. I've never been anywhere like it. I ask a young man if he speaks English. Of course, he says. I ask an old man if he speaks English. He just points out the window. Outside the bar, beneath the ornate clock tower of the town hall, I talk with Alfie from Norway and Emre from Turkey. They insist I get out of the hotel and move into their hostel, where I can mix with internationals and speak in English. I don't want that, I explain. I want to get the wrong end of the stick. I want the quiet and disquiet. I want to speak in black and white. I want to see things starkly. I want not to know.

I want to see Citadel Park, where a battle was fought at the end of a war. Once seized, Hitler designated the citadel a *festung*: a crucial fortification to be defended at all costs. Thousands perished fighting over it. I seek the park at dusk, find it at length and enter by a hundred steps, at the summit of which stands an overwhelming memorial, a testament to disaster, to a Europe at odds. I want to locate the headless people – a mindless sculpture that remembers those taken by war – but find only tanks, perhaps the very ones that blew off the heads. I clamber onto one of the tanks and enjoy sitting astride a lethal snout and watching my breath. I cross the park alone. Occasional couples on benches pause their conversations until I'm once more out of their lives. I fear the subject of their talk is of a serious nature. Why else would they come out here in dark winter to talk?

At the end of the day, I have not done enough. I do not know how to describe the architecture, the habits of the people, the colour of the eyes, the history of the city, the political situation. I have formed an impression but little more. Too much of Poland has gone over my head, when I might have reached up, intercepted it, pulled it down to my level. I'm supposed to be inquisitive. I have read some of Moran's book and some Norman Davies and their grave erudition makes a fool of me.[2] These chaps were serious gringos, serious fish out of water. Neither of that pair would miss the hotel breakfast. They would have it at 7.00 and then go to an early service at the Franciscan Church to get a look at the devoted, before strolling around town as the shops started to open. I have not seen either of the castles. I have not entered a museum or gallery. I have not taken a photograph. I have not seen the goats that are supposed to emerge each day at noon from the clock tower. I have asked few questions of people and the questions I have asked have tended to be vague and boring. *Do you live here? What's that? What time are the goats?* Instead of seeing things and forming opinions and asking questions, I have drunk and smoked liberally. Such are my thoughts on this, my second Polish night, just before bed.

---

[2] Norman Davies is a pre-eminent historian of Poland.

10 March. I'm woken by the sound of a crowd protesting in the square onto which my hotel room looks. I open the window, ready to remonstrate, to tell them to put a sock in it. An angry Pole is blasting something through a megaphone about the cost of lemons or the recent visit of David Cameron.[3] I have missed the hotel breakfast. My nose is out of joint. I have a hangover. It is midday. Oh, wouldn't they just be quiet! But then I remember that I have an interest in the welfare of all people, no matter their nationality or class or colour, and no matter the time of day or the extent of my headache. And so I put myself in the shower, experiment vainly with the vanity pack, then dress in the clothes of an ordinary person to go and inquire about the disquiet of ordinary people, and perhaps lend a hand.

The thousand-strong throng is arranged on Freedom Square, outside the neo-classical library. I approach a young couple to ask what all the fuss is about. Tessa tells me in perfect English that the protest has to do with the newish, right-wing, ultra-Catholic government, which has been ignoring the country's constitution on a daily basis in an effort to destroy liberty and antagonise the EU and thwart a Russian invasion and bring back slavery and deport all

---

[3] Cameron, then prime minister, visited Warsaw to ask the Polish prime minister if she minded if he made life a bit harder for the Poles living in the UK by cutting their benefits. This was part of a wider effort on his part to 'get a new deal' for the UK in Europe ahead of the forthcoming referendum. The idea was that a 'new deal' with the EU would make it harder for the public to vote to leave. In the event, the 'new deal' wasn't up to snuff. 'Cameron promised a loaf, begged for a crust, and came home with crumbs,' wrote one columnist.

WE ARE HERE TO GO SOMEWHERE ELSE

non-Catholics and make it illegal not to have one's forehead or forearm (whichever is more spacious) branded with the Polish eagle. Phew. I look forward to hearing the other side of the story, I say. There isn't one, says Tessa.

I am introduced to Tessa's father, who sounds like the headmaster of an English boarding school, and then her mother, who doesn't. They are all going for pizza to discuss the general folly of the government. I am told to come along. I do as I'm told and I'm glad for the fact because before Tessa's parents are halfway through their pizza, and despite the fact that I have barely said a word and am quite obviously hungover, I have been offered a teaching position at the school they run. It turns out they need someone to stand in a room of Polish eight year olds four times a week and say things in English. Can I manage that? Can I start on Monday?

'But I've got no experience.'

'Irrelevant.'

'And I'm not very good with kids.'

'Irrelevant.'

'And I'm not very well behaved.'

'Irrelevant.'

'I don't live anywhere.'

'Irrelevant.'

'I've not told anyone I'm here.'

'Irrelevant.'

'Would you employ an English-speaking goat?'

'Almost certainly.'

I take the job.

2

What's the point having a home if it means nothing to you?

12 March. I walk to the address. It is below freezing. I don't know the streets. Their names are reminders of my status – out of place, unknowing. *Sienkiewicza. Słowackiego. Bukowska.* I don't know if the names refer to fish or trees or dead parliamentarians. I notice the registration plates. If the car was born before 2004, when Poland joined the European Union, the plate bears a little Polish flag. If it was born after, the flag is European. An incidental detail perhaps, but one that argues a redirection of the patriotic spirit. Polishness, at least superficially, and in this small way, has been made subordinate to Europeanness.

I don't know how to pronounce the name of the young European I am on my way to see. *Jędrzej.* That's how it's written. What a queer set of letters. Surely the word is an expletive or imprecation, the noise Poles make when something goes wrong. A Pole drops a platter of dumplings – '*Jędrzej!*' A Pole hears disappointing news on the radio – '*Jędrzej!*'

Jędrzej is a friend of my new employers. Like me, he is looking for a home. Having heard of my arrival he has invited me to look at a four-bedroom flat that has two rooms available. I don't much like the idea of living with a civil engineer but am sufficiently open-minded to at least take a look. The flat is in a rough neighbourhood put up by the Germans in the late 1800s, when Poland was having time off from being a country. The district is Jeżyce. The street is Szamarzewskiego. Hardly rolls off the tongue. What's the point having an address if you can't articulate it? What's the point having a home if it means nothing to you? I arrive at the building – 36 – give it a good look through the fog. It is elegant but tired. I know the feeling.

'Hey there!' says an American tourist tethering a bicycle.

'Hey.'

'I'm Yen-Jay. I'm a civil engineer.'

'That's nice. In fact, I'm supposed to be meeting a Polish civil engineer right now.'

'Yup. That'll be me.'

'It can't be. I'm meeting a Polish civil engineer who isn't American and has a very, very different name to you.'

'Let's just go take a look, shall we?'

I take the room. It's the smallest of the four. There are no curtains but plenty of motivational framed posters from IKEA. My favourite, probably owned by half of Europe, encourages the viewer to embrace their individuality.

Jędrzej is happy with his room, too. He has reason to be. It is three times the size of mine but the same price. When I point this out to him he looks delighted, not at all abashed that he's on the right side of a massive injustice. I notice that Jędrzej smiles a lot. After signing a twelve-month contract, he goes to the kitchen window and smiles out of it for ten minutes. 'Don't ya just love the rain, Benny?' It is hard to say if we are going to get along.

I sign a two-month contract with the option of an extension. I don't want to commit to longer, not with Jenny about, or whatever his name is. The contract's terms and conditions mean nothing to me. For all I know I can keep seven pets in my room, apart from at the weekend when I can have as many as I want. It hardly seems worth asking for a translation. Jenny is evidently quite good at English but it is mostly a sort of cartoon-English taken from the Disney Channel and I don't think he'd cope with the legal terms.[4] I pay the first month's rent and another month's worth for the deposit. I'm handed a set of keys. That's all there is to it. The potentially troublesome bureaucratic procedure of finding a place to live has been dealt with. Compared to Paris and London, where it's easier to get malaria than a roof over your head, securing accommodation in Poland has proved pleasingly simple.

In the evening I go to the local convenience store. I inspect the place as if it were a precious archive of exotic oddities. I am amused to find a pack of ground coffee beans called 'Family'. The coffee's packaging shows two adults and two children – the eponymous Family – sat around a table upon which stands a steaming percolator and four expectant cups. That's fair enough, I think, depicting people looking happy in response to the commodity in question, but the children look no older than eight or nine. At what age do they start drinking coffee in Poland? The Poles in the UK have a

---

[4] Henceforth, and without his consent, Jędrzej became Jenny.

reputation for being hard workers. Perhaps I have stumbled upon the explanation. Perhaps it's because they start drinking coffee before they've hit puberty. Either way, I put a pack in my basket and continue shopping: the number of gherkins is astonishing; there's no beef or chicken to speak of but about a kilometre of sausage all things considered; and milk comes in two qualities, 2.4 per cent and 3.2 per cent, which may, this being East Central Europe, refer to alcohol content.[5]

18 March. Tony and Marietta (my employers) met at a disco in Billericay, back in the 80s. Marietta had gone to England to find herself. Instead she found Tony. This must have been quite a shock. At any rate, and with no clear idea what she would do with him, when Marietta's holiday in the Free World ended she returned to Poland with Tony on her arm. She hasn't been back to England since, in case the same thing happens again.

The couple opened The Cream Tea School of English – which is also their house – in the mid-90s. It is a small, independent school that provides extra-curricular tuition to young Poles whose parents want their children to leave the

---

[5] I regret this flippant comment about Poles being heavy consumers of alcohol. By suggesting that the Poles drink a lot I was lazily recycling one of those clichéd, often fallacious ideas about this or that group. The Irish eat potatoes. The English drink tea. That sort of thing. It is exactly this sort of clichéd thinking about the Polish – about Others – that I hoped to counter or complicate by moving to Poland. One reason for moving to a new place is to challenge one's attitudes and intuitions, to destabilise one's common sense. As evidenced above, old habits die hard.

country as soon as possible. The school is in the Starołęka district of the city, south of the centre on the east side of the River Warta. From my flat it takes two trams and a bus to get here, which is a bit of a pain. Also a pain is the idea of teaching. As Tony and Marietta introduce me at length to each of the trees and plants in their garden, and then their dog Pirate, I can't help thinking that the time might be better spent telling me what (and how) they expect me to teach. In lieu of such instruction I am given tea and biscuits and told exactly how my tax contributions will be spent by the government. Some will go on infrastructure, a small bit will help Poland remain a member of NATO, while the lion's share will help fund the 500-zloty monthly baby payments that are issued to parents to encourage breeding.[6] 'Now for the good news,' says Tony, 'your pension!' Apparently, explains Tony, if I put in some decent hours over the next year I can expect to draw a pension of 10 zloty a week when I reach the age of 75 – enough to get a hotdog. There is little in the way of paperwork. All Tony requires of me is my

---

[6] The 500-zloty 'baby payment' is a divisive policy. It is essentially a child benefit. The government's detractors insist that in the run up to the 2015 election the policy was dangled in front of the electorate like a reckless carrot. It is not inherently regrettable for a government to support families with more than one child, and yet if you were to ask any Pole who is against the governing Law and Justice Party for an example of its misbehaviour, they will most likely cite the 500-zloty baby payments. Why? Because they feel the benefit makes people reliant on the State when they should be reliant on themselves. And they don't like the idea of people being paid to have sex.

British National Insurance number. It is frustratingly easy to enter the Polish tax system.

My first lesson is with D1. D, I quickly discover, stands for diabolical. The students, aged between eight and ten, are not in a cooperative mood. I have lost my patience before I've finished listing their names on the board.

'You. What is your name?'

'You just wrote it.'

'Which one?'

'Top one.'

'How do you say that again?'

'I've forgotten.'

'At any rate, you are playing up.'

'What does it mean?'

'To play up is a phrasal verb. It means—'

'What is a phrasal verb?'

'You will learn about phrasal verbs when you start behaving yourself.'

'So how are we supposed to understand you in the meanwhile?'

'If you are able to heckle like that, I'm sure you'll understand well enough.'

'What is heckle?'

And so it begins. Sensing an alien out of his depth, a wanderer beyond the pale, the students are openly and joyfully defiant from the word go. It stands to reason. I can't speak a word of Polish and they could speak Polish fluently when they were five. Ergo, I must be stupid. The people they have learned to respect and obey and defer to – parents, teachers, adults generally – know Polish to an advanced level, and are able and ready to manipulate their use of the Polish language, their tone and diction and syntax, in order to win arguments and appear awesome and earn authority. But the adult before them, supposedly a teacher, can barely say hello. He is either stupid or lazy, neither quality deserving of respect. This is the conclusion they all silently draw. When I step outside to hyperventilate, the ringleader, Lucas, briefs the others. 'He is either stupid or lazy. In either case, he neither deserves nor shall receive our respect. Not until he pulls his socks up and finger out and gets up to speed. Agreed comrades?' When I return to the classroom, Gosia and Basia are actively attempting to escape through a window, while another pair have begun to argue and tussle noisily, having failed to reach an agreement as to which of them is the greater nuisance. There is misbehaviour in front of my eyes and behind my back. When I ask for an example of the present continuous tense, Nella starts jumping on the table.

'I am jumping!' she shouts (which, to be fair, is an example of the present continuous tense). When Marietta pops in to check on my progress, D1 briefly settle and feign interest in what they did last weekend. Marietta is all smiles, is pleased with how it is all going, is proud of her gang of brats. Alone with me again, the feigning stops and the rebellion resumes. I try to be patient. I try to be philosophical. I even try to *empathise*. I tell myself that these kids have already spent the day at school, that no kid, not a single kid in the world, not the nerdiest, gawkiest, most scholarly child in the solar system wants to go to school after they've already *been* to school. When these kids get to Cream Tea they are ready to burst. If they are met with anything other than an iron fist – with me for example – they detonate. Their answers are nonchalant and sarcastic at best, hurtful and upsetting at worst. The kid who is normally easy-going becomes stubborn and obnoxious, while the kid who is normally a bit shy starts actively trying to sabotage the lesson. It is easy for all this to sound mirthful and harmless, to sound as if I'm playing it up, but I'm not. The lesson with D1 is actually stressful. I won't name names, but Lucas is almost certainly related to the devil. Olivia, on the other hand, is devilish one moment and angelic the next, which is even more intimidating because there is no legislating for it. You can put Lucas in the cupboard and be done with it. But you can't put Olivia in the cupboard and be done with it because she'll turn into an angel in that cupboard and start to sob and bleat like a gorgeous cherub in the unfair dark. It would be like putting Joseph Stalin in solitary confinement only to discover upon his release 30 years later that it was actually Jesus. Besides, the cupboard wouldn't even scare these kids. They'd sit down and play on their phones. They'd call their grandparents and explain how rewarding further education is. By the lesson's end I am ready for retirement, ready for my pension, ready to book a vasectomy that I might assist the teaching fraternity by keeping class sizes down. I can't possibly carry on. I must seek alternative work. I want to deliver pizzas. I want to deliver newspapers. I want to stack shelves. Now that I think of it, I bet most of the people stacking shelves in supermarkets are ex-teachers.

After a five-minute break spent in the garden trying to understand who I am and why I am here, I head upstairs to face M17, hoping M doesn't stand for malignant and 17 for the size of the group. The students are aged between sixteen and eighteen. They are receiving extra tuition in preparation for their final high-school exams, the equivalent of British A-levels. Mercifully, the group are less inclined to get under the table, or on the table, or out the window, in part because the classroom is on the second floor. Unlike Lucas, M17 do not think it reasonable to take my journal and start reading it to the class in an affected English accent – 'I was am-bi-va-lent about the dump-lings' – and nor do they think it reasonable to make jokes about me in Polish, to the amusement of the rest of the class and to the detriment of the scholastic atmosphere and my self-esteem. As well as being altogether less demented, M17 are also more self-conscious, with the result that keeping a conversation going with them is a challenge. They care what I think of them. They care what their classmates think of them. In Freudian terms, D1 were light on superego, heavy on id. M17 have enough superego to sink a ship. When I ask what their motivation for studying English is they all insist they have none. I take that as my cue to wrap things up.

23 March. I spend my first wage packet in a pub called Dragon. I spend too much time here. It is proving an extension of the flat, a distant living room, a boozy en-suite. It has a homely quality and takes a varied crowd. A suit at the bar with a beer and newspaper. A pair of skateboarders sharing a pack of cigarettes in the courtyard garden. Students from Southern Europe talking quickly in mother tongues, asking when the weather will turn and where the wine is. Eighties pop music from the UK and the US plays as loud as the bartender wants, while conflicting music videos run on a TV above the bar next to a protruding dragon's head. It's a very social place – for me at least. I am sociable here because I am always alone and open and willing to practise Polish or English and so on. Moreover, I've been more or less in a good, gregarious mood ever since arriving in Poland (apart from when in a classroom), and such a mood can make anywhere social. I consider the corner shop a social place, and the trams, and even the public toilets. I spoke to my mum last night and she asked if Poland was a friendly place. I quickly answered that it was. But on reflection perhaps it isn't, perhaps it's *me* that's friendly – buoyed by being away, apart, abroad – and perhaps it's my friendliness that forces it out of others in a sort of unnatural way. All that is not to say the Polish are *un*friendly – I'm sure some are and some aren't just like everywhere else – but rather that I am probably not the best barometer. If you sent a deprived child into a toy shop and then asked them for a report, no doubt it would be glowing. Poland, for the time being, is a bit like that for me. I'm out of place here and it suits me.

I'm here for a date. I'm meeting Tala, who I connected with on Tinder.[7] To be candid, I am less interested in Tala as

---

[7] Dating application millennials require to fill their weekday evenings. I

a potential romantic partner and more as a pedagogue. This, I know, shouldn't be my opening line. In the event, we have a good, solid lesson. I am introduced to Polish history (one thing after another by the sound of it) and then the Polish case system (distinct from the Indian caste system, which is a lot more fun believe me), which requires all nouns, even the most trivial, like carrot, to take fourteen different spellings, depending on what mood it's in. When the subject drifts off learning Polish as a foreign language, Tala asks me what I think about the attacks in Belgium. I ask her what attacks in Belgium. She tells me that members of ISIS detonated themselves at various places across the country to make a point about something, but that the 'something' can't be agreed upon. 'No matter what,' she says, 'it will make it more likely that you leave Europe.' I tell her I'm going nowhere, that I'm not scared. 'Not you,' she says, 'the UK. In the referendum. Such events get distorted, are used to make people fearful. It happens here in Poland. Half the country is scared of Russia, the other half is scared of Muslims.' I will almost certainly see Tala again, though next time I should offer to pay an hourly rate.[8]

---

used it a bit in England, and then a bit in Poland. It makes you a worse person in both countries.

[8] I never saw her again.

3

Love is blind

24 March. I follow the blue-and-white scarves onto a green-and-yellow tram and then, about ten minutes later, off it and towards a stadium that looks expensive and rather like a giant metallic turtle. I buy a ticket and a scarf and place a bet that Poznań will win 3–1, which they haven't done since 1655.[9] The home fans, even before the match has commenced, are more vocal and tenacious than any set I have previously witnessed. It is a Tuesday night, an inconsequential league fixture, a mid-table clash and the stadium is barely a quarter full, and yet the noise! It is aggressive and militant, suggestive of an army going into battle. These supporters would make a good set of nationalists, a committed and indefatigable home army, buoyant and bellicose no matter the opponent, no matter the balance of power, no matter the odds and no matter the stakes. If it is a corner to them or a penalty to us (how quickly one sides), a tactical switch or the captain down with cramp, the noise alters not. In the context of a football match such fervour is, for the most part, harmless; but in a different context, a less sporting one, it could prove murderous. Flares are lit by the pocket of undaunted away support, answering

---

[9] Coincidentally, it was in 1655 that the Swedish Deluge began in Poland. The Deluge was brutal. The Swedes swept across the country butchering and burning and buggering indiscriminately. Poland lost half of its population. These days, Swedish presence in Poland is limited to a dozen IKEA outlets.

those of the locals. Smoke fills the arena. The ball can no longer be seen, and nor can the players. All is one. It is an armistice of sorts, an impasse, a blank slate. The lack of clarity, that friend can't be distinguished from foe, doesn't bother me a jot, but you'd think it might bother the referee. Not at all. On they go invisibly, and still the crowd roars, not caring a bit that the match is no longer apparent. *Love is blind.* Perhaps it is less the match and more the idea of a match that gets them going, that keeps them going. A giant flag is unfolded and spread above the heads of 5,000. For those trapped below, the game is freshly obscured for a further fifteen minutes, but it matters not, for still they roar. There is a war on and that is all. The detail is beside the point. When Poznań score the fans celebrate by turning their backs to the action. The semiotics of it all, the encounter's many meanings, are impossible to pin down. I am cold and almost alone in the west stand, quietly at odds with the raucous banks behind each goal. My bet does not come in. The battle ends in a draw, and the armies go home.

25 March. By now the flat is full. As well as Jenny there is Mariusz and Anna. Anna is a beautician. She carries out her work from home. Half of her bedroom is given over to equipment designed to increase people's self-esteem by manipulating their appearance. The stream of customers is unrelenting. When I'm at the kitchen window smoking, looking over the dusty courtyard, I hear the shrieks of men having their armpits waxed. Besides a beautician, Anna is also something of a *Matka Polka*, a Polish Mother, which is to say she cooks sixteen meals a day, puts a lot of things in jars, and makes an effort to keep things clean. This last mostly involves making sure Jenny and I keep things clean. Mariusz doesn't need to be told. He likes to clean. He likes to clean and is tall. That's all I know. He doesn't say much generally, and says even less to me, perhaps on account of the language barrier between us, which is higher than the one between Anna and I, which is about two metres high, and much higher than the one between Jenny and I, which is about half-a-metre high and much too low for my liking. Besides being tall and clean, Mariusz works as the manager of a café somewhere in the old town. He appears to work 140 hours a week. In his rare moments of liberty, Mariusz will put a pizza in the oven and vacuum the flat in his underpants. The jury is still out on Jenny. He's an unorthodox character. Maybe paradoxical is a better word, or incongruous. I've seen him wash pots and pans in the shower, and now here he is washing socks in the kitchen sink. There is a severe, monastic quality to him – he likes to sleep on a bed of walnuts and will only eat steamed garlic and spinach – and yet he makes Mickey Mouse look like a manic depressive. He goes off to work each day, something to do with French windows, then comes home to gaze out the window and play the cello and generally goof around. I asked Anna the other day if Jenny is representative of the modern Polish man. 'I hope not,' she said. I don't want to be unkind about Jenny. In part because *he* isn't unkind. Jenny is always keen to share – his food, his opinions, his time – which is either good or bad depending on whether you want those things to be shared with you. He spends time with me at the kitchen window playing I spy in Polish – *samochód, trzepak, drzwi, niebo*. In many respects I think we're on a similar wavelength. I know Anna thinks we're on a similar wavelength, which is why she directs her domestic opprobrium at the two of us collectively, as though we were conjoined twins, were much of a muchness. Yeah, he's not bad. I went into his room the other day and said, 'Sorry to ask but have you got a pair of socks I could borrow?'

He stopped what he was doing, kind of smiled apologetically, then said, 'I was just about to ask you the same thing.' If great minds think alike, then like minds aren't always great.

27 March. They embrace the coming of spring. The men are quickly in shorts, big milky calves unveiled to the sun. Girls, too eager perhaps, over-exhibit long-hidden forms. It is a long winter here, and it can be severe, so no wonder their haste. By donning little they remind themselves of their bodies, of their meaning and pull. Two handsome boys are currently wearing little outside the café on my street. One is waiting for Anita, the manageress, who I've been avoiding eye contact with for ten days now, for fear she'll detect my fondness for her. I instantly and unfairly dislike the boy waiting for Anita. (It is unfair because one doesn't dislike another person for having a likewise taste in books, but then there is more than one copy of the same book.) I eat a salad and drink an espresso and rehearse some phrases from my book, useful and everyday according to the cover, stuff like 'Are guide dogs allowed here?' and 'Can sir tell me his birthday?'[10] When Anita comes to clear my table, I am cold with her. I am cold because of the handsome boys, and in particular the one waiting for her to finish her shift so, I imagine, they can ride their bikes to a poetry pop-up together and do lines. Anita is undoubtedly prized, and by the look of it involved elsewhere, but sooner or later I'll let her know of my fondness nonetheless, notwithstanding my fondness for the woman who drives the number 13 tram, and the girl who works at the shop at the end of the street. Am I behaving unfaithfully by idly admiring in several directions, for preferring to stay at the junction and dreamily ponder the ways? Men prize the thing ungained more than the thing itself, said Shakespeare, so maybe I'm best where I am, going nowhere, all things ungained.

4 April. I instruct D1 to write letters to hypothetical pen-friends, outlining exactly what that penfriend can expect to happen during their forthcoming visit to Poland. Maciej, not given to hard work, lays down his pen and folds his arms. I give it a minute before satisfying him with atten-tion. 'What's the matter, Maciej?' He gives me a long look, and then his classmates a glance. He has something up his sleeve, that much is obvious. 'Have you something up your sleeve, Maciej?'

---

[10] Honestly, that phrase book was a joke. If you've got a city-break in Poland coming up and you're planning to hire a donkey or telegram your second-cousin, then I'd recommend it. Otherwise invest in some-thing genuinely useful, like a wireless vacuum cleaner.

'I don't want to write to my penfriend about what we are going to do.'

'Oh? Why's that?'

'Because I don't want to destroy the surprise.'

After this has gained a small applause, and after the hypothetical letters have been hypothetically sent, we play Monopoly. It is amusing watching them while I carry out the duties of banker, collecting fines and dealing properties. I try my best to keep some English chat going.

'Julia. Will you build a café at Liverpool Street station?'

'I think not.'

'Why not?'

'I do not like coffee.'

'And Marcin, do you like living at Trafalgar Square?'

'I like this house. It is a good shape.'

'Life in jail must be difficult, Lucas?'

'*Takie życie.*' (C'est la vie.)

8 April. I had planned to go to the zoo but it started to rain so I go to the café on my street to drink green tea and pretend to read a book. When the moment is right I go to the counter to ask Anita for more hot water and whether she'd be willing to teach me Polish. (Nothing better to cower behind than a pretext.) She says yes to both, but in exactly the same way, so that I don't know if Polish tuition is just another thing on the menu, asked for several times a day. I rip a page from my book (the page I was reading: twit), put my contact details on it, hand it to Anita as nonchalantly as possible, then leave before she can change her mind. The page is from *A Country* *in the Moon.* Walking back to the flat, I remember what was on it. *On a balustrade in the gardens of Wilanow Palace, Warsaw, there are four statues symbolising the stages of love: Fear, Kiss, Quarrel, Indifference.* I owe a debt to the afternoon's rain.

4

The city doesn't shut up

10 April. Taking public transport unnecessarily is one way to see a place – its odd crumbs and loose ends, each vital to the whole, and no less alive for being less seen. I take the 10 tram from the Theatre Bridge and go south through Wilda. I watch a fridge-freezer being delivered to a language school, a range of protein powders being arranged in the window of Muscles Mental, and the Slavic chefs at Sultan Kebab getting lunch ready. At the end of the line there's a crib in the bushes, and 'I think I would like to die' has been written on the body of a spare carriage. A cyclist trails us as we swing round and head north up Roosevelt Street and past the Hotel Vivaldi, where a man slams his hand on the tram's window because he's late by a whisker. We slip by an unorthodox church that looks like a chicken – a paltry part of God's unreal estate – then conclude on the fringe of a housing estate. I get out and wait for the 4. A baby in pink points at me then looks to its mother for an explanation.

The 4 covers old ground – the queer church, Vivaldi, Roosevelt – then turns left on Saint Martin, passing a film-screening castle and a Danish fashion outlet, whose bare window suggests the Danes are wearing little this season. On Gwarna, Second Hand London is a towering outlet pushing jaded bottoms and washed-up brollies. A man with crutches gets awkwardly off at Greater Poland Square. He's offered help but waves it away, preferring a tricky dismount. The 4 wants to head south, but I don't, so I switch to the 6, which goes east past Porsche and Volvo dealerships towards Russia. On our right is Malta Lake, ordered by the Nazis and dug by their prisoners. I get off at the end of the line, where there happens to be a cemetery. As I wait for new wheels, a young woman joins me and then, using her self-effacing phone as a mirror, proceeds to remedy what she imagines is wrong. When the 6 finally shows, the girl is made-up.

I ride as far as Ostrów Tumski, the cathedral island, where I get off and walk to a new shopping centre. In the entrance hall, a public pianist plays to an audience of four, Pizza Hut is chock-a-block, and the window of a bookshop promises '*bestsellery!*', which has me wondering if it specialises in books that are like bestsellers.[11] The shopping centre's slogan is announced in purple neon above the food court: *#allaboutlifestyle*, it says, which is just as well if you're one of the developers and have skin in the game. The Dalai Lama said he likes to go to shopping centres to be reminded of all the crap he doesn't want. I draw the attention of a peacekeeper when I start to photograph window dummies.

The 16 clatters back into town. We cut across a shopping street and then under the nose of the industrialist Hipolit Cegielski, whose workforce threw its dummy out of the pram in 1956, and so doing changed the course of history.[12] Up

---

[11] It doesn't. *Bestsellery* means bestsellers. As *burgery* means burgers, not something burger-like, as I first thought.

[12] The protests of June 1956 in Poznań were conceived in the factory

past the Hotel Rzymski, where I leant from a window on my third morning in Poland and wondered at the fussy din below, not knowing, not believing that my future was down there, among the pent-up crowd on Freedom Square. Right onto Roosevelt and then quickly north, rising above the earth, gliding over cars on a brief tram highway. After an estate of towers in peach and pink, whose balconies bear pots and plants and bikes and washing, we finish at the university, or a part thereof. I get off and read. I read from the rough surface of the city's endless text. I read the walls and panes and sheets and boards: a piece of new writing called *The End* will play for four nights at the cathedral; a fading promotion for sparkling teeth; an invitation to exercise. If you listen carefully, the city doesn't shut up, and nor does the crowd of infants wearing hi-vis tunics (the better to be avoided) that is being led back to school by teachers across the street. Behind them, an old lady limps along at an inch an hour. I watch her put her shopping down and check her wristwatch in case she's late and ought to hurry. I board the same 16, stand beside a pram and poke my tongue at the occupant, a boy of two or so, who *ding-ding-dings* the stop button in alarm. The mother tries to stop the boy's music,

---

that Hipolit founded a hundred years earlier. The cost of living was punishing. The price of staple food items was put up another 10 per cent. A delegation of workers walked to what is now Plac Mickiewicza (then Stalin Square) to vent their spleen. Authorities reacted with undue force. Seventy or so of the demonstrators were killed. The seeds of a wider rebellion – that would finally lead to the Solidarity trade union and the fall of the Soviet Union – had been sown.

THE CITY DOESN'T SHUT UP

but he's evidently determined so she relents and lets him do as he wants. Nobody on the tram seems to mind the kid's racket, which makes me smile. I sit behind two toddlers – Polish-African-American, says their mother. A young photographer, drawn to their relative difference, tries to snap the children on the sly but gets rumbled by the grandmother. The snapper explains his purpose in broken Polish. The mother doesn't mind, but the grandmother is evidently less persuaded, for when the photographer gets on the floor for a better perspective, she fakes to kick him in the back of the head. When I start photographing the photographer that's too much for her. She gets to her feet and gets in my face and nips my meta-instincts in the bud. 'Photography is one thing,' I imagine her saying, 'but photography of photography is just smut.' I move to the other end of the tram, where a boy's jumper says 'I'd Rather Be Mining', and a girl's T-shirt says 'But I Mean Just Coffee'. Most of those being carried along read screens in lieu of daydreams, and I don't blame them: the screens are quick and smooth and knowing, and besides, they've seen real life before.

5

They wouldn't leave if they didn't have to

16 April. She is an hour late. She said the cathedral at noon but has been delayed by the sudden arrival – as opposed to gradual arrival – of an electrician. I don't mind. I'm happy waiting. The nave offers a beneficent space in which to compose both myself and some opening remarks. Ordinarily I don't mind what comes out my mouth, but with this girl I do; I worry about coming across, about seeming, about leaving a mark. When she arrives and sits next to me on the pew and I am finally given the chance to come across, I say nothing, do nothing, don't even look at her, just keep my eyes on Christ and try not to sweat – which is one way of coming across, I suppose. Without saying a thing she gives me her headphones. It is good music – electronic, instrumental – and improved further by the context: the church, her. I listen with my eyes open. The scene before me makes an odd music video. The son of God, three years my senior, is unmoved by the cleaning lady who goes patiently along the pews, disinfecting. All things considered it is a poignant scenario – the music, the cleaner, the crucifix – and so when the song is done I mention the fact to Anita, hoping to appear sensitive and poetic. She responds by asking what I'm doing in Poland. I tell her the Poles were going the other way and I wanted to know why. It's money, she says. They wouldn't leave if they didn't have to, she says. So now you can go home, she says. I get up and make to leave, which makes her laugh, but only just. She asks how I'm getting on. I say the language is a puzzle and I'm drinking too much, but more from an excess of happiness than anything else, which may be hard to believe, but there it is. And what about you, Anita? She sighs, twice, then tells me she was living in Iraq until recently, that she was happy there despite the illiberal climate, and that she no longer has contact with her family because she doesn't share their values. No wonder she sighed. It is hard to really look at her. I see her eyes one at a time, twenty minutes apart. They are between blue and light blue. I think of complimenting them if only because I know these colours in Polish. Her hair is up in its usual way, a high-rise nest of snakes like Medusa. I think: *should I say that?* She says: 'Will you eat with me, Benjamin?'

We cross a bridge whose railings carry padlocks and coat hangers, the former to signal commitment, the latter contempt for a proposed law to illegalise abortion in all instances. The bridge leads to the district of Śródka, where the walls are colourful and full of poems. I have Anita translate one but her effort is in vain because rather than listen I can only watch her pointing up to the words in question, giving them a stab. When she turns and asks what I think of the poem I say emphatically that it was memorable. We eat noodles in a café renowned for its cheesecake. I ask her to sit next to me, rather than opposite. This way we don't have to look at each other, I say. We drink Vietnamese coffee

– that sweet thick milk! – then, remembering our pretext for meeting, practise large numbers and important verbs – *spotkać, podejść, zdać*[13] – until she gets a text from the electrician and must go. I watch her push her bike across the cobbles until it feels ridiculous to still be doing so.

22 April. I read online about Barack Obama's recent visit to the UK. He says that if Britain leaves Europe it will be at the back of the queue. According to Cameron this is good news, because come the referendum it will deter potential Leavers from voting to do so. I can't help thinking that Cameron is making a blunder by forgetting how stoic the British can be in the face of a queue. At any rate the story has legs. It gets a second airing when Obama's use of the word queue is put under the spotlight by correspondents who reckon something fishy is afoot because he didn't say line, and then a third airing when Obama and Cameron play a round of golf together in Hertfordshire, during which Obama is forced to queue for a bacon roll at the halfway house. When pressed by Jeremy Paxman on the details of the round, Cameron's caddy admits that the PM only lost one ball. Much media speculation ensues as to whether, in the context of the referendum, this is a good omen or not. I don't often read the news.

---

[13] If you've an eye for portents and wish to know how these verbs relate to my evolving relation to Anita, look them up.

23 April. I buy drinks for a couple of men at Dragon, thinking we could discuss the government's stance on abortion. Marcin and Marcin are happy to talk on the condition that we do so with the support of a bottle of flavoured vodka. We find a table outside in the courtyard garden, where Marcin 1, who has Italian or Persian ancestry, I forget which, quickly gains the attention of a tall man with no hair who thinks that Marcin 1 looks out of place.

'Don't worry,' says Marcin 1, 'he is just a tracksuit.'

'A what?'

'A *dres*, a tracksuit. He doesn't like the fact that I don't look like him. Just ignore him.'

Ignoring the tracksuit is made more difficult when it comes over to introduce itself. When Piotr arrives at our table he says, 'Are we English? Oh, I say! What a jolly idea! A spot of rain on the cards, is it? Shagged your mother, did you? Jolly good!', before turning to Marcin 1 and accusing him of being from Pakistan. When Marcin 1 says in Polish that in fact he's never been outside of Poland but thank you for the interest, Piotr frowns, looks about the courtyard, sort of laughs, then restates his opinion that Marcin 1 is from Pakistan, and therefore a Muslim, and therefore a threat to Poland and Catholicism and perhaps the entire continent of Europe. It is obvious that Piotr – who, on top of hair, is also missing most of an ear – doesn't post enlightened things on Facebook, and so I ask him if he wouldn't mind telling me about how he came to acquire his English over a drink at the bar – where, I conjecture, he is less likely to attack someone. At first Piotr doesn't say anything. I think he might even blush. Then he says, 'Alright,' and leads me through to the bar, where, over the course of an hour or so, he grows slowly less offensive, and slightly more likable.

It is an odd hour of my life. The same conversation loop happens several times. Piotr will tell me something about living in Luton and soften while doing so, forget what he's saying and what he's doing with me, remember the sort of things he normally says, and then start again with his favourite accusations, i.e. that I am English and Marcin is Pakistani and that neither of us should be in Poland, at which point I will apologise for being English, explain that I didn't have much say in the matter, establish that Marcin is Polish and Catholic and has never left the country, and then offer Piotr a beer and ask him about his time in Luton, whereupon he will tell me something about living in Luton and soften while doing so, and so on. Eventually he wants to go back to the courtyard to smoke. He says I should come with him. When we get outside he offers me his pack then realises there's only one cigarette in it. He looks at the pack uncertainly. I reason that he's probably seeing two of everything, including Pakistanis, so can't be sure how many are left in the pack. To get to the bottom of it, Piotr turns the pack upside down. Indisputably, one cigarette falls out. He picks it up and holds it out to me. I refuse. You must, he says. Take it, he says. It is the last one and it is for the Englishman, he says. I haven't smoked for a month but decide in the interest of mankind that I should do so now. Besides, it's not an easy thing to offer someone your last cigarette, not when you're out drinking, not when you're Piotr. In its own small way, the offer is a significant one. It hints at something peaceful in the man, something kind. After two drags of the cigarette Piotr takes it off me and then leaves. I return to Marcin and Marcin and say that beneath the many thick layers that Piotr habitually adorns – so habitually that they are like a skin – there is a not indecent guy. I don't suppose anyone sees much of that guy, I go on, and I don't suppose Piotr cares much about the fact, but he's there in any case. The Marcins beg to differ.

30 April. Tony needs me to cover B4. He tells me the class will be sitting an exam and I'm to be watchful for cheating. It's endemic, he says. They just can't stop themselves, he says. They gang up on the system, he says. I assure Tony that I'll stay alert, ready to pounce on miscreants, on malfeasance, on careless eyes and furtive whispers. Then I do nothing of the sort. I let them get on with it. I read *How to be an Alien* by George Mikes while they cheat as much as they want. I am not here, I reason, to meddle with the local customs. That would be chauvinistic. I let them whisper.

6

Was your mother happier under communism? (Katowice)

2 May. Katowice's reputation invited me. An industrial city in the south, it is generally held to be ugly and disappointing. I buy a second-class ticket for 64 zloty, about £13. The train has a restaurant car, staffed by two amiable Polish women who, on the face of it, must be nearing retirement. One will take the orders, the other will bring them to life. Strictly speaking the two women are never in the same room, and yet they never stop talking. A small hatch in the wall of the kitchen means the chef can keep up with the hostess. I am impressed by their untiring talk. No number of customers or degree of pressure – and bear in mind that this is a busy little restaurant car – will interrupt their dialogue. I should like to know what it is they talk about. I prefer to think they stay off the bigger themes – love, mortality, politics – and settle instead on smaller matters, like the unreliability of the coffee machine, and the questionable decisions of their children. It's possible these two women rarely work with each other, and so have a lot of ground to cover when they do, but I suspect not; I suspect they work as a pair all the time, have done for years, and go at it like this each hour and each mile of each journey across Poland. They might discuss me. They might – the cook turning a cutlet, the hostess clearing a table – briefly discuss the strange gentleman who chose to introduce himself ungrammatically at the counter, before, somewhere outside Wrocław on the return journey, forgetting him altogether.

After a plate of scrambled egg and gherkin, I go to my compartment, which constitutes two cushioned benches, facing off. There are two other passengers in situ, a girl about my age and her mother. The layout seems right for interviews, so I ask the girl what the time is and what station we just passed. When these questions go nowhere ('half-past ten', 'Leszno') I ask if her mother was happier under communism. The girl says she can't be sure. Might you ask her for me? After a quick back and forth with her mother in Polish, the girl turns to me and says that her mother thinks people have more but are less friendly these days, but that I should bear in mind that back in the day people were less helpful and more suspicious, on account of the unforgiving regime, and the mindsets it induced. I nod several times to indicate that I follow, that I understand, but to be frank I'm confused. I want to ask how back in the day people were at once friendlier and less helpful, but gauge from the mother's demeanour (she is asleep) that the Q&A is over. When it is announced that we are approaching our destination, I think with regret that I have barely looked out of the window. Of the landscape and settlements that we have passed on our journey, of those five hours of Poland, overtaken and unseen, I can say little. Let's say that what passed outside was unremarkable. Flat mostly, at times built up, arable on occasion, generally overcast – as most places. This isn't a country on the moon, after all. I get off the train at Katowice wondering whether, generally speaking, one is liable to learn more from the land or its people.

The train station at Katowice is an attractive structure, neither classical nor Soviet in style. In fact, it manages to suggest both styles without conceding to either – a stylish compromise, you might say.[14] The station is enveloped by a glass shopping centre and a spruce pedestrianised area. It is plain that money has been spent 'regenerating' the centre. It's a familiar tale. A town loses its industry (in this case coal mining) and by way of compensation gets an art gallery, new benches and a hundred succulent plants. Katowice's centre isn't the only thing that's been restored. So has my mood. I feel enlivened by leaving. I was starting to grow complacent in Poznań, whereas here I feel daft and dumb and infant again, beady-eyed and greedy. I am tempted to approach a couple outside a café and ask for their opinion on something – the Pope, post-industrialisation, the paintings of Edward Hopper – just to get a sense of the tongue, the jib, the gab. I give in to the temptation and ask where the tennis tournament is taking place. The woman nominates the man. 'Tennis?' he says, 'How should I know?'[15]

---

[14] In *The Architecture of Happiness* Alain de Botton says that we like certain buildings because they embody qualities that we value in people, and I think he has a point. I don't mean to say that I like compromised people, or even stylish ones, but I do like people that are confused, mongrel, unashamedly various, peacefully at odds etc.

[15] A friend of mine worked for the World Tennis Federation at the time.

I pay attention as I search for the stadium. A lady is leaning well out of a window, as if ready to take questions. Under the portico of a theatre, a display of old photographs shows people queuing outside shops for whatever was going. (What stopped Poland having enough? Did the Soviets skim the cream?[16]) Opposite an abandoned library is a travel agent, its window full of threats to whisk me away. Allegedly, I can get seven nights at a four-star resort in Bulgaria called The Garden of Eden for 1,700 zloty. (Only four stars for The Garden of Eden? God knows what's to be done for five.) I take a step back from the window and think cynically that if prospective travellers want a cheap getaway they should lobby for the library's renaissance, and then read its books and travel thereby. I take a photograph of a vending machine selling fur hats, and then another of the longest single block of flats I have ever seen, titanic in scale, a province *per se*. The block is incongruous. Most of the downtown buildings are Germanic-seeming rather than Soviet-seeming, which stands to reason, for this part of the country was German until the end of the First World War.

He mentioned in passing that there was a tournament coming up in Katowice. I said I'd go, because I'd heard the place was disappointing.

[16] Because 40 per cent of Poland's wealth was destroyed in the Second World War, it's fair to say the country's socialist experiment was handicapped from the word go. Even Marx said socialism was the stage *after* a successful round of capitalism, once productive capacity was sufficiently advanced and so on. Giving it a go when you've only got a couple of tractors and a decimated, demoralised population wasn't ever the idea.

If I thought the titanic block was incongruous, I had another thought coming. The stadium is something else. I hope it's one of a kind. It's called *Spodek* – flying saucer – and with reason. The saucer's interior is pleasingly down-to-earth, however. Unlike North American stadia, where you can do a week's shopping between touchdowns, here you can get coffee, sausage and lager, and that's it. Believing in a balanced diet, I get one of each then take my seat. There are about seventeen of us in attendance. There is a South Korean couple a few rows in front who, from what I can tell, have got mixed up and were expecting a pop concert. Another lady is with a guide dog. When the players begin warming up it is clear the Latvian girl has an issue with her thigh, because she keeps rubbing it and wincing. I put a bet on the Latvian's opponent, for as pleasant as it can be to watch professional tennis it helps things along if one has something at stake. Not long into the first game I realise there's an obvious Polish lesson available to me: the numbers 0, 15, 30 and 40. Over the course of the first set each number is announced by the umpire about a dozen times, and yet on each occasion, even deep into the set when I ought to be up to speed, I have no idea what the umpire is trying to say. He may be saying 40–30, or 15–40, or 0–15. Whatever the score, Camilla Georgi, the Latvian's opponent, an Italian with a degree in Medieval Literature, is after my heart. She has everything going for her until she somehow contrives to lose the match and in so doing scuppers my bet. She's cost me money before I've even asked her out – an ill-omen if there ever was one, especially for a writer, who even at the top of their game can expect to earn about 40p an hour.

I leave the saucer and walk east in a light rain and a coming dark. I pass a squat red-brick concert hall, raised with EU dough, gathering early-evening ears, and then continue towards a collection of coal mining relics; shafts and cranes and nodding donkeys, jutting out of the earth like fractured bones through skin. The old coal mine is now a museum, its once dirty concern scrubbed up and hung out to dry, so day-trippers and ex-miners might come to pay their respects. I'd love to provide more information about the region's industrial decline, and what it gets up to these days, but I can't, because I don't have any.[17] In any case, it's a good view from up here. Katowice slopes in a way Poznań doesn't. Its contours and gradients throw things together visually – aesthetic compositions spawn from the

---

[17] A more serious travel writer would have read up on the city's socio-economic situation in advance of going to Katowice. But I tend to think that too much pre-emptive research takes away some of the joys of travel – surprise, revelation, chance – and because I am a traveller before I am a travel writer, I prefer to remain mostly ignorant of where I'm going, and so doing lend a bit of mystery to my wandering. If I miss crucial or interesting stuff along the way by dint of this approach, then I can fill you in later. Now, for example: There is still coal mining in the city and its environs, but far less than there was. In the 60s there were 400 mines roundabout. Now there are fourteen. These days, most of the city's residents work in the expanding service economy, serving T-shirts and hot drinks and cinema tickets. It's not an altogether disagreeable reorientation, though I am sure there are plenty who would beg to differ, the bulk of them, like me, never having spent a minute down a mine.

urban scrap for space – whereas a flat city gives so little at a time. Office and residential towers appear to take the motorway in their midriff, to rub shoulders with church towers, to sprout bridges. From where I'm stood, up on the hill in the rain, the city is positively photogenic. Crossing a bridge that spans the motorway, I look down at the rushing cargo, blinking and wet, going where needs be, running this and that to here or there, children to Krakow, ink to Gdańsk, cabbage to Slovakia, the latter just four hours south beyond the mountains.

I take a single room for 200 zloty, about £40. I can't be bothered to search for cheaper. The hotel – Diamante on ulica Dworcowa – is opposite the old train station. After some pointless television, I lie down and close my eyes and remember my walk in the rain. I want to reinforce its points, download its detail – the urban confusion, the quiet concert hall, the shiny saucer, the industrial graveyard and the colours of the motorway. Then I go to a bar along the street called Absurd, where I order a burger and a beer and then settle on a couch to peruse my phrase book. I am usually open to casual interaction. But not tonight. I am spent and selfish and so when Agatha sits next to me to say that she saw me alone with my phrase book and wants to lend a hand, I really wish she hadn't. She is drunk and unabashed; indeed, she behaves as if we've been dating for weeks, patting me when I make mistakes, saying that the best way to learn Polish is through a lover. She assumes I'm enjoying all this. She expects me to play along. When I don't, she asks what the problem is. I shift, squirm, then say that I'm spent and selfish and hope to be in bed before long, which, I instantly see, only serves to encourage her. She tries and fails to kiss me. (Her drunkenness makes her easy to dodge.) Mistaking defiance for shyness, she has another go, with the same result. When I announce that I'm leaving, she insists on walking me to my hotel. In front of the hotel she says: 'Am I coming in?' I explain as best as I can that sometimes one simply wants to be alone, no matter the alternatives. She hails a taxi.

7

Sure there was equality. Everyone was screwed

6 May. I meet Anita at a Mexican restaurant in the old town. We sit in the garden and watch Zorro dramatically enter the scene each time cheesecake is ordered. (One of the kitchen porters keeps a mask and cape in the storeroom so that each time cheesecake is ordered he can transform himself and charge through the restaurant and toss the dessert across the offending table while calling for a revolution.) It is entertaining every time it happens. Usually such antics – like romantic encounters – are subject to the law of diminishing returns. But not the appearance of Zorro upon cheesecake orders at the Mexican restaurant in Poznań.

Anita looks normal: beautiful, unflappable, inscrutable. I want to mention the fact but worry that to do so would be to display a basic, shallow, even misogynistic instinct, as if she could only be beautiful, as if beauty were her limit. We speak about our scars and her tattoos, and then a philosophy professor with whom she had an affair at eighteen. She tells me that her family only care for themselves so she ran away as soon as she could with a backpack and 60 zloty. I express sadness at this state of affairs. 'It's fine,' she says, 'I wouldn't change it. Either I left my family or I killed myself.' It is difficult to hear such things, and I say as much. She smiles in the way she does – in a hurry, unnaturally, more a clenching of the face than a smile. She suggests a soft drink at one of her favourite bars; I suggest we go home. She picks up on the ambiguity. 'To our separate homes,' she says. She waits with me at the tram stop. It feels indecent to want more than her confidence, her company, and so I kick desire aside. But I watch where it lands, just in case.

10 May. It is hard to learn Polish on foot, on the street, in the field, for each word, even the simplest and most quotidian, like banana, can take up to twenty different forms – quite a slippery banana. This is the Polish case system that I have been trying to avoid. It is a grammatical conspiracy, designed a millennium ago to make life unnecessarily difficult, and so doing give Poles a common adversary around which they can cohere. I used to stay alert when walking the city, keeping an eye open for recognisable words, hunting for connections or resemblances between something I had ordered for lunch and something for sale in a shop. I thought I knew the word for bread but then I heard it being called something else, and then written down as something different again. I began to think that the Poles were just very bad at spelling. And that would have been all right, preferable to what's actually going on, which is that the appearance of banana will vary depending on whether you're ordering a banana or addressing a banana or undressing a banana or accusing a banana or whatever it is one is inclined to do with a banana. The upshot of all this is that, after nearly two months of endeavour, my Polish is still the Polish of a baby. My favourite Polish TV programme is *Bolek and Lolek*, because the characters don't say anything. If it is a meaningful conversation in Polish I'm after, I really ought to be hanging out with Poles under the age of two. We could toddle around pointing at things and taking it in turns to have a stab at the noun in the nominative case. It's unlikely to happen though, for obvious reasons, so I'll have to persist with adults – or Jenny at least – and hope for the best.

16 May. The 24-hour convenience store across from my flat attracts a regular congregation, usually in the evening and sometimes through the night. At all times, each member of the congregation appears to be waiting for an arrival or a delivery – wide stance, darting eyes – and yet nothing ever comes. Sometimes the men drink and smoke, but for the most part they just stand, sharing jokes and observations and making loud, demonstrative phone calls (sometimes to each other). The phone calls are a charade, I feel, designed to communicate to the street that each of the men has dependents, sycophants, dealers, acolytes, interlocutors, a thick reliable phonebook of touchpoints, of ready ears, with each point and each ear evidence of their membership and vitality and identity. But the overall paralysis of the scene, of the routine, night after night before the same unclosing shop, gives lie to the idea of urgency, of vitality, and argues for a lack of options, a dearth of alternatives, a net deficit of status. I don't know. There is something pathetic, in the noblest sense (in that it is moving and human but sad), about their pointless vigils, their manly posturing. For it is a posture. They are a menacing prospect but give no grief to passers-by

SURE THERE WAS EQUALITY. EVERYONE WAS SCREWED

or the shop's keeper, who years ago might have feared their presence, but now values their familiarity. If a shopper is struggling with their load, or if someone has a puncture across the street, one of the men will be the first to attend. The group's integrity usually starts to unravel about the time I'm trying to sleep, when the chorus will start to sing and quarrel, perhaps to distract themselves from the cold, or the fact that there is nowhere else to go apart from home. For many of the men, home is overbearing, is on top of them: many live in the flats above the shop. The windows of the uppermost flats are mere portholes, manholes, no bigger than the heads that stick out of them, to check on the weather, the traffic, the scene, to watch out for news, to wait for Godot or winter or the Russians. I would paint the scene if I were able. I would have the heavy, aimless congregation on the street, and then duplicates of each at the windows, humanising the stone façade of home. Sometimes, when I'm watching the chorus from my window, I call Jenny in to translate what the group is saying. He says, 'I don't want to know what they're saying, and nor should you.' Perhaps it is easier for me to appreciate the men because I don't understand them.

24 May. B4 sat an exam, if you remember. I return their papers, which all earned more or less the same grade, which shouldn't surprise anyone, given the spirit of collaboration and consensus in which the exam was carried out. That done, I show the class a section of a BBC documentary about the migration of Poles to the UK. It is called *The Poles are Coming*, or something equally alarming, as if the

Poles were a criminal outfit from another galaxy, ready to wage war with sour cucumbers and pork knuckles. After showing a twenty-minute clip of the documentary I ask the students questions about what they've seen – about the town of Peterborough and the European Union and the migrants' motivations for leaving Poland – before chairing a more general discussion about the film. Timothy thinks the portrayal of Poles in the film is unfair. Zosia, who is always quick to disagree with Timothy, says that maybe the Poles that go to the UK are simply like that (which is to say, unruly characters with a fondness for alcohol). In which case, says Barbara, it is sad that British ideas about Poland are formed in response to such a narrow 'delegation' – that's the word she uses – whose members are often in difficult economic situations. How do you know they are in difficult economic situations? asks Zosia. Well, says Barbara, if they weren't then why would they leave Poland and go looking for work abroad? Someone suggests that all television is propaganda and I ought to be ashamed of the BBC. After the screening and discussion, I set a grammar exercise. You might have thought, from the collective groan, that I'd sentenced them to ten years' hard labour. Some of the groans carry accusatory tones, as if I had betrayed them, gaining their interest and trust by showing the documentary only to go and stab them in the back with a grammar exercise. And yet, despite their protests and moans, I sense that at some level the class is pleased to suffer this reversal of fortune.

I ask M17 to nominate ten famous Poles and tell me why they are famous. This exercise is as much for my benefit as theirs, but then I don't see why teaching shouldn't be mutually stimulating. Top of the list is Copernicus, who said the sun doesn't move. A close second is Robert Lewandowski, who is the leading scorer for the Polish national football team. Others on the list include Marie Skłodowska-Curie (scientist), Adam Małysz (ski jumper), Lech Wałęsa (shipwright turned president, responsible for the capitulation of communism), Dorota Rabczewska (eye-catching singer better known as Doda), Roman Polanski (director), Joseph Conrad (writer), Reksio (animated dog) and Arthur Rubinstein, who, I'm told, played a slow, powerful version of the Polish national anthem on the piano at the inauguration of the United Nations in 1946, in protest of Poland not having a delegation.[18]

27 May. I haven't been in a canoe since I was seven, when I had a lower centre of gravity and less anxiety. Most of the

---

[18] And that was fair enough; to be irked by Poland's treatment after the Second World War, I mean. The Polish government in exile in London had been told that in the event of an Allied victory Poland would be independent and the government in exile reinstated. In part, the hundreds of thousands of Poles who fought for the Allies did so with this in mind. Squadron 303 of the RAF, formed in Blackpool and made up exclusively of Poles, was the safest and most effective squadron throughout the war. And yet at Yalta and Potsdam and Tehran, when the future of Poland was on the table, Stalin was given what he wanted, which was most of Eastern Europe. The Polish government in exile were delivered the news over afternoon tea at the Ritz in London. 'Er, now listen up, would you. That thing we said, about you getting your country back, well it turns out it was a silly idea all along, so we've given Poland to the Soviets, who say they'll do a smashing job of it. More tea?'

group I'm with are paired up, so to divide the responsibility and labour, so they might lend each other support and counsel and reassurance, or make life saving interventions should the canoe flip. Marietta, knowing of my inexperience and anxiety, decides I'm better off in an individual canoe, 'so I can have a real experience'. Lowering myself into the canoe is like trying to rest a pint of milk on a bobbing apple. Marietta enjoys my attempt to embark. You'd be forgiven for thinking the sight of my struggle the essence of comedy, the very peak of wit, such are her giggles and guffaws. In the end I board the canoe on dry land and demand to be pushed in. After an hour or so of nervous flapping and wobbling the going improves and my mood lightens. After several hours we come to a big lake. I am at the front of the pack when I make an ostentatious U-turn and start paddling the other way, towards the start. As I pass the other canoes, the occupants turn their heads and look to me for an explanation. I bide my time and then say, 'It's alright. I left something in the car.' I am alone in being impressed with this tomfoolery.

We stop to eat something and rest. Fixed to one of the trees is a memorial to John Paul II, who used to muck about on this river when he was a lad. By all accounts JP2 was a popular pope, and by all accounts the Poles were rather proud that their man got such a big job abroad. I understand their pride but wonder if it sometimes goes too far. I mean, if the Poles are prepared to commemorate a river John Paul once jollied on, what else are they prepared to commemorate? Is there a memorial on the forecourt of John Paul's preferred petrol station in Katowice, and another outside the supermarket where he got bitten by a dog as a teenager? I keep such thoughts to myself, where they are undoubtedly better off, and instead watch Tony swimming pedantically in his Y-fronts. I am invited to take part in a tree-climbing competition – Marietta promises it will be another 'real experience' – but I refuse. My reasoning, happily shared, is sound enough. 'Look, there are things we are better at, things we are worse at. I happen to be bad at Polish and lovemaking and climbing trees. Because I am not totally without a spirt of adventure, I am happy to give Polish and lovemaking a go, a good go even, because even if my attempt is unsuccessful there is no chance that I will die or break my neck. The same cannot be said of climbing trees.' By the time I have reached the end of my reasoning, the competitors are out of earshot, are at the top of the tree celebrating their ability and supremacy and daring, comparing grazes and routes, pointing out landmarks in the offing – the Palace of Culture in Warsaw, Brandenburg Gate, the docks at Gdańsk. From where I am sat, the view is just as memorable.

After the day's paddling, we go to a traditional village for a traditional meal in a traditional restaurant. I enjoy the *golonka* (pork knuckle) for the first twenty minutes but then grow tired of the thing. I try and hide what I've left under my sour cabbage. To encourage digestion, I get a bit of political talk going. I turn to Dominic (Tony and Marietta's son) and say, with my tongue in my cheek, that communism was a good thing because it provided equality. Dominic snorts. 'Sure there was equality. Everyone was screwed.'

8

What would you say if I said that I often think about kissing you?

29 May. I miss my mother. Because without her my life lacks the pleasure she gives, and there is no replacement for that pleasure. New friends and new experiences, as well as alcohol and cigarettes and all that rot, are poor substitutes for a mother's love. I am not a person inclined to solitude. I can cope with it, and sometimes aim for it, but raised on love as a child, and then carried through on it into adulthood, it comes as a harsh ration to be without it now. I don't always feel this way. Days and sometimes weeks go by without my feeling any lack of love at all, for curiosity and novelty and adventure are themselves great loves of mine, and between them have the ability to support and nourish me. But moments come – this morning for example – when I would give my right arm for some time with my mum, not to gain anything in particular – news or food or reassurance – but to be thoughtlessly surrounded by her easy and lasting love. It's invisible, such love. It doesn't need form, or indicators, or obvious expression – though doubtless my mum wouldn't mind a few more postcards. It's invisible and yet I see it and need it and am better for it. A friend once told me about a book called *Promise at Dawn* by Romain Gary. The book's main idea is that a child will spend the rest of their life searching for a love that lives up to the one given to them by their mother.

With this in mind, I am almost certainly barking up the wrong tree by looking for love in bars and pubs and discos and other such juvenile places. I'd be better off asking Tony and Marietta to put me in touch with any single mothers they know. But say I did ask Tony and Marietta and they did put me in touch and I did enter a relationship with a single mother able to love me as my mother did when I was a child, what then? If history were to repeat itself, I would spend the first stage of the relationship being generally defiant and obnoxious, before escaping abroad at the first opportunity. No, it's a bad idea. It wouldn't work. A mother is only able to love like a mother when they have no choice in the matter. As a result, the only mother in a position to love me like my mother is my mother, and I can hardly go out with her.

1 June. Anita invites me to meet her halfway. When I arrive she is drinking pink lemonade and doing paperwork. I order nothing, just sit next to her and lean backwards into the sun with my eyes closed because I feel awful. Minutes pass, and then several more, and just as I begin to make my peace with the fact that we have nothing to say to each other, she asks what I want to do before I depart. It's daft, and pompous, but all I can do is quote William Blake, because I love the lines and they are as true as anything else.[19]

'I kind of meant what do you want to do in Poznań before you leave,' she says.

---

[19] 'He who binds to himself a joy / Doth the winged life destroy. / But he who kisses the joy as it flies / Lives in eternity's sunrise.'

I smile, still with my eyes closed, still leaning backwards so my hungover face is in the way of the sun. What do I want to do in Poznań? I want to express my feelings for you, Anita, which are outgrowing, it feels to me, the present shape of our relation. Because we can't always do what we want, I say: 'I would like to spend an entire afternoon walking this street, back and forth, until I know it like the back of my hand.' I smile again, laugh almost, thinking how little I know the back of my hand. 'And then I want to photograph all of Poznań's churches, for some are plain and others monstrous, and then I want to visit all of the city's statues, to learn what Poznań chooses to remember.'

Anita looks at me, or at least I think she does, and says, 'Well you can do those things alone, so please go ahead.'

And then I let it go, let it out. I take a mental run up – while she sips her pink lemonade – and then say, 'But in fact the first thing I want to do is ask you something.' She says nothing. I take a deep breath, a deep cliché breath to buy time and draw composure. I guess this is the end of fear.

'Anita. What would you say if I said that I often think about kissing you?'

'I would say stop thinking about it.'

2 June. Down in the courtyard there is a step that gets the sun for a good portion of the day. I go there this morning with green tea and two rolled cigarettes to move on with Laurie Lee. I am reading his *As I Walked Out One Midsummer Morning*, which recounts the author's teenage jaunt from Gloucester to Spain in 1936 or so, on the brink of that country's civil

war. My favourite bit in the book so far is when the author's landlord in London, having seen a poem of Lee's in the newspaper, says to him, 'I didn't know you had such beautiful thoughts.' Every few pages or so I pause to watch a tireless ant for some minutes, or to drain the pool of sweat that has formed between my foot and sandal. A dog enters from the street with the intention of pissing on as much of the milieu as it can manage. It is pursued by its owner and best friend. 'Daisy! … Daisy! … DAISY!' Daisy pays no attention; I'm quite sure she would answer back if she could: 'What now, woman? Can't you see I'm busy?' More than anything else, it is such moments on the step, or at the kitchen window, when a happy inertia keeps me still and quiet and ponderous, that make me feel at home in Poland, rather than away or apart or merely passing through. Odd that *a part* suggests inclusion, whereas *apart* – so nearly the same – means the opposite.

3 June. To the step once more, where I take the sun and read. Laurie isn't as good today, and nor is his landlord. I resent the sweat that pools between skin and sandal. The tea is bitter (I left the bag in too long) and the courtyard smells weakly of urine. I was here yesterday and felt fine, glorious even, wanting nothing. Today I could stamp on the ants and want everything.

5 June. I enter a room on the sixth floor of the university's humanities department and there listen to the poetry of Vona Groarke, who I know loosely from my time at Manchester University, where she writes poems about the rain and Gary

Neville. I enjoy the reading. It is a bit like being in a yoga or meditation session. There are all these words buzzing around, like soothing gentle flies, landing on shoulders and earlobes before leaving via a window. It is nice to be led out of my own world of words (both said and unsaid) and into someone else's, someone who makes word-worlds for fun, for a living, for life. I reproach myself between poems. *Why don't I listen to more poetry?* I know that it does me good. I know that it removes me and improves me and makes me feel better and calmer. And yet I never make it a recurring thing in my life. Instead, in the gap provided by poetry's absence, I routinely poison myself until I can't think or talk in order to spend the next day in a state of subdued idiocy, a lazy moronic torpor, of which no good comes, of which no good *can* come. Yes – I will drink and smoke until the cows come home (and even after they've come home) and will do so knowing that such behaviour will make me worse, make me dull, make me ordinary and idle, but I won't listen to poetry for twenty minutes twice a week. Gosh no. Hell no. Poetry's got nothing over petty intoxication. Fool.

After Vona has finished her reading, someone asks about her writing process. She says she's suspicious of anyone who says they require certain conditions in order to write – ambient music, chai tea, a mistress – which encourages me to raise my hand and remember out loud the words of Mark Twain, who said he was unable to write unless he had a cigarette in one hand and a cup of coffee in the other, a remark I reckon unusually funny, and one that isn't a million miles from my own thinking on the matter. At the end of the event I speak to the Polish professor that had chaired the reading about whether I could be of use to the department. She asks me to be more specific (which strikes me as impertinent), so I say something about being English and coming from England and being able to speak English (things that were sufficient to get me a job at Cream Tea), and therefore a potentially vital additional to the Department of English Philology. Professor so-and-so clears her throat or stifles a laugh, then encourages me to visit her during office hours, before rushing off down the corridor in pursuit of the poet, having given no indication what those hours were, and where that office was.

6 June. Anita comes over to the flat. We share a beer and revise fruit and numbers and the words for frost and spring. Despite (or perhaps because of) the confidences that were shared the last time we met, when I said that thing about thinking about kissing her, things feel no easier between us. Indeed, I am in a hurry to be rid of her. I feel anxious, quietly beside myself, at ill ease. But why? Why this fearful state? Jenny said that I just need to relax and be myself. But I *am* myself. How can I be otherwise? Myself is nothing more or less than the sum of my thoughts and words and behaviour at any given moment. To become self-conscious and timid is not to depart from one's personality, but to show another aspect of it. She says she has to go. She stands, adjusts a few things, buttons a few others, clips this, tucks that, but doesn't otherwise move. She is unquestionably ready to go but instead of going she just sort of stands there,

hands together and chin down. Her inaction might be a gentle, passive invitation to kiss her, or hold her, but then again it might not, so I err on the side of caution and move past her and lead her out of the flat and down the stairs to the building's entrance. At the threshold, having considered a dozen alternatives, I offer her my hand, as if she were a functionary or a friend's aunt. She refuses it, thank God, and says goodbye another way.

9

Do you want to go to Gdańsk?

8 June. A friend sent me an email a few days ago. I'll paraphrase it: 'Ben. Your campervan didn't start. I don't know what's wrong and I'm not interested to be frank. I missed the ferry. I'm not taking the van to Spain as planned. I've booked a ticket to Poland instead. Can I stay for a few weeks?'

Richard is a nice boy. He is dead against all forms of tribalism – nation, religion, race – except when Arsenal are playing. Given the choice, Richard wouldn't have an identity at all, would rather be recognised as a nameless sack of atoms due to expire *circa* 2060. He is a recovering academic – hence his whimsical arrival on my doorstep, which we celebrate with duck and beer at the café on my street.

'What do you think then?'

'Bit overdone.'

'I mean Poland.'

'It's alright.'

'It's alright? Aren't you meant to be a professor of political thought?'

'I'm on holiday.'

'You say the van didn't start?'

'Fate.'

'My dad said it was a flat battery.'

'Depends how you look at these things.'

'How do you look at the forthcoming referendum?'

'Not voting.'

'You're too aloof to vote.'

'Let's not do this. How's your duck?'

'My duck is voting to remain in Europe.'

'Your skin's crispier. Give us a bit.'

'No. Do you want to go to Gdańsk?'

'Gdańsk?'

'Yeah.'

'North, right?'

'Yeah. On the Baltic. Home of Solidarity.'

'Who?'

'Trade union. Brought down the Iron Curtain.'

'Fair enough. When?'

'1980s.'

'I mean when are we going?'

'Tonight. Jenny's girlfriend is there. Her friends are having a party. We're invited.'

'So let's go.'

When we arrive at the party in Gdańsk the host is barbecuing in the living room, which is also the kitchen and bedroom. We are instructed to sit somewhere and eat something and watch out for the rat. We chew the fat over dinner – Poland doesn't have a middle class because it never got around to it; Polish donuts don't have holes – then play a game called Psychiatrist, wherein one member of the party is sent out of the room so the others can contract an invented condition that the returning psychiatrist must diagnose by interviewing the sufferers. When I am sent out as psychiatrist everybody starts suffering from being me. I ask Richard if he is happy. 'When people like my Facebook posts,' he says. I ask Pawel if he is good looking. 'Not at all,' he says. I ask Jenny if his condition gives him pain. 'I would put money on it,' he says.

I spend dawn on the balcony, above the old tree and the playground, opposite a thousand neighbours, watching night calling it a day. I have not slept, am not ready to do so. It is six miles to the centre of town. I leave a note, step over Richard, quit the flat, down the stairs. The sides of the high residential blocks are covered with murals, fantastic ridiculous depictions, epic abstract flat-faced portraits. Together they make a marvellous exhibition, out here in the suburban sticks, miles from polite society, from sanctioned gallery space. A good kind of art, the better for being out of place.

It is 6.30am and already hot. I feel good despite last night's intake. I follow a construction worker out of the estate and across a bridge over the railway, where I pause to look and smoke in the early sun, unfelt by most of the city. A minor station below. *Gdańsk Wrzeszcz*. I'm glad I didn't arrive there. I wouldn't have known what to say. I find a main road: its six lanes are still stretching, still yawning. The road seems to run beside the old shipyard into town. I'll keep it in sight, that I don't miss my mark. I buy a bottle of water from a baker, use the toilet in a neighbouring hotel, then smoke again in a children's playground overtaken by high grass. I continue to the Polytechnic University, sit on its front steps, watch students arrive one at a time, here, judging by the last-minute notes and the gulped energy drinks, to sit an exam. I am not fit for examination. I would collapse under the weight of the lightest enquiry – of my knowledge, of my intent, of my worth. Back to the main road. The cranes of the shipyard grow greener by the minute. The clock towers of the old town rise with each step, the slow effect of my pedestrian approach. I listen to the sound of my progress, of my tread, and remember Laurie Lee and that walk of his through Spain, on which he was always in need of a drink. I come to the city.

By now it is too hot to stand, so I sit in the shade of a church and watch it receive a wedding party. The church is the biggest building I've seen in Poland. Its recipe (for we should remember it is a confection rather than something sent from on high) called for a billion bricks, a million back-breaking shifts, a thousand fatalities. The priest arrives behind time and switches outfits in the car. I think of Clark Kent becoming Superman in a phone box.

I walk the length of a pedestrianised street (Długa) then through a hole in the wall and onto a river or canal, once a lifeblood but now mere scenery, a cute excuse for waterside ice cream and coffee. A few cafes are putting out menus and ashtrays. I take a seat at one and there watch an old-fashioned ship being set upon by old-fashioned tourists, to be taken down the river or canal and into the Bay of Gdańsk, where the first moves of the Second World War were made. My situation is nice enough, what with the water and the gentle weekend commotion, but all I can think of is my fatigue and the heat. I eat a breakfast of eggs and olives and toast, then sit motionless until the waiter tells me to order something else or move on.

Whatever gumption I had at dawn has gone. I need a place to sleep, to lie down at least, but Gdańsk has no such places, no six square feet in the shade, and so the city becomes a perilous place, a sauna with standing room only. Yes, it has tall and slim Dutch-seeming architecture but what good is architecture if it doesn't facilitate my recovery? Yes, it has thin, uneven streets where you can get amber keepsakes and complicated coffee, and yes it has churches to die for, and yes it has authentic women sat on pavement crates selling plucked chickens, but does it have a cool park with a few benches and some privacy? I search in vain for a place to capitulate but everywhere is open for business, all space is accounted for, including the Hilton hotel, where I enter and ask for a nap. There's room at the inn, she says, but you'll either have to check-out in an hour or check-in in six.

Then I find a park. I'm being unreliable. It is less a park and more a bit of grass between busy roads, but for me it might as well be Eden. Never has a place benefited so much by comparison – by comparison to every other plot of this poaching metropolis. I am due to meet the others at 1pm by Neptune's Fountain. I set an alarm then sleep in the shadow of a billboard promoting sun screen. I am woken not by my alarm but the heat. My fingers are sunburnt. Dark orange homeless faces eye me as I come around. I watch them target passers-by for cigarettes. They don't ask those that look well-off but those that don't, knowing something about the mechanics of compassion. I shuffle back into the shade. The feeling of being trapped outdoors, of heat and fatigue, and the knowledge that I'd brought it all on myself – this is Gdańsk. I'm sure it has a history but for the time being I couldn't care less.[20]

I go to Neptune at one. By two it is clear no one is coming. My phone has an alarm but not the ability to reach out to others – I'm unable to roam. I go east without purpose until I reach a celebration of gay pride. The celebrants are fenced in, boxed in for not thinking straight. I photograph the unnecessary quarantine, and the hundreds of coppers manning it. There must be five police for every proud person. What on earth do the celebrants have up their sleeve to warrant this level of containment? Then a few hundred straight-talking Catholics arrive to demystify the situation. They get as close to the pen as the Law will allow, then start carrying on like football fans in the face of the opposition: the martial chants, the mean routines, the open spleen. Odd to get so worked up by a peaceful minority. I am tempted to get among the strait-laced gang and ask a few questions, but then wonder what sort of questions my limited Polish would enable me to ask. *Are you not gay? Are you not happy? Are you not happy because you are not gay?* Instead of going behind enemy lines I enter the pen, join the encamped. I accept a

---

[20] The city was Polish from the 980s, then Danish, then Russian, then Prussian, then French for about a fortnight when Napoleon was in town, then German, then an independent quasi-State under the auspices of the League of Nations, then German again when Hitler decided he needed more *Lebensraum* in the east. Danzig became Gdańsk after the Second World War, a name it's gone by ever since.

rainbow flag from Janek, slip it through a button hole like a poppy, then borrow his internet so I can contact the others and discover where I'm meant to be.

I'm meant to be at the European Solidarity Centre, down by the shipyard. I find my friends outside of said, beneath a monument that is both cross and sail, god and work, old man and sea. Nobody asks about my walk, or my suffering, or my nap in the shade of a billboard, or my rainbow flag, or the priest that got changed in the car. Nobody asks a thing. My return to the group is as unceremonious as my departure from it. My fatigue and hangover have sufficiently subsided to allow me to move around the museum with genuine interest and enthusiasm for about an hour, in which time I learn that John Paul II got shot in the face and instead of being angry went to visit the gunman in prison to tell him not to worry about it, that it was water off a duck's back, which seems a pretty noble and mature thing to have done, which is why he was the Pope I guess, because he had that sort of thing up his sleeve, that kind of extravagant, inexplicable decency in him. I also learn that when Poland played the Soviet Union at the 1982 World Cup, the two teams were squaring up in more senses than one. In 1982 Poland was still under the thumb of the Soviets. Martial law had been imposed in Poland less than a year earlier at the behest of the Soviet Union, chiefly because Lech Wałęsa and his unmerry men (i.e. the Solidarity trade union) were doing their best to bite off the aforementioned thumb. All of this was reduced and sublimated to a football match, which ended in a nil–nil draw by the way, a stalemate which suited neither country. Beside the Pope and the football, I see and read plenty of things during my lap of the museum, but only the odd name and the odd date have taken root, and what good are they in the long run? In truth, the museum offers an overdose of information. One needs a week, a month, a lifetime to process it all. Instead one gets an hour, and so moves quickly, scanning and snapping, grabbing and gawping, aware all the while that the bulk of their download will be forgotten by dinner.

The city is better by night. The cobbles are softer, the crowds gentler, the terraces and patios more inviting. Only a few hours have passed since I thought the city hellish. I've had a nap, drunk some water, eaten a fish, taken on a bit of knowledge. As remedies go it's uncomplicated, and yet I feel like a different man on this second lap of town. The buildings are more obvious in the dark: Gdańsk is a mongrel city, drawn from Europe's wide example, from Holland and France, Belgium and Italy, anywhere but Germany in fact.[21] The atmosphere is urbane and sophisticated. A barrister walking his dog. A singer on a boat. A fiddler under a bridge. A pair of professional women sending the wine back. Everything is lightened in the dusk. Gdańsk – unbeknown to itself – is playing a late hand to win me over, or so it feels.

---

[21] When the town was rebuilt after the Second World War the consensus among the planners and architects was that it could look like anything but Germany.

10

I'd rather be a man of the world than a man of merely England

10 June. We sit outside a fashionable vegan restaurant in deckchairs wrought from rhubarb. She eats curry, I eat pâté and pickles. It is the first time we have been alone since she briefly kissed me when I tried to shake her hand. I remain unsure in her company. I eat the pickles painstakingly and think of casual things to say. There is a moment when, done eating and having mounted our bikes, our pedals knocking, jostling, flirting, I could conceivably move a knight into harm's way, could move my eyes closer to hers until they're as close as they can be, and then let physics do the rest, but I don't. Instead I pick up a pawn, waggle it briefly, then put it down again, and the moment passes, the window closes, the game freezes, and we go off – she easily, I with difficulty – in opposite directions.

11 June. I meet Richard at a bar called Tandem, a small place off Saint Martin, where an international meeting is held every Wednesday. Upon entry we are given stickers to indicate which languages we can speak. Most of those present are wearing four or five stickers. Even Richard requests three – unprecedented for an Englishman. While I attempt to negotiate a second sticker on account of my Polish, Richard spots someone with a Chinese sticker and heads over for small talk. I take a seat on the edge of things and study myself. One sticker. What's the point? I peel off my ice-breaker and put it in an ashtray. I would rather be a man of the world, blind to flags and boundaries, than a man of merely England. I regret doing so immediately, because people have started to approach Richard with friendly and interesting questions, having spotted his fluency in English. His enjoyment is unabashed. I have never seen him so happy, so popular, so in demand. It's difficult to watch. A small queue has formed to speak to him, as if he were a version of Harry Potter. I go back to the doorman issuing stickers and demand another orange, another stab at England, then get among it. I mingle with a British-Indian (his appellation) called Shanks, who doesn't like the Polish food (too starchy) nor the weather (too inconsistent) nor the language (too much). I mingle with Piotr, an ebullient local, who invites me to his house for board games and *smalec*, which he cannot believe I haven't tried. (*Smalec* is lard, which is why I haven't tried it.) I mingle with Sam Wilson, a tall, handsome, United States of American. I mingle with a Norwegian who is studying dentistry. I mingle with a Mauritian, and a Russian, and a Dane, and am warmed by the indistinct chaos of it all, warmed to see Poland – so often reckoned closed and grey – a leaning tower of Babel, half-cut and catholic, loose-tongued and all over the place. I buy a round of vodka shots for this rum league of nations, for all the do-gooders and rascals, all the Yanks and Finns and Chinese-Canadians, all accidentally gathered in Poland this June. *Na zdrowie!* The shots rise and fall. The call comes for more. Because I'm feeling mawkishly global, I oblige. My second purchase draws a round of applause – I am Gorbachev whipping away the curtain, Blair pacifying Ireland, Woodrow Wilson announcing his fourteen points, each one pointing us in the right direction, to love and life and hygge and Zen. And where is Richard? Where is my indisputable brethren? We were born in the same hospital, mere moments apart. We were put in neighbouring incubators to relax. I turned my head to weigh up his humanity (6lb 4oz). He was asleep, snoring. I tapped on the dividing plastic, the invisible barrier that kept us apart. He turned to me. He looked familiar. Even then I knew we'd one day be in Poland together, raising glasses and voices, raising a rabble, feasting on life, apparently adults but still indisputably infant, our arms in the air, our arms about each other, about the others, about the world. Here he is, 30 years later, stood on a table dancing like a robot. By now he has nine stickers on his blazer and I've two on my forehead, and yet when we are finally put in a taxi by Shanks and Piotr neither of us can say where we're going in any language.

12 June. I wake up at 6pm. I was due at work two hours ago. I send Tony a message: 'First chance to contact. Obviously I'm not there. No good excuse. Will call later to explain. Am very sorry.' I had also been due to meet Anita at lunchtime. I wanted to talk to her about being bad at chess. I call her and explain there was a problem with my phone. Was it drunk again? she says. I feel ill and weak and angry and ashamed. To have let down Tony and Marietta, to have missed Anita, to have got into such a state again. There's no sign of Richard. He might have woken me up before he went. I go outside to the front of the building to stand in the sun and smoke the remaining cigarettes from last night. The sun makes me think of Diogenes, the Greek cynic. I should take a leaf out of his book. He lived in a barrel and wanted nothing more than peace and quiet and a bit of sun now and then. I was told by a friend (who died soon after) that I had the world at my feet and it looked that I meant to leave it there. I don't think there's any more of the world at my feet than the next person's, but whatever is there, and there must be something, I'm not so much leaving it as spitting on it. Or so it feels this evening, having missed what I've missed, having let down what I've let down – and for what? A bit of bogus bonhomie? Sometimes I tell myself such binges are a way of staying sane, that there's something cathartic about them, something necessary, that they aren't all bad. I tell myself that maybe letting people down, and letting yourself down, is the price we pay for moments of unusual emotional weight. However inelegantly, pathetically, destructively and painfully, being unreasonably drunk strips us back, down to our essence, so we might weep and hug and reminisce, and dance and laugh and long, so we might feel fully alive, fully sensible, fully vulnerable and fleeting. Being unreasonably drunk is a bad way of getting at good things. Maybe. Sometimes. In the last of the day's sun, I send the same text message to several people I love, about wanting to live in a barrel like Diogenes, hoping, I guess, for affection and consolation in reply. My dad replies with a link to a barrel that's for sale on eBay.

15 June. It is my last day at the school. I am rested and clear-headed – an out-of-body experience for me. For once, the lessons are something to relish rather than survive. I'm in a playful mood so I climb under the table, bang on the window, sit on the edge of my seat and throw my hand up desperately in a bid for attention. I am pretending to be Nella. The class know what I'm doing. They know what the game is. Everyone is laughing and smiling apart from Nella, who pretends to be deeply offended by it all. And they are listening too. I know they are listening because when I make a mistake on purpose – 'I bang the window, present simple, I banged the window, past simple, I was banging the table, present continuous' – they are quick to correct me. 'Past continuous!' they shout. When I quit being Nella they make me do someone else. I choose Lucas, the devil-child whose good behaviour of late can only be explained by absenteeism. He doesn't flinch. He takes it in his stride. He doesn't blush or balk or bark or bite when I make stupid faces or poke people or take their pencils or randomly walk out of the room or pick my nose or heckle the teacher or feign stupidity or foster rebellion or draw inappropriate things on the white board with a permanent marker, a swastika for example, or mammary glands. Then Lucas decides enough is enough, that I need some of my own medicine. He puts on my jacket and my sunglasses and says, 'Hello my name is Ben and I am from England and I can't speak Polish but everybody knows this because it is *very* obvious.' This gets applause from his classmates. 'Sometimes I must leave the room and be lonely for five minutes because in my opinion the children are *too* bad.' He's revelling. I don't mind. He can say what he wants if he says it like that. The others in the class watch through their hands. Olivia, hardly a stranger to misbehaviour, can't believe what she is seeing. Lucas writes a few Polish words on the board – the words for road, bridge, pasta – then asks the class, '*Please* help me. Polish is no easy. How *do* you say this words?' I bring the curtain down on Lucas's performance when the words he writes on the board – judging by the reaction of the class – become unpleasant. I tell Lucas that I prefer Lucas how he is, rather than how he isn't. He doesn't let it show but I can tell the remark sneaks under his defences and makes an impression. I can see a little bit of pride in his face, in his eyes. He's fighting back a smile. The class has run over by five minutes. The children waiting outside are doubtless wondering what the hell's going on in there. Lucas comes to me with the dog-eared sheet of A4 on which his behaviour is monitored. If he is too frequently bad then his parents are informed. I write that he was very good, then correct this to *is* very good. He offers a fist-bump then walks out of my life, and I can't help but look upwards and thank God. Following Lucas' example, Martyna offers a fist-bump and asks if she was good. Very good, I say. Then Maciej wants to know if he was good, and Marcin, and Julia and Nella. All very good, I say. Paulina wants to know if she was good then gives me a plant to mark the end of term. Just a small thing. Had she known that it was also the end of my teaching career it might well have been bigger. In any case I am touched by the gesture. Olivia is the last to file out. She doesn't want a fist-bump or an appraisal – she knows too well what she is. Instead she pauses in the doorway and turns to me and almost makes me cry by saying, 'You are very good.'[22]

---

[22] I later discovered that Paulina had issued half-a-dozen such plants that day, which altered the quality of the gesture somewhat. Just about everyone got a plant, including Marietta's father, who's not even a teacher.

11

Do you want a job making fish and chips?

16 June. 'Ben.'

'Anita.'

'I want to ask you something.'

Okay … 'Sure.'

'I don't how to put this.'

Holy cow she loves me. 'What?'

'Do you want a job making fish and chips?'

Do I want a what? 'Say that again?'

'I need someone in the kitchen.'

'Bloody hell, Anita.'

'What?'

'Nothing.'

'For the summer.'

'Where?'

'A place by the river.'

'Fish and chips?'

'Uh-huh.'

'At what rate?'

'As quickly as possible.'

For the love of God. 'I mean how much is the pay.'

'Ten zloty an hour.'[23]

---

[23] This is more or less the minimum wage, about £2.

'You know I have no experience?

'It doesn't matter because you're English and it's fish and chips.'

'You know fish and chips isn't something one has in the blood, right?'

'What?'

'It isn't a hereditary sixth sense unique to the British.'

'Julia says it will be fine.'

'Julia?'

'My boss. That's her there. She's coming over now.'

'For a blood sample?'

'Try not to say anything.'

If anything, Julia shows even less interest in my working background than Anita. It's perfectly obvious she's only bothered about one thing – my origin. I reckon she'd put a rabbit in the kitchen if it could prove it was British. I say: 'Doesn't this contravene equality legislation, Julia?' She shrugs and tells me to practise peeling potatoes over the weekend. Anita looks happy.[24]

18 June. The bar is on the east side of the River Warta. Hence its name: *Brzeg Wschodni*, East Coast. Two old freight containers – one for the bar and one for the kitchen – have been placed perpendicular to each other in the grounds of

---

[24] I was happy as well. Sort of. I had been planning to get a job for the summer that paid the minimum wage in order to gain a truer taste of the cost and standard of living in Poland, and thereby better understand why so many Poles (6 million) have left the country since 2004. This was my opportunity.

a rowing club. An artificial beach has been fashioned and deckchairs planted so customers can pretend they're not 200 miles inland. This summer will be the venue's second season. Last year the kitchen served good but complicated Middle Eastern food that nobody knew what to do with. I suppose the chef was Iranian, with hummus in his blood. I sit down in one of the deckchairs and wait for the barman to arrive and open the containers. It's peaceful. There is a delightful absence of children. For this reason alone, I decide, East Coast is objectively a nicer place to work than the Cream Tea School of English.

Then I start working there, and my decision falters. My first task is to peel 30 kilograms of potatoes. I am established in a small no man's land between the containers. I have a stool, a bin for skin, a pan of water for rinsing and cooling sore flesh, and one of the fifteen kilogram sacks. The first potatoes take five minutes apiece, a rate which, if maintained, would see me still at it next Tuesday; but by the end of the first hour the peeler is a feature of my hand, a sixth digit, an extension to the articulacy of my body. Soon I am peeling a spud every five Polish seconds. My task is simple enough to allow the mind to go elsewhere. Damned are those whose labour asks just enough of their minds to preclude it from escaping. I take advantage of my freedom and count to 100 in Polish, in time with the peeling; each stroke a number, apart from the difficult numbers like *dziewięćdziesiąt-dziewięć*, which sometimes require four or five strokes, and on the odd occasion the whole potato. Then Philip arrives. Philip's the head chef. When I forget certain numbers – *trzydzieści*, *szesnaście* – I call to Philip for clarification. He doesn't mind. He must be a father, I think; he's used to ignorance. Bored of counting, I play a word association game, starting with peel: John Peel, Robert Peel, the repeal of the corn laws, lbw appeal, appellation, *comment t'appelles-tu*, Tutankhamun, *Carmen* by Bizet, bidet, David Baddiel, Baddiel and Skinner, potato skinner, me, and so on. Without meaning to I always return to myself. Perhaps I'm a closet narcissist. After three hours I ask Philip if I can take five minutes to think about where my life has gone wrong. He says not yet, *nie jeszcze*.

You can see a fair amount from the bottom. What you can't see are those at the top: five hours into the shift and still no sign of manager or owner. Anita will probably make an appearance when the staff begin to have ideas above their station, and Julia when there is money to be counted. I am growing more cynical by the minute. After years trying to forget him, I start to remember Marx. All those terms that used to appeal to me when I was a retail assistant, or a waiter, or an intern at the *Chichester Observer* – surplus value, alienation, means of production – are newly alluring.[25] By the middle of the second sack, by kilo 24, I am having revolting daydreams, am privately unionising, am fantasising about another great potato famine. I lift a spud aloft as if I were Hamlet and it were Yorick's skull. This potato, and this one and this one – they all have nothing to do with me.

---

[25] Two things led me away from my teenage commitment to Marxism: my first encounter with income tax and the discovery of the means of reproduction.

I am a cog, a tool, a means to an oily end. The potato has become my starch-enemy. I shift between despondency and stoicism, thin and thick skin; between ironic satisfaction (look at me peeling spuds! What a hipster!) and simple discomfort; between a sense of novelty and a sense of nothingness. During the final stretch of sack, I can't bring myself to count or play games. My mind goes nowhere, bound to its lot, hitched to its maturing distress. The bar staff pass my station every so often, to fetch something from the storeroom or to smoke in the small garden area behind the kitchen. They don't make a fuss of me. In hospitality the turnover of staff is high and quick because the work is inhospitable. It is a transient community. That isn't to say there isn't kindness or intimacy. There is. But it grows slowly. It comes over weeks and months on the job, of mutual hardship, late nights and double shifts, common complaints and shared foes. If the kitchen porter survives a month the bartender will offer a cigarette. I quit smoking two days ago for the nineteenth time.[26] I am fully persuaded that the habit is wholly asinine. But now, here, smoking seems less ridiculous. It isn't the nicotine I crave but the pause, the brief halt, the ceasefire. I call for a cigarette break. Philip approves, only I don't have any cigarettes. I ask Philip if he has a spare and he nods to his pack on the shelf. While smoking I consider throwing in the towel but then decide that I've made my bed and although it smells of fish and misery, I'll sleep in it for now.

---

[26] Mark Twain said, 'It's easy to quit smoking; I've done it a hundred times.'

It takes me another hour to finish the second sack. I think of Alan Sillitoe's novella *The Loneliness of the Long-Distance Runner*, then begin composing a sequel called *The Loneliness of the Large-Amount-of-Potatoes Peeler*, which I will self-publish in my mind.

When I finish at 7pm I make a note of my hours on a timesheet that's kept in the locker. Anita sent me a message earlier saying she would be coming to the bar at 8pm. I drink a couple of beers then leave at about 7.45pm, which is telling. I meet Jenny and some others at a place called Sphinx, an ugly chain restaurant on the corner of Saint Martin and Gwarna that is showing the football. There I spend the rest of the day's wages, a pint of beer costing an hour's work. I share my complaints with the table. I show the irretrievable dirt beneath my nails. I speak at length of the dull ache at the base of my thumb. Then I go home and sleep like I've never done before.

19 June. Sensing my beef with potato, Philip asks me to remove the bones from five kilos of cod. I pretend not to understand what he has said, hoping he'll give up and do it himself, but to no avail. This much can be said for the task of boning cod: it will stop you picking your nose. It is a deeply fiddly business because the skeleton of your average cod is all over the place, is about as regular and intuitive as the Polish language. It can seem that each of a cod's bones has been positioned arbitrarily, with no regard to how it relates to the others, how it is part of a team with a shared goal. Frankly, it's as if God gave up on cod. Because a cod's bones are wherever they please to be, the task of removing them requires a more or less constant mental engagement. No chance for the mind to wander so much as a metre. As well as being mentally strong, a decent boner must be dexterous and fastidious and imaginative and quick. Never in my whole life have I been all those things at once, and now here I am being told to be all those things for six hours on the spin. The fish isn't the only one whose spine has seen better days. The work is actually back-breaking. Even with the fish laid out on an upturned pot, to sufficiently get among it one has to stoop, which soon becomes painful. If I tell myself to just think of the money the pain is even worse. I don't want to get too cod-philosophical about it, but in order to remotely enjoy the work I have to put myself in the shoes of my subjects, to take an interest in their lives – had they loved? did they know happiness? – and their deaths – who caught them? to what bait did they succumb? By enlivening the fish, by fleshing them out, I'm able to lessen the pain of unpicking them. For about five minutes. After which point it's dreadful again.

20 June. After my third shift Anita asks for a word.

'How is the work for you, Benjamin?'

'*Skomplikowane.*'

'Please don't speak Polish. Is there a problem with something?'

I want to take her face in my hands and bring it towards me and say: *YOU. You are the problem.* Instead I say: 'I guess with everything really.'

'I don't understand. Is there a problem with the equipment or the staff?'

'It was the potato peeler on Saturday. It gave me a blister here and a bruise here. And then it was the fish on Sunday.'

'What's wrong with the fish?'

'What's wrong with the fish? The bones are everywhere for a start. The skeleton of a cod—'

'Cod?'

'*Dorsz.*'

'Ah.'

'The skeleton of a *dorsz* is … Oh forget it. I'm not used to this sort of work. It will take time to adjust.'

'But we don't have time.'

'Don't we?'

A pause, then a half-smile. 'Just try not to take so long, okay?'

12

I said nothing at all

22 June. It's meant to be my day off but I go to East Coast because Anita asked me to be there between 10am and 3pm to receive a delivery. When I arrive I'm surprised to see her there. She explains that Julia had slept on the matter and decided I wasn't up to the job, that I needed to be more fluent in Polish to watch a man deposit twenty boxes of tonic water and fruit juice. I ask why she hadn't called me. She says: 'I was thinking you could keep me company.'

The idea of keeping Anita company isn't as appealing as it might once have been. Whatever is going on between us has become sufficiently confusing as to be stressful. We kissed once about three weeks ago but since then have reverted to shaking hands. When I heard a lyric of Leonard Cohen last night about the gates of love budging an inch and then nothing else happening, I nodded dementedly in recognition. I am almost fully persuaded that Anita isn't interested in falling in love with me. I'm okay with the fact. I'm phlegmatic. These things happen.

We stand in the sun, waiting. There's no room between us. She looks the only way she can look. No amount of fatigue or disarray could lessen the effect of her face. I want to say: 'For God's sake do you understand the extent to which you occupy my mind?' Instead, I put my hand on her side, just above the hip. It takes some nerve to do so. I want her to read the gesture as a polite appeal to come closer. She looks at the hand and makes a doubtful, disappointed noise, as a mother warning a child. It sounds like a perfect rejection. The noise humiliates me in the strictest sense of the word – I am made humble by it, low, weak, small. I had anticipated her doing nothing, but I hadn't anticipated her being disgusted. Her reaction suggests that she's sure: sure that she doesn't want my affection, sure that I won't be getting hers. I withdraw the hand, wish I never had it, say absolutely nothing as loud as I can. Some minutes pass – ten? fifteen? – and then she says: 'I am going to my home town this afternoon. Do you want to come? We can take a bus.' I have to supress a laugh. There's a danger that my response will be impolite. I take a moment, sigh ostentatiously. 'Sure,' I say, matter-of-factly. After handling the delivery, we go to eat something vegetarian. She eats quickly, anxiously. I'm halfway through my okra and buckwheat when she abruptly stands, announces she must go straightaway, and then does so. I make no protest or query. Suddenly alone in a shopping centre food court, involved with a meal I had pretended to enjoy in order to appear virtuous, I realise that I am always confusing the verbs *chcieć* and *lubić* in Polish – that is, what I want and what I like.

23 June. I work with Kuba in the kitchen. Kuba is eighteen, looks about seven, and is somehow related to the owners. He tells me that he is a keen historian, likes volleyball, and is 'unprecedentedly fluent in English'. I become fond of Kuba the moment he agrees to bone five kilos of cod. While he gets on with that, I chip potatoes. There is a contraption for the chipping, which is nice. I used to consider myself a luddite but now I advocate mechanisation come what may. There aren't customers so we're able to talk as we work. I decide to treat Kuba less like a person and more like a learning resource.

'Thanks for learning my language,' I say.

'Don't sweat about it.'

'Can you tell me about the partitions of Poland?'

'Yes.'

'Go on then.'

'Prussia, Austria, Russia. Late 18th century. Poland was off the map for 124 years.'

'Who is your favourite Polish historical figure?'

'Piłsudski.'

'Again.'

'Piłsudski.'

'Slower this time.'

'*Pi – ł – suds – ki.*'

'What did he do then?'

'He beat the Russians.'

'At what?'

'At what? Jesus and Mary. Let's say it wasn't gymnastics. Can you pass me the— Thanks.'

'When?'

'Nineteen-twenty. Outside Warsaw. The miracle on the Vistula I think it is in English. He believed in an omnifarious Poland.'

'A what?'

'A multicultural Poland – a home of nations, recognising numerous ethnic and religious nationalities.'

'How did that go down?'

'He died of liver cancer.'

'Anyone else?'

'Andrzej Tadeusz Bonawentura Kościuszko.'

'And what did he do?'

'He beat the Russians.'

'Am I right in thinking the best way to secure your favour is to beat the Russians?'

No answer. Kuba is hell-bent on the fish. I understand what he's going through.

'I understand what you're going through,' I say.

'I don't doubt it. It's because you understand what I'm going through that you were quick to land the fish on me, so to say.'

'Well you better get used to it. There's plenty more where that came from.'

'You mean there's plenty more fish in the sea?'

'I suppose.'

'That would have been a wittier thing to say.'

'I've better things to do than be witty.'

'Like work in a kitchen in Poland for 8 zloty an hour?'

'Ten zloty an hour.'

'What?'

'Ten zloty an hour.'

'Why am I being paid less than you?'

'Because you're seven years old and know nothing.'

'Oh, I see. Forgive me for asking.'

'I'll speak to Anita about it.'

'Thank you.'

'No bother.'

'By the way.'

'What?'

'Aren't you supposed to be voting in a referendum today?'

'I don't want to talk about it.'

I don't want to talk about it because I'm supposed to be voting in a referendum today. What I went and did was book a flight for the day after the vote – for tomorrow morning, crack of dawn – believing the referendum was on 24 June. By the time I'd realised my mistake it was too late to organise a postal vote or sort out a proxy. Granted, I could have booked another flight, but the prices had shot up and I was scheduled to work and, to be frank, all the polls have been calling a Remain victory so I figured it wasn't as if my straw was going to break the camel's back. I've had a shocker, I know. Whoever invented democracy – Herodotus? Cleisthenes? – is probably turning in their grave. Having said all that, if one considers what the American satirist H.L. Mencken said about democracy – that it's a pathetic belief in the collective wisdom of individual ignorance – perhaps I'm doing the result a favour by keeping my ignorance to myself.

On my way home from work, I stop at Freedom Square. I don't normally stop at Freedom Square in case I get offered another teaching job. A crowd has gathered to enjoy an arts and culture festival. Perhaps feeling a certain amount of guilt about not voting, I decide to behave in an overtly political manner by asking 50 people what they would do if Poland were in Britain's shoes. Opinion is split. Some want to see Britain leave and so doing provide an example to Poland. Others say they would vote to leave because the EU is just Germany really and hadn't Germany been a bully for long enough? One young man, with his tongue in his cheek, says he'd vote to leave because there's too many British immigrants in Poland. On the flipside, there are plenty who think the idea of leaving preposterous, given the opportunities and investment that come with membership – Poland, let us remember, has had more money from the EU than any other member state, and by some margin.[27] One intrepid woman asks for *my* opinion on the matter, and soon wishes she hadn't. I say something about the people who go on about sovereignty but who are unable to nominate a single piece of EU legislation with which they disagree. I say something about the misinformation and propaganda – the claim that Britain sends £350 million a week to the EU, the poster that said all of Turkey was going to move to Britain. I say something about the democratic process, and referendums especially, which are by their nature divisive and reductive, which reduce wild complexity to a straightforward binary, which distil a thousand unknowns down to a straight yes or no. I say something about the bigger picture, the underlying principles, the overarching ethics, about the long-term virtues of cooperation and sharing and

---

[27] Poland has seen a good slice of the European Regional Development Fund because, in short, a lot of its regions needed developing.

integration, and the need to remember what a disunited Europe is capable of: 100 million killed in the last hundred years because civilians were goaded by patriotic fruitcakes to loathe each other. I say a lot of questionable, sentimental, half-baked, half-arsed, self-serving, well-meaning *stuff*, and I say it because, when I had my chance, when push came to shove, I said nothing at all.

13

The morning of Britain's detachment (London)

24 June. I go to the airport at dawn. I sit at the counter of a café-bar and watch the rolling Polish news. I deduce that the official result isn't in yet but that the final poll, like the ones before it, had the UK staying in Europe: I got what I wanted without breathing a word. I finish my cappuccino, my strudel, my *woda niegazowana*, then board the Wizz Air flight to London Luton.

At the border there are two men in uniform. One wears glasses and the other wears a turban. They are cut from different cloth but both have proper London accents. 'What was the score?' I say. The one with the turban looks up from my passport.

'We're leaving, son,' he says. 'Welcome home.'

I hadn't planned for it to happen like this. I hadn't planned to get the news off the country's doormen, surrounded by incoming Poles, whose relocation to the UK was one of the reasons there'd been a referendum in the first place. If I were a novelist and had set things up so the protagonist learns of the result on the border alongside 200 implicated Poles, it would seem indelicate penmanship, too bad to be true.

I buy a couple of yesterday's papers – the *Mirror* and the *Guardian* – because today's aren't out yet. I read them outside the terminal on a bench. I am shocked and want to know how it happened. A bus is idling nearby. 'Last call for London Victoria!' That'll do. I pay 50 zloty for a ticket: that's five hours' potato work for a one-hour bus ride. And for what? I feel like I'm bound for a funeral, or if not a funeral then a wake, or if not a wake then some kind of socio-political purgatory. The coach driver has the radio on, but the awful reception obfuscates reports of a fallen pound and sunken shares.

I get off at Finchley Road. I have nowhere to be. It is early, 8am or so, but already warm – people go to work in confident tops, without contingent cardigans or brollies. I find an ordinary café – there's no other sort on the Finchley Road – and there take a coffee on the pavement and continue with the papers. It is a cliché to talk of a palpable atmosphere, but I like clichés on occasion so will come right out with it and say the atmosphere is palpable. Never have I heard a city's conversation so dominated by one topic. A lorry passes noisily.[28] Hope Construction, it says. There'll be want for their services, I'm sure.

I walk the short distance to Swiss Cottage. There is a market in train outside the theatre: Italian cheeses, Turkish bread, Corsican olives, French pastries, Korean hand rolls. That'll be right, I think, on a morning like this, Swiss Cottage showing off all its culinary variety, all its tasty diversity, the yummy goodness of sharing stuff. And then, outside the public library, where the written word is pooled for the common good, a paddling pool has drawn a crowd of bright

---

[28] How else is a lorry to pass? Gingerly? Like a mouse?

fearless children of all kinds, whose splashing and chasing is lifeguarded by various smiling parents. Yes, I think. That will be right. Go on London. On the morning of Britain's detachment, show me the good-looking, heart-warming, encouraging charm of community.

I enter the library to use a computer. Everyone is after the same thing. *What now? Can I still go on holiday? What if I've changed my mind?* Cameron has already resigned. Fifteen minutes before I entered the library, while I'd been watching London's children splish-splashing in the sun, Cameron had given a parting declaration outside 10 Downing Street. He said he could no longer lead the country without doing it injury. Further injury, more like. Cameron had said he'd stick around to steer the ship no matter the result, but he was plainly only joking. A queue has already formed to jump in Dave's grave. Gove and Boris and May are all chomping at the bit. For my money, Boris is bound to win by a head, if only on account of his being bigger than most. I read that the pound has taken its biggest pounding since Black Monday in the 80s – down 10 per cent in a matter of hours, which although generally disastrous does mean that I'm now on £2.20 an hour. The old lady to my left wants to know if the Channel Tunnel will close, while the old lady to my right is ordering something from IKEA while she still has the chance. I sit back in my chair and stare at the BBC homepage, waiting for breaking news that it was all a joke.

The Bank of England doesn't appear to be trembling. It appears as taut and august as ever. Its columns haven't buckled under the pressure. Inside there must be madness and panic but the bank's face is brave. I am handed a copy of the *Evening Standard*, and then a slim emergency version of the *Financial Times*. I sit on the front steps of the neighbouring Royal Exchange and read. Traditionally, it is on these steps that royal proclamations are delivered by a herald or crier. Perchance someone will emerge with a trumpet presently and announce the rebirth of Great Britain. The steps are replete with workers coming up for air. Sandwiches and salads, shop gossip and referendum talk, all watched over by the 1st Duke of Wellington, up on his horse, fresh from duffing the French at Waterloo. To my left is a statue of James Greathead, railway engineer, who spent his life building bridges, while above Bank junction, where Princes and Poultry collide, a rainbow flag has been raised, which I read as a gesture of tolerance and inclusion.[29] It feels to me that all things are pointing to the bigger story, that all items are commenting on the context. I half expect an Anglo-Polish couple to break up before my eyes.

I wait for a friend in the courtyard of the Guildhall. It was here, just hours ago, that the London referendum results had been announced. London's rump had voted to Remain, but its outskirts – Romford and Dartford and Barking and Basildon – had not, which needn't surprise us, for doesn't it make sense for the periphery to be on edge, to be unsure? Whereas the centre is secure, immured, the edge is by its

---

[29] The flag had nothing to do with the referendum result. Pride festival was scheduled for the next day.

nature precarious. The Leave campaign, mendaciously or otherwise, promised control, assurance, revival. If you don't have such things, or feel you don't, you are wont to want them. What's more, the edge is a contested space. It attracts the newly arrived, who, in good faith and in all humility, compete gamely for its fruit, its school spots and surgery slots, its work and shelter. For many on the edge, the status quo left much to be desired, and here was a throw of the dice. But that's there and this is here. This is Zone 1, kilometre zero. This is the country's heart of gold and it isn't easily perturbed. A marching band is due on court, to serenade a round of graduating cadets, and so I'm told to clear off, whether I like it or not.

14

I just don't want any more to come (Boston)

26 June. I go to Boston, Lincolnshire, an old market town of about 40,000 people, because I read in a newspaper that it has the highest concentration of Leave voters and the highest concentration of Polish migrants, and I fancy the two are connected.

At Boston train station there is a Thai restaurant where the ticket office used to be, and a sports day is in progress in the playing field of a neighbouring primary school. Egg and spoon race, sack race, long jump – the competitive din is lovely and menacing; I can't hear a child for the children; it is all chorus, a shared noise that sounds like fun and fear at once, the sort of noise you might expect from Britain's most unsettled town.

West Street is known as East Street round here, because it carries a number of businesses run by Eastern Europeans. I pause outside one such business to look for evidence that Boston is the least integrated, most murderous, most obese, most European, most anti-European town in the country, as the papers have claimed, but I can only see John. John isn't obese. He wants some milk and reckons I might be the man to get it for him. He's just been hit by a car. Just? I say. 'Well, a few months ago,' he says, 'but I'm after some milk at any rate.' I make to go in for his milk but he stops me. He's remembered something. 'Make sure it's soy milk, yeah?'

Opposite the shop is the local cinema. *Independence Day 2* will be showing tonight. The timing of the film's release is appropriate. Nigel Farage, one of the Leave campaign's chief stokers, called 23 June Britain's 'Independence Day'.[30] Next to the cinema is The Corner Shop. I go in and find things I recognise from Poznań. So here is a British institution – the corner shop – filled with tasty Polish sausage and chocolates and salty snacks like *paluszki*. The owners might have called the shop *Polski Sklep*, like most do, but instead opted for something quintessentially British – a small nod to the host nation. I quite like the compromise. I buy a few chocolates then ask the cashier for hotel options. She says she has never required a hotel in Boston and doesn't know anybody who has.

In total, there are eight or nine shops on West Street called things like European Delicatessen or Euro Stop or Global Quickie. Almost invariably, the shopfronts display both European and British flags, in an effort, one assumes, to demonstrate that although the produce is from elsewhere, the owners aren't arrant nationalists, here to impose their culture on England's green and pleasant land one bag of shopping at a time. Outside Global Quickie I ask a tough-looking, Slav-seeming lad where I might get a bed for the night. 'Try The White Hart, pal. It should be a girl called Marianne on reception. You can tell her Kieran sent you. She'll like that.'

---

[30] In *Independence Day 2*, London is destroyed by those it won independence from twenty years earlier. Just saying.

It is Marianne on reception, and I do tell her. 'Ordinarily I'd say pay no attention to Kieran. He's a bit of a knob. But on this occasion, he did well.' Marianne proposes a single room for 50 quid with breakfast and a view of the River Witham. 'The River Witham was busy until it wasn't,' she adds. I take the room, if only for Marianne's manner of putting things. I reckon all history should be presented in such a way. King George VI reigned until he didn't. Poland did communism then stopped. Before Europeans went places and called them things like America and Australia and British Hong Kong other people already lived there but that didn't matter. That sort of thing.

I drop my bag in the room then go to the bar downstairs. I ask for something local, but the most local thing was brewed in the Netherlands.[31] Both the barmaids voted to stay in the EU and think that anyone who didn't is a bit daft. Coincidentally or not, both girls live outside Boston in cute villages with professional families. 'We're not yellow-bellies,' one says. Yellow-bellies? Is that a political term? 'It's what the locals are called,' clarifies the other. 'I don't know why they're called that. They just are.' *They just are.* Again, I'm impressed how things are put around here. It reminds me of the Leave campaign. How will Britain benefit from detaching itself from the biggest trading and security block known to man? *It just will.*

---

[31] As it happens, Boston is closer to Amsterdam than it is to most of the United Kingdom, which makes me wonder what the word local means.

Across from The White Hart is a pub called The Moon Under Water. George Orwell wrote an essay about an idealised pub called The Moon Under Water. I try to recall the details of Orwell's pub now but can only think of liver-sausage sandwiches and stout on draught.[32]

I stick around the bar at first, looking at the old photos of Boston that decorate the walls, back when the bellies were a brighter yellow and the sky a brighter blue. I want to ask questions of the old boys around me but don't have the nerve. My sense of decorum isn't as sharp as it might be, but I know nonetheless that it's a faux-pas to go up to a stranger and ask how murderous they are. So I fabricate a pretext, something plausible and disarming, then take it to a native-seeming couple in the corner. I tell them that I'm considering property in the area because I've just landed a job at a nearby university.

'Which one?'

'Oh, you know. The nearby one.'

'There ain't a nearby one.'

'Well it depends how you look at it.'

'Does it?'

'Anyway, what part of town should I avoid?'

'All of it,' he says.

'You'll want to buy on this side of the river,' she says.

---

[32] I looked up that essay by Orwell. In The Moon Under Water 'everything has the solid, comfortable ugliness of the nineteenth century.' I fancy Orwell might have voted for Brexit.

'And what side is that?'

'*This* side.'

'Yeah but what's that – left bank, right bank?'

'This isn't Paris, duck.'

'Just don't cross the river!' he says. 'Then it doesn't matter about names, does it. Take it from me, if you cross the river you'll be beeling.'

'I'll be what?'

He lowers his voice, comes in closer. 'There's a load of gofers that side.'

'Golfers?'

'*Gofers.*'

'What Jim means to say,' she says, 'is that in certain parts of town – not to name names but Fenside especially – there are people new to the area.'

'It's not about your Polands and Latvias,' he says. 'It's *gofers full-stop.* You can't 'ave a town the same for hundreds of years and then double it with gofers in the space of ten and reckon it will have nothing to say about it.'

'And what does it have to say about it?'

'It said it, duck,' she says.

'You said it, duck,' he says.

'Sorry?'

'In the *referendum,*' they say.

'Independence Day?'

'It weren't Independence Day,' he says. 'It were waking up day.'

'And now we're awake will the gofers be sent back to … *Gofer-land?*'

'Look,' he says. 'Don't misunderstand me. I've had enough of that. I don't want anybody to leave. I just don't want anybody else to come. The gofers work, they go to the church, they have a drink, they take the kids to school. Fair enough. It is what it is. But if you're asking me by means of a plebiscite if I wouldn't mind a bit of control going forward with regards the numbers, then I'm sorry but it's a no-brainer.' He finishes his pint. She finishes her half. 'And I'll tell you another thing, young man,' he says.

'What's that?'

'I better get home or me wife will kill me.'

We all have a laugh at that.[33]

I err right (topical) then enter a pub called The Folly (ditto). I have to spend at least a fiver if I want to pay by card, so I buy a round for a guy called Ratty and a few members of the pub's staff that have just finished a shift. I ask Ratty the best way to spend an evening in Boston.

---

[33] This is not exactly how the conversation went. Of course not. I did use that pretext and it did get us talking about this and that side of the river. They did call each other duck quite a bit, and they did once or twice employ terms that baffled me. And the sentiments were more or less as presented: the speed at which the town had changed was felt to be too fast; they didn't desire anybody to be repatriated but given the choice they would like the British government to have more control over levels of immigration from the EU. The couple were warm, conservative, well-meaning. I liked them. For the record, I've still no idea about the etymology of the term 'gofer'. If you can enlighten me, do get in touch.

'Just don't get murdered, mate. Boston's been voted the most deadly place in Britain.'

'By who?' I say.

'What?'

'Voted by who?'

'Nah I mean – not voted but selected like. Statistics. Boston has the most murders per capita.'

'I see.'

'But I can't help wondering, like – when they are working out the per capita statistics, yeah, do they take the murdered person into account? Because if they didn't that'd be unfair.'

After thinking about this for a while, I still don't know what to say, so I ask: 'Who's committing these murders then?'

'Nobody knows. But I know what you're thinking. You're thinking it's gofers. Well it ain't. Or it ain't only. Some of 'em are dodgy. Like people from anywhere. To be honest, I'm no angel myself. That's not to say I've murdered anyone. I wouldn't wanna be just another statistic.'

Ratty drinks up and leaves. After a minute's silence to mark his departure, someone says: 'Statistics have also shown that Boston is the fattest town in the country. But I don't believe it. I don't ever see obese people.'

'That stands to reason,' says someone else. 'They're all inside. That's why they're fat.'

'Yeah maybe they *can't* go outside,' says someone else. 'Because they don't fit, like.'

I like the notion of somebody being so big that they don't *fit outside*.

'Yeah, maybe,' comes the reply, 'but, like, if they're all stuck inside, then how can the statistics have seen them?'

For me, this is a terrific question, and it gets a terrific answer.

'Because they're so *big.*'

My attention is drawn to three boys sat watching the football. I fancy the boys are Polish, so ask if I can sit with them for the second-half. Turns out they're from Lithuania and only arrived yesterday, having been sent to Boston by a sort of work abroad agency that must know something about where the jobs in the UK are. The boys will be working in a factory for the summer before going home to begin their studies. They will be sharing a room in a three-bedroom house on the wrong side of the river, with eight other EU citizens. They explain that by working in Boston for three months, they'll be able to focus solely on their studies upon their return. I ask if they can tell me more about their new jobs, but all they know is that they'll be working in a factory outside Boston and that they will earn £6.70 an hour. 'People think we are being paid below the minimum, yes? They think we are taking jobs because we will do them for peanuts as you say? But it is not true.' I say that although it's true they'll be paid a legal wage, it will be the minimum wage, when really such jobs should be paying more in real terms in 2016 than they were twenty years ago, not less. The fact that migrant workers will accept the minimum wage and less favourable working terms and conditions, in a country whose unions and parliamentarians and what-not have been fighting for better wages and better working conditions for centuries, gives people cause to link the mass employment of EU citizens in the UK with falling standards of living. When it's apparent I've thoroughly taken the fun out of our encounter, I leave the boys to it and move on to Goldfinger.

I go to Goldfinger because Ratty had said it was the only place open late on a Sunday. I buy a drink then go outside to smoke. The narrow lane smells faintly of excrement. A yellow-bellied plumber is up a ladder trying to unblock the pipes. At the bottom of the ladder is a younger apprentice holding his nose and hoping for the best. A woman walks past and shouts up to the plumber that her husband was always blocking the toilet. 'This ain't the Gents!' says the plumber. 'Oh no – this is the Ladies! They put too much crap down the loo!' From his accent the younger man seems to be Polish or thereabouts. So here is the fabled Polish plumber driving down prices and causing a stink. He is dressed quite smartly given the job in hand. I go up to the apprentice plumber and ask if he's an apprentice plumber.

'I'm the owner of this place,' he says. 'It's my toilet.'

With the old yellow-belly above pushing and pulling and keeping us all updated – 'Cor, I've never had this much before' – Henrik and I have a little talk. I ask how integrated the town is.

'You get fights,' he says. 'Last week I was attacked by a group of Lithuanians.'

'And where are you from?'

'Lithuania.' Blimey. 'They get jealous. I own this place and the club next door and they work in a packhouse.' I ask

if the natives fight the gofers. 'You know, it is normally the
Polish fighting the Lithuanians. It's easier for them to fight.
They have more in common. When they can be bothered
the English prefer to fight each other, but mostly they can't
be bothered because they're not working in the factories or
in the fields. Sometimes the foreigners will fight the English
if the English go after the foreign women. But it's a nice club
generally, you should come.' I thank Henrik for his invitation,
then call it a night.

15

An important day for the whole country

28 June. The last time I was on stage I was fourteen and in a boyband. We were called 4U2NV. Before *X-Factor* there was a talent show on the BBC called *Steps to the Stars*, hosted by H and Claire from Steps, a pop group successful for about eleven weeks in the late 90s. We were the first act on the first show. You might say, without straining the truth too much, that we launched the modern talent show. For doing so, we got two days off school to film in Manchester. There were eight of us in the band and, on paper at least, we all sang and danced. But when it came to the BBC recording, it was decided by all stakeholders (including my mother) that it would be best not to turn my microphone on and position me somewhere near the back. If you are one of those people that like to watch utter crap on the internet, our BBC performance is on YouTube. We didn't get past the first round.

I mention being on stage because I'm due on one tonight. My friend Magda sounds like a member of the British royal family and works for an organisation (FKA) that puts on cultural events in Poznań. Magda got wind of my reverse-migration and asked if I'd be willing to read a selection of the notes I'd made so far in front of a small audience. Magda said she'd chair the meeting, that there'd be a venue, that a photographer would be present, and that a few pop-up signs promoting the host organisation would be popped-up to suggest formality and professionalism. With this evening's reading in mind, I spend the afternoon refining observations about coleslaw, pedestrian crossings, and looking out of the window, then send the text to Magda to be translated.

It is an important day for the whole country. It is the anniversary of the 1956 uprising in Poznań, when unhappy workers were put down by 400 tanks. The day before, on 27 June, a delegation of workers from the Cegielski Metal Works had been sent to Warsaw to negotiate with certain Party helmsmen. The workers were given short shrift. The following morning, the staff back at the factory in Poznań downed their tools and made their way to Stalin Square to let their disaffection be known. Doing so, rumours circulated that members of the delegation sent to Warsaw had been interred, and before long a section of the crowd had stormed the prison at Młyńska Street. Hundreds of prisoners were liberated, while arms were seized and distributed among the furious. Meaning to nip the rebellion in the bud, 10,000 troops and 400 tanks turned up to the party. About a hundred of the workers were killed in the resultant fighting. The prime minister soon arrived and announced that any person that raised a hand against the people's government would have that hand chopped off, which went down well I'm sure. In the wake of the uprising, hundreds of arrests were made. Although the government failed in its attempts to coerce the detainees into stating that the strike had been provoked by foreign agents, this became the official government line for years to come. In 1980, one of the first actions of the recently formed Solidarity trade union was to raise a monument to the events of June 1956 in Poznań, so the official line could be monumentally corrected. The twenty-eighth of June is now a national holiday in Poland. Commemorative events take place each year. Consequently, as I prepare to take to the stage in a side street bar to address seventeen people on the matters of coleslaw and looking out the window, just around the corner on what used to be Stalin Square, the current Polish prime minister and his Hungarian equivalent are taking to their own stage to address a crowd of several thousand, all of whom would surely have been at my event had there not been a clash of dates.[34]

When I arrive at the bar (Andalusian Dog) I am nervous. I grow less so when it becomes clear how little Magda cares about how the evening unfolds. What if only a few people come? I say. Then they'll have more space, she says. And what if they find it dull? I say. Then they'll never bother you again, she says.

In the event, about 50 people turn up. Anita is not one of them. She said she'd come but she's said she'd come before and hasn't, as I've said I'd come before and haven't. Maybe our mutual unreliability is telling. Maybe it tells

---

[34] The Hungarian president was in attendance because Hungary saw its own share of strife in 1956. Thousands of Hungarians were killed in fighting, and thousands more fled as refugees. Taken together, the '56 uprisings were the first major test of Soviet control over the Eastern Bloc countries.

that we simply don't care enough. Anyway, Magda has said something and people are laughing, and now she is looking at me for an answer. I have to do something. I can't not react. If I admit I wasn't listening, that I was thinking about a girl who hadn't come, everyone will take me for a fool. 'Obviously,' I say, in Polish. *Oczywiscie*. People laugh. Magda frowns but moves on. I get away with it.

I read sections from my diary. Magda reads her translation after each one. The reaction to the English and Polish versions is identical – silence. Below is a very abridged version of what I read. It ought to have been very abridged when I read it to be frank.

1.   In my country we only have coleslaw, which, as I'm sure you know, is a raw salad of carrot and cabbage and onion, dressed with a bit of mayonnaise. I am very fond of coleslaw but in Poland the appreciation of coleslaw – or surówka, as it's known – is at another level. The first time I went to a big supermarket I was not surprised to see a special section of the supermarket's delicatessen offering a range of meats, and another a range of fish, and another a range of cheeses. I was surprised however to see a special section offering 50 versions of coleslaw. I spent half an hour trying to ascertain how the coleslaws were different from one another, which caused me to be late for a job interview.

2.   The large majority of Poles will wait for up to an hour to cross the road. It doesn't matter if a vehicle hasn't been seen in the area since 1962, still they will wait for the green man to signal his consent that it is now okay for them to cross and resume their lives. I have been told that Poles tend to be rebellious, quick to protest and disobey, and yet the average Pole will wait a month

before crossing the road. If the truth be told, I rather like this cultural trait, but fear it may be one of the reasons why Poland has never evolved into a global superpower. Simply put, its people are always at a crossroads.

3.   I see a lot of people looking out the window in Poland. It seems to be a kind of national sport. Even the children do it, animals also. I have never seen so many cats and dogs looking out the window. There is a man living opposite my flat who has been looking out the window for eleven years. (How I know this needn't distract us.) This man has seen the gradual gentrification of the street, the rise and fall of governments, the changing of 44 seasons. Without fail, every time I go to my window the man is stationed at his, shirtless and smoking, waiting for Godot or the Russians or winter. Sometimes, when he is called away on some piece of business, his grandson, a boy of eight or nine, takes his place. If the boy is unavailable, the budgerigar does it.

I'd hoped these readings might get the occasional laugh or the occasional noise suggesting recognition. As it was, I was forced to wade through the text in silence. Maybe the memory of June 1956 was on everyone's mind, weighing down the collective consciousness. Although the reading is over nobody is moving. Nor are they talking among themselves. They are still staring at the stage, looking at me, and then Magda, and then me again, convinced there is more to it, convinced there must be a final section that somehow rescues and explicates what has come before. Magda stands and gives me a little clap but it doesn't catch on. It's like everyone is asleep with their eyes open. I step off the stage and walk through the audience to the bar.

Walking home later, I stop on Plac Mickiewicza, site of the '56 disquiet. I join the crowd in waiting for an act to come on stage. I get talking to someone who tells me about an incident that had occurred earlier in the day. Along with the names of those who died in '56, the government wanted to read out the names of those 'murdered' in the Smolensk plane crash in 2010. The plane was carrying former Polish President Lech Kaczynski, and nearly a hundred other Polish politicians and dignitaries. The crash is believed by the current government – the Law and Justice Party, whose leader is the brother of the late Lech Kaczynski – to have been the doing of the Party's political opponents, namely Donald Tusk and the Russians. To read out the names of those who died in the Smolensk crash at a memorial event for those who died in '56, says my informant, would be to wilfully confuse the two tragedies, to co-opt and appropriate the latter's political and historical significance to service the government's conspiracy theory. It is the politics of remembering, she says. With that, the act everyone's been waiting for comes on stage. It's not someone reading from their diary, thank God. Instead, it is a ballet. The dancers are all in white, playing at war, gesturing at peace. The atmosphere is reverential.

16

I love Others. I am one, for heaven's sake

5 July. I arrive at work and find a note instructing me to have 30 kilos peeled by this evening. The prospect is so unappealing (if you will) that I make a desperate phone call to Julia, wherein I wax lyrical about a set of chips I ate the other day whose skin had been left on. Not only did leaving the skin on make the chips healthier and tastier and crispier, I tell Julia, it also made them more profitable because nobody had been paid to peel the potatoes. (I didn't eat such chips, but that's why we have imaginations, to spare us from grief.) Julia is prepared to give it a go. I celebrate my reprieve by burying the peeler in the garden. Then I get on with washing the spuds. I fill up the sink with cold water and then pour in a few kilos. I plunge my hands in the water and turn and shift my potatoes – yes, *my* potatoes – so they clash and rub and rid themselves of dirt. The gradual discharge browns the water until it becomes a muddy broth, wherein the spuds steadily ricochet, each coming-together prompting a partial cleansing. Running my hands around the opaque basin is like trying to read enormous, vivacious brail, its starchy signifiers hopping and dancing and evading comprehension. It's fair to say the experience of washing the potatoes is unexpectedly pleasant, and it makes me wonder if any task can be made remedial, restful, sensual, if one has a mind to make it so, before deciding, after washing the sixteenth, seventeenth and eighteenth kilos, that it can't.

Anita is here, for the record. We haven't spoken much since that time when she left me at the food court. We aren't cold with each other. We're friendly, professional. We're colleagues now, and I suppose that'll have to do. I'm not perplexed by her rejection of me. After all, I'm no Renaissance man. And even if I was a Renaissance man there's no guarantee I'd be irresistible. Consider the case of Leonardo da Vinci. Leo was arguably the most diversely talented person known to man – a prolific painter, sculptor, engineer, astronomer, anatomist, biologist, geologist, physicist, architect, philosopher and humanist – and yet he couldn't get a girlfriend for love nor money. You'd think if you were Leo all you'd have to do is show up to the date and put your CV on the table, but evidently not. Perhaps da Vinci spent so much time being diversely talented he was simply too busy to woo. I'd love to claim the same for myself, that I'm too busy being diversely talented to woo Anita, but the real reason things aren't escalating between us is there's an inequality of stature – that is to say, I'm just another person, whereas Anita isn't. As far as I'm concerned, there has been no miscarriage of justice – which makes the whole thing easier to deal with. In fact, I'm feeling so sanguine about the situation that when she occasionally comes into the kitchen for a chat – like now for example – I'm able to enjoy the exchanges far more than when I was after her heart. In a sense, I like Anita more since I stopped liking her, if you know what I mean.

'Are you happy, Benjamin?'

'Yeah, I don't mind making the salad.'

'I mean generally. Being in Poland.'

'Definitely. I like being away.'

'Away from what?'

'Away from the familiar, I suppose.'

'What's wrong with the familiar?'

'Oh, you know. There's something a bit repulsive about all familiar things.'

'That sounds severe.'

'I don't mean repulsive as in disgusting. I mean repulsive as in having the ability to repel. No matter if the familiar thing is sweet and wonderful and good, we are apt, after a time, to desire its opposite, to want the unfamiliar.'

'I see. And is there anything in Poland that's too familiar?'

'I'd say yes.'

'And what would that be?'

'I'm looking at it.'[35]

12 July. On the train back to Poznań from a neighbouring town, a pregnant academic invites me to the sixteenth conference of the International Association for the Study of Forced Migration she's on her way to. I like the sound of the conference – I'm a migrant myself and it's on my doorstep – and so when we alight at Poznań the three of us proceed to the appropriate university building on Plac Mickiewicza, where we are just in time for the welcome

---

[35] I was looking at a pile of cod.

reception. I help myself to canapés and wine and partly enjoy a pair of violinists working through a piece of Schubert. I am unable to fully enjoy the fiddles for two reasons: first, I wasn't subjected to a classical education and so have no idea whether the music has nuances or not, and second, I have to watch out for conference officials whose job it is to eject anyone that hasn't paid to be here. After the concert, I get talking with an English girl and a group of Italians. The consensus is that there's no wine left and it would be nice to go on somewhere. I extrajudicially appoint myself social coordinator and force a group of ten to migrate to Dragon, where we get a good table in the courtyard garden. When I'm finally asked about the research that I'll be sharing at the conference, I tell my story about meeting the pregnant professor on the train (and where have those two got to, by the way?) and not being able to fully enjoy the music. I'm asked if I plan to attend any of the lectures tomorrow. When I say that I couldn't possibly because I haven't paid anything, they all laugh and say not to worry, which is all the persuading I need.

13 July. I arrive during the morning break. Through the building's glass exterior, I can see steaming pots of coffee and ornate biscuits. I daren't go in. Yesterday's bravado owed to a disturbing hangover which made me careless. (It is easier to be bad when one feels so.) I draw back from the window and sit on a bench, where I read some abandoned literature about the conference. It would appear that much of it will be spent addressing the ongoing migrant crisis in and around the Mediterranean, which has seen hundreds of thousands of people attempt to enter Europe from Africa and the Middle East. I know a bit about the crisis. You'd have to be an ostrich not to know something about it. I know there are suspicions that some of the asylum seekers are actually charlatans jumping on the refugee bandwagon. I know there are concerns that it is overwhelmingly men of working age that are undertaking the journey, which might look a bit odd to some but makes sense to me: in short, men of that age stand a better chance of surviving the ordeal, and they know that in the event of asylum being granted they'll have the right to be reunited with their family. I know that reports of some migrants falsely claiming to be Syrian or younger than they are in order to receive favourable treatment are making it harder for people to warm to their cause. I know that my thinking on the whole thing is simple: anybody who pays a smuggler the equivalent of a year's earnings to attempt a potentially fatal crossing of an unforgiving body of sea in an improvised vessel so that life for them and their beloved might be less punishing is deserving of respect and sympathy and support. I also know that before my simple thinking is ten metres down the track it runs into a load of questions of a practical and philosophical nature. It's easy for me to say that anybody in need should be helped, but where do you draw the line? One way I like to think about the problem is to conceive of Europe as a house, a house that sits on a street that is the world. The word on the street is that the European set-up is decent: a better stocked pantry, bit of a garden, and maybe a pool. For one reason or another (rogue landlords, weak foundations), certain other houses on the street aren't in such good shape. They require more maintenance, there's less in the cupboards, and no central heating. One day someone from one of these houses risks their life by walking up the street (it's a dangerous street, full of sharks) to knock at Europe's door. They explain their situation, their motivation, their wish. I'm decent, they say. I'm human, they say. You might not be aware but it's actually pretty effing hard down the street, they say. I want to live here, they say. Europe shrugs, then says, 'Sure, why not, so long as you don't mind cutting the grass every other day and cleaning the pool once a week.' The next day there's another knock on the door, and the day after that there's another. Some of the European household start to feel that the door should be left open so there's no need to knock, while others want to fortify the property and evict the latest arrivals. In the meanwhile, with confusion and uncertainty rife, and while signs of damp start to appear on the walls and the basement is hastily converted into bedrooms, the knocking at the door persists. You're a tenant of this house. What do you do? For my part, I'd be tempted to move to another street.[36]

A bell rings. It must signal the end of morning break. Those inside are jostling about confidently, last minute

---

[36] Douglas Murray alludes to a similar scenario in his book *The Strange Death of Europe*. The gist of the book is that Europe is tired, vacuous and nihilistic, which makes it masochistic, gullible and guilty, and thus a danger to itself. In order to prevent Europe self-harming, Murray prescribes migration control, obligatory integration, and a Christian renaissance.

banter before heading to this room for that paper, or that room for this one. I am disinclined to ask for guidance from one of the volunteers, lest they start wondering why I haven't got a clue what's going on. In the end, I follow a brace of women up two flights of stairs and along several corridors, only to discover they have nothing to do with the conference. I head back on myself and find a lecture theatre wherein a discussion on how the countries of Europe (or their governments, rather) have responded to the aforementioned migrant crisis is in progress. It is generally agreed that Britain's response has been negligible and Germany's exemplary. The Polish response isn't mentioned at all, which is odd given where we are. The silence might have to do with the fact that when Poland was asked by the EU to accept its fair share of asylum seekers, it said, 'Nah, you're alright.' Poland's uncompromising stance will have come as no surprise to anyone even slightly conversant with contemporary Polish politics.[37] If Poland's refusal to take its 'fair share' was to be expected, less expected was the panellists' unwillingness to mention the fact. Surely it would have been both appropriate and salutary for Poland's attitude to migration to be discussed. *Discussed*, mind you, not rounded upon or attacked. After all, there are many reasons why Poland might be unusually averse to immigration, not least among them the historic tendency of other countries to

---

[37] To explain its negative position vis-à-vis refugees and multiculturalism more broadly, the Polish government claims that it is protecting Poles from both an imminent security threat and an unsuccessful social model.

invade, ransack and subjugate Poland whenever they felt like it. The title of a book by Norman Davies about Polish history – *God's Playground* – hints at the number of times Poland has been the site of international contests. If it wasn't Austria, Russia and Prussia taking Poland off the map for a century and attempting to annihilate its culture and language, it was the Nazis prospecting for an extended living room in 1939. If those two experiences weren't enough for Poland to grow somewhat cautious, somewhat cagey, somewhat paranoid regarding outsiders, then 60 years under the heel of the Soviet Union, which saw the country practically sealed off from the rest of the world, certainly was. When compared with Britain, which hasn't seen an invasion since 1066, Poland's unfortunate track record helps one understand why the country might be less than enthused at the prospect of being forced to open its doors to what is foreign and unknown. By saying all this, I don't mean to excuse Poland's position vis-à-vis asylum seekers and migrants. What I do mean to say is that a conference being held in Poland that is ostensibly concerned with issues of migration and asylum and tolerance and prejudice, really ought to have asked itself how Poland has behaved in relation to these issues and why it might have done so. All that having been said, it is worth remembering that I am an interloper at this conference, and that beggars can't be choosers.

We are dismissed. Walking south on Independence Avenue, I reflect on the matters at hand. It would be hard not to. I tell myself that when a person arrives in a new place, they come with a dowry of habits and manners, of airs and graces, aims and intents, beliefs and gods, foibles and fancies, and that these dowries are benevolent more than they are malevolent by a factor of a hundred. Then I tell myself that maybe it's easy for me to champion migration and diversity because I have never suffered by its hand, have never personally witnessed its uglier side – the clash, the clamour, the scrap, the tussle, the irreconcilable dispute. But then I tell myself that during my life I must have passed, crossed, needed, seen, heard and served *circa* 50 million people, and not once during all that crossing and passing and seeing and needing and hearing and serving did a single human being of any stripe or any land harm me or injure me or threaten me or impact my life in an appreciably negative way. What am I to do with this fact? I am to conclude that people are overwhelmingly peaceful, overwhelming good. My mother sometimes chastises me for trusting people I don't know and putting myself in dangerous situations. I can't help it. I'm convinced they deserve the trust. It is the same with migration, with multiculturalism, with the supposed threats and imminent dangers presented by Others. Others have never bothered me a jot. I love Others. I am one, for heaven's sake, and so are you. As far as I'm concerned, migration is the movement of decency, and always will be.

17

About lechery

17 July. I am speaking with a girl at Dragon about lechery. We fell on the topic because I was sat alone reading a book and the girl used to love going to bars on her own to read but stopped doing it years ago because she couldn't be alone ten minutes before being made to feel uncomfortable by a man. She is now of the opinion that it is unethical for a man in any scenario to look at or approach a woman just because they're attractive. Because this would make me unethical, and I'm not sure if I am unethical, I say: 'But people look at things. Buildings, nature, road accidents, paintings, other people. Aesthetically speaking, people are just things that can be looked at, studied, ignored, interpreted. Of course, people are sentient and have feelings, which complicates the matter. Landscapes and buildings can't let it be known if the experience of being attractive – of having people clamber over them, gawp at them, photograph them, merchandise them – is disagreeable. People are different. People can let it be known, and so the looker must listen and pay heed, must be sensitive to the degree to which the person they are looking at is made uncomfortable by their doing so. It can be hard to judge the degree to which a person is made uncomfortable by our looking, of course, which complicates the matter further still.'

At this point the girl looks at me (the pest!) as if to say: *and your point is?* 'My point is I don't think it is always unethical for one person to discreetly appreciate another, while admitting that it often is, and that the matter is complicated.' The girl laughs and then says: 'I am sorry but it is hard listening to a man talk about these things because frankly men haven't got a clue because they have never felt uncomfortable being looked at. However *discreet* such *appreciation*, it nevertheless reveals a basic instinct which more or less covers men in shame. Men fall on women as if by gravity. And so does their gaze. It is unoriginal, unflattering and, yes, basic. If you want to be impressive as a man, then do something else. Be un-manlike. Have different priorities, different sensibilities. Appreciate other things, be distracted by other things, compelled by other things, preoccupied by other things. Be otherwise attracted. That would be attractive!'

'So you're saying, in short, that men need to get over women?'

'Yes. Exactly. Then they might stand a chance of impressing them.'

20 July. The barman and I lie on picnic benches in the sun and smoke. At least an hour passes before a customer appears on the horizon. While I scuttle back into the kitchen to appear professional and willing, Lucas merely sits up, lights another cigarette, and resumes playing a game on his phone. It isn't until the customer politely asks Lucas whether anybody is around to pour a drink that he acknowledges his existence, and then only with a surly glance. Lucas finishes his cigarette, pockets his phone, hops off the picnic bench, returns to the bar and then cups a hand around an ear as if to say, 'I'm listening.' The customer, for his part, doesn't appear to be bothered by the horrendous customer service he's getting. If anything, he looks almost pleased with how he's being treated. When I mention the episode to Anita later, she doesn't understand why I'm bringing the matter up. 'I don't understand, Benjamin. What did you expect Lucas to do?' I decide that Anita's indifference to Lucas's indifference provides sufficient grounds to claim with some authority that the Poles, all of them, are not in the habit of giving, or wanting, customer service that might be described as bubbly.[38]

Anita says there'll be a party in the evening, that a DJ is coming from Berlin, that a famous Polish actor might turn

---

[38] Imagine a woman sat in a lay-by behind a makeshift stall selling strawberries. Imagine she's been sat there for days with her strawberries and not a single car has passed. Her strawberries are wilting. She is wilting. Her business is wilting. Imagine this woman staked her late husband's life insurance pay-out on the stall and the strawberries and the vendor's licence and the one-way bus ticket to this godforsaken lay-by. Imagine all this and now imagine that, lo and behold, a car pulls up, and out jumps a wholesome family saying things like, 'Gee could I do with some strawberries,' and 'What I wouldn't do for a couple dozen punnets of strawberries, ma,' as they approach the stall of the sad and lonely fruit seller. Now imagine the vendor not giving the slightest discernible toss about her sudden, miraculous, biblical change of luck, and you have an idea of Polish customer service. Not Polish hospitality, mind. That is a different matter. If you go to a Pole's house there's a chance you'll never get out. And if you do get out, you'll have put on a few kilos. No, the sort of behaviour shown by Lucas and the strawberry seller is reserved almost exclusively for the *customer*.

up, that the whole event is being sponsored by an ice cream company, that I'm obligated to wear a T-shirt bearing the company's witless mascot (an anthropomorphised ice cream), and that there's a strong chance we'll be very busy and I won't enjoy myself. In the event, she's spot on. Philip and I are flat out for hours. After the third or fourth of these hours, the workload starts to wind me up. I start to involuntarily kick and punch things, and, in delirious snatches, recite passages from a book by Roddy Doyle called *The Van*, wherein two mates in Dublin open a fish and chip van, grow increasingly sick of it, and then drive the bugger into the Irish Sea. Watching the chip oil froth vengefully, and bits of salt creep into a cut on my left thumb, I fantasise about doing similar, of somehow getting the container back on its wheels and pushing it into the Warta. Not that the party's guests seem to be having much fun. Their pleasure, if it can be called such, looks like hard work to me. The music is repetitious and so is the behaviour of those that have come to hear it. There is something mindless and robotic about the fun they're having. Maybe they all have tough jobs, or demanding relationships, next to which any trance-like experience is an indisputable tonic. I remember a Marxist, one of the Frankfurt School, saying that the culture industry is as much a factory as the metal works, wherein popular distractions are confected as nails and screws, as cakes and buns, each conforming to type, each to be gormlessly gobbled over the weekend before returning to work on the Monday. Anyway, less of all that because something's up with the fryers. They've given up behind our backs, called it a day in the middle of a large order, only neither of us noticed, which means that a load of cod and chips have been bobbing around in dirty lukewarm oil, drinking its slick yellow indecency for about ten minutes. It seems that the main power supply has gone off. Philip is in a panic. About two-dozen customers are waiting for their food at the counter and the orders are still coming through. Several of the two-dozen start firing advice at me in Polish – clean the sockets, reset the mains, rinse the fish, give it a whack: they might be saying anything. All I can do is smile and shrug and say, *Nic nie wiem, moje panie* (I know nothing, ladies), and then point to Philip. Despite knowing of our troubles, the bar staff are *still* taking food orders, so the gallery at the counter keeps growing. I feel uncomfortable being looked at. If only that girl was here to see it. I argue to close the kitchen. A closed kitchen, I say, is better than a bad one. My superiors disagree. Keep taking orders! Keep taking the money! The whole palaver is a potential parable, the story of a capitalist who kept on taking money for what they could no longer produce, before finally being set upon by unfulfilled customers and slung into the river with a bag of profit hitched to their ankle, to the sound of a DJ from Berlin playing robotically to no one. Oh, boy. Two quid an hour.

We get through it. It takes an intervention from Anita, and about two hours of hard work, but we get through it. Around 1am I draw down the shutter. Seconds later, someone has the cheek to knock on it and call for service. Neither of us moves. They knock again. Philip pulls up the shutter. It's the famous Polish actor. He and Philip talk in Polish. I ask Philip what the man wants and he says that the man is wondering if it's too late to eat something. Without thinking twice, I turn from the sink and say, '*Tak, późno, bardzo*' (Yes, late, very), but Philip is kinder than I am so tells the man it would be our pleasure. As I get on with the order, Philip tells me the actor's name is Andrzej Chyra. Despite not knowing the guy from Adam, I tell Philip I've never liked the guy's films and like them even less now, which makes him laugh. Anita drops in to take something from the communal locker. As she turns to leave she puts her hand on my lower back for a moment. I can't help but think about the gesture. Philip puts on 'Zadok the Priest' by Handel and we work for another hour then go home.

22 July. I write to Meg Dobson, a friend from university, requesting permission to bring a guest to her wedding. I have Anita in mind. I have Anita in mind because she put herself there. She put herself there by asking, upon learning of the occasion, if she could be my guest. You'd be right to consider this a further twist in an already twisty narrative that I would be wise to draw a line under, and yet before the words had even left her mouth, before her unexpected request had been fully voiced, I was imagining her looking glorious in red, with me on her arm, either arm, in red, at the wedding, in Yorkshire, as my guest, and saying: 'Yes, Anita, yes.'

18

I miss the bus to Auschwitz (Wrocław)

24 July. I look out the window and see broad beans climbing up a wall, old track stacked like forgotten waffle, a neon crucifix above the treeline, no hint of lift or lilt in the land, and then, beyond Leszno, just darkness and my reflection.

At Wrocław station, a pianist plays a nocturne. She has a vagrant at her shoulder, conducting and advising, skipping and dancing at her side. He is a nuisance, surely, but she glides on nonetheless, untouched by his performance, immured by the music. As she plays, her feet shift a skateboard to and fro. At the song's end, the man finds a coin from somewhere and makes sure the pianist takes it. Some scenes defy photography. Some scenes have to be told.

I move thoughtlessly towards the centre, as if drawn by a centrifugal force designed for tourists. I pass a woman selling flowers in front of a wound-up casino, then a Nespresso emporium, its halls decked with a billion capsules, pointless variations to keep pod lovers competing. I cross the road for a better look at a statue. Bolesław Chrobry is your man on top, your man overall, and I wonder what he did to earn his likeness in stone, and then stop wondering because it says on his plinth that he was king once. I'll struggle to remember Bolesław Chrobry unless I bastardise his name. I go for Coleslaw Chob.

The Monopol Hotel looks a class above. It boasts of being a Party hangout in the 70s, when blunt functionaries in sharp suits met here to talk shop. The receptionist gives me a form to complete. I'm asked to nominate my social class: working class, intelligentsia, nobility. It would appear the categories are mutually exclusive, that one can't be a noble peasant, for example, or an intelligent noble. I tick nobility for a laugh, then hand over the form. The rate is 370 zloty for a single. The receptionist enjoys delivering the price, enjoys giving a figure I plainly can't rise to. Perhaps it makes him feel better, or better off, to be associated with such a sum. I try at the Moon Hostel up the road, but it only accepts groups, a measure against dodgy loners who spend unfit periods watching coffee capsules in the rain.

It's 10.30pm and I've not eaten, so I pause my search and enter a place called Setka on the main ring road. I sit at the bar and consider my options. A flattering photo of each dish is displayed above the bar, doctored or workshopped to curry favour – *żurek*, *pierogi*, something that looks like dog food: vague brown chunks and bits of carrot in colourless jelly.[39] On my neighbour's advice I order *żeberka* (ribs) and a Tyskie beer. Marek is friendly. 'Have you tried *smalec*?' he says. I explain that I'm doing enough damage to my body as things stand, and don't need to introduce unadulterated fat to my diet. Marek listens to my explanation and then orders two portions. I hope to God that one's for him to eat now and the other's to take home and grease his bike wheels with. No such luck. To be fair, the stuff isn't bad. It has little nuggets of meat in it, not that I bother chewing; I prefer to get the

---

[39] *Galaretka*. Basically pig's head in jelly.

thing down asap, as an oyster. Satisfying some dark sadistic impulse that he was probably born with, Marek then orders me a plate of *śledź*, of which the less said the better.[40]

Marek says he knows a vodka bar I'll like. To get there we cross the old square, which, as Poznań's, has a striking town hall and perimeter tenements with elaborate façades. Marek says the city was put up in stages by Bohemians, Austrians, Prussians and Poles, then brought down in one fell swoop at the end of the Second World War, during the Battle of Breslau, as the German city was then known.[41]

Marek was right. I like the bar. Too much perhaps, because it's getting late and I still don't have a room. Each time I say this to Marek, he says, 'The hotels aren't going anywhere. Let's have one more.' With each one more my concern loses weight, so that by the time Marek leaves at

---

[40] Raw bits of herring, paddling in oil. It tasted like fishy *smalec*.

[41] That was the extent of my history lesson. If you'd care for a potted history, entirely strewn with error, then keep reading. If you wouldn't, forego the following. There was a Slavic settlement in the area from the 6th century. In the middle of the 12th century the Mongols turned up looking for a fight. They got one, won it, but didn't stick around for long. Then the Germans turned up looking for a fight. They got one, won it, then stuck around for 600 years. As the Soviets approached from the east in early 1945, the city, like Poznań, was designated by Hitler a *festung*, to be defended at all costs. It was all but obliterated during the ensuing Battle of Breslau. After the war the city became part of Poland under the terms of the Potsdam Conference, which was when the map of Europe was redrawn according to the whims and wants of Stalin, Churchill and Roosevelt. The city's new population was for the most part shipped in from Polish lands annexed by the Soviet Union in the east of the country. Phew. Get me a drink, Marek.

4am to go to work at a casino I've reached the conclusion that I'm better off without a hotel, that I'm better off staying here until dawn and then getting on with it. An English banker about my age sits at the table next to mine. He says his name is Charles and is in town on business. I ask him what he thinks of Poland. 'The women are all seven out of ten – it's great!' Charles wants me to know another thing, bless him. 'And you know another thing – they all find me funny – it's great!' When Charles goes out to smoke, I return to the bar to order something to eat. A guy turns to me and asks why he shouldn't kill me. From the look of him, the question isn't rhetorical. He's heard my accent and he's upset that I'm English. He's a cage fighter. He has scars all over his face and a shaven head. He reminds me of Begbie from *Trainspotting*. It's obvious to both of us that should Begbie wish to, he could significantly reorganise my appearance, or do away with it altogether. He gets a little closer.

'Why not I kill you? In your country they are killing my people.'

He's referring to a murder in Essex and a general spike in hate crime since Brexit, both of which I know quite a bit about. I think about challenging his perceptions, then stop thinking about it, reasoning that the last person who challenged this guy's perceptions probably no longer has perception. 'Why not I kill you?' he asks again. I say: 'Because I like Polish people and I like Poland and I haven't killed anyone. Now do you want a drink?' We drink a vodka together, then he pushes me away, but in a nice way. At this moment, I see Charles noisily entering the bar with a couple of girls. I intercept him, believing that if Begbie got so much as a whiff of Charles, all hell might break loose.

≈

I wake on the floor of a flat. The flat belongs to the grandmother of one of the girls that was with Charles. She is Canadian, or Polish-Canadian, studying in Wrocław for a term. Her grandmother is now in a retirement home. The balcony looks over a derelict building used by Spielberg in *Schindler's List*. That's what she says, handing me some tea. I stare at the derelict building, and the pupils playing basketball in the proximate schoolyard, and she says, 'Charles left his number for you.' I say, 'Well you know what you can do with that.' It is afternoon and she has to take a train so I'm hurried up and then returned to the street.

I am somewhere northwest of the centre. The streets take me to Budapest; they have that city's lapsed classicism, its dirty good looks. I walk east without purpose, across bridges, past islands, then enter a large civic building, the Ministry of the Interior, or similar. The place is rammed. Long queues are snaking everywhere. I ask a woman what's up and she explains that everyone here wants to be Polish. *Sorry?* They are Ukrainians seeking Polish citizenship, she clarifies. The sight of several hundred Ukrainians waiting for a stab at Polishness is beautiful. The scene has colour and severity; it is hopeful, restive, and all too human. The youngest children tear about on scooters, not caring a jot for their official identities. The woman tells me she is entitled to Polish citizenship because she has a Polish grandparent. 'Poland wants its blood back,' she says.[42]

I cross the River Odra then take a right on Oławska Street, which returns me to the main square. Just off the square, heading south, I trip on a pair of golden gnomes. The gnomes are pushing the same boulder in opposite directions. The small sculpture is called *Sisyphus*. The very sight of its implied futility makes me tired: I take a bed at the next hostel I come to. It's above a fast-food restaurant on the corner of a street named for Kazimierz the Great, an old monarch who was made tolerant by lust.[43]

I take a nap then go out for the evening. In a traditional Irish pub on Plac Solny, a guy sits next to me at the bar and orders a vodka made from rye, not potato. The man is from Grimsby. We reel off spiels. I tell him I work in a chip shop and keep a diary. He tells me he oversees a chocolate factory on the edge of town, visits once a month to dip a toe in. Then Willy Wonka has an epiphany. 'Sod it. You know what? I'm going to throw caution to the wind. I'm due in at seven tomorrow morning but I'm going to take you out for a nightcap. *Carpe diem* and all that.' In my experience

---

[42] A quarter of modern Ukraine used to be Poland as recently as 1945, so there are lots of Ukrainians with one Polish grandparent, keen to change their spots, earn their EU stripes, and at the same time plug a hole in the Polish labour market caused by the westward exodus.

[43] I was told by someone that Kazimierz the Great took a tolerant attitude to Jews in the 14th century because he was in love with one. Which is fine by me. Did Romeo not overlook his ancient grudge for the sake of a kiss? Bridges ought to be built on love.

people who play the *carpe diem* card tend to do so between the hours of ten and midnight, when there's barely any diem left to be carped. Willy takes me to a place called Mother's Kitchen. 'It's an institution,' he says. 'Everything used to cost 4 zloty, but then Poland joined the EU and now it's eight. I don't want to tell you what the rising zloty's doing to my blood pressure! It used to be peanuts to run a chocolate factory in Poland. I might have to keep going east – Bulgaria, Romania … What's east of Romania? Anyway, I'm sure they know how to put a biscuit together.' We eat steak tartare – raw beef and egg, strewn with onion and gherkin and mustard, manoeuvred with bread – and there is more beer and vodka. Willy says Brexit and Polish women are the same: 'Both bad decisions. Both complicated. Both costly.' I tell Willy he shouldn't talk about Brexit like that.

By now it's three in the morning – time I regained some focus. Walking back to the hostel, I am approached by a girl.

'You don't look like you're from here. Are you English?'

'Very, darling. How are you?'

'I love the English language. Are you busy?'

'Not in a great rush, no.'

'Could I buy you a beer and speak English with you?'

I smile for about ten seconds. 'Of course. *Of. Course.* Lead the way! *Carpe diem*!'

About three hours later I am naked in what I believe is called a safe room. It is certainly very padded. I can see the shape of two women in their underwear trying repeatedly to get somebody's debit card to perform. My feet have turned black. What have they done to me? Hang on. Wait. I'm still wearing my socks.

One step back.

Upon entering the language-exchange bar I am presented with a glass of beer and positioned on a sort of chaise longue, where I am joined not by the girl who took a shining to me on the street but her friend, also a keen linguist. I don't catch the girl's name but we are getting on well enough so when a waitress asks if I'd like to buy my friend a drink I say, 'Sure why not, get the girl half a lager.' I am encouraged to consider something from the cocktail list. While scanning the list for something under ten quid I notice somebody undressing in the corner. When I discover that the cheapest drink on the menu is a vermouth-based cocktail called *Mama Told Me Not To Come*, costing 350 zloty, or 70 quid, I am all but convinced that something is up – or will be before long, at any rate. I inform the waitress I'm not in a position to treat my friend to a cocktail on account of outstanding student loan, at which point a gentleman resembling Maximus Decimus Meridius appears at the waitress's shoulder to lend credibility to her suggestion that it's ever so important that I be a good sport and buy a cocktail. I do what I have to, then get up to leave.

Only I don't leave. My next memory is being naked on a banquette, peering gormlessly down at my own shortcoming, then spotting a pair of g-strung polyglots trying to hack my HSBC account. British to the core, I try to be a gentleman by lending the girls a hand in the buff. One of the girls – the better student of the two, if I remember, comfortable in all tenses – hands me my bank card and tells me to put on my clothes and wait for her outside. This sounds like a reasonable plan, so I do as I'm told. It is a lovely morning.

Walking back to the hostel, the key exchange goes something like this.

'What hotel are you staying at, Benjamin?'

'I'm in a youth hostel actually.'

'Okay, see you later.'[44]

⤚⤙

I miss the bus to Auschwitz. I'm told not to worry because I can get the next one. It's the worst thing I've waited for.

The town itself seems to carry some of the atmosphere and historical burden of the camp. Fancy living in such a town; just working in a shop or at the petrol station, or running the kiosk next to the museum carpark, where I buy a roll and a coffee, and before which I have a disrespectful cigarette. Everything one does here feels disrespectful, every gesture inappropriate. It feels arrogant and unfair to be alive.

Tickets were sold to Auschwitz-Birkenau. Passengers were told to bring one suitcase weighing no more than twenty kilos – valuables only, efficiently commandeered. They emerged from the cattle carts breathing a sigh of relief. They drank the ditch water greedily, having not drunk a thing for days, and decided that nothing could be worse than that. Selection

---

[44] A few things are obvious to me now. 1) I am a fool. 2) Something was put in my drink. 3) I couldn't remember my PIN number so ended up only paying for the cocktail. 4) The young lady who escorted me home planned to rob me. 5) She picked the wrong guy to mess with.

began immediately. Only those who could be usefully laboured to death were not led directly to the gas chambers, which were disguised as shower blocks to deter panic. At Birkenau – the purpose-built extension to Auschwitz, which was originally a military barracks – a railway runs through the main gates and up to the crematoria. Israeli schoolchildren, draped in light fog and the Star of David, walk its sombre length, kicking stones and talking about lunch. A man – God I could have killed the guy – takes endless photos as we are led around the two camps, honouring some queer instinct to – to what? Some things, surely, aren't meant to be taken. The shoes. A thousand pairs displayed in a glass case, the shoes of the final intake, a mere week's worth. Next to the shoes, the suitcases, labelled carefully by their owners so they could be easily reclaimed when that time came. The rollcalls at five in the morning that went pointlessly on for hours in winter, the barely standing prisoners all but naked, the temperature below freezing. Some died on their feet. Others ran for the electric perimeter, knowing they'd be shot. The shorn hair that was spun by those who'd lost it into profitable fabric, the sale and use of which aided the war effort against them. Photographic portraits of the final 5,000 are displayed in one of the workhouses. Their faces. How can I look at one, and be open to its tragedy, and not look at the others? Our guide, a Polish lady in a red hat, whose parents had been arrested by the Nazis while at church (she didn't elaborate), tells of a visitor who saw the face of their mother among the gallery. The medical experiments of Mengele. We are told about these in detail. Can eye colour be altered without the use of an anaesthetic? Everything bombards you, but odd things anger or confound. The priest who pleaded with a Nazi guard to spare the life of a man about to be shot. It is his life or your life, was the guard's reply. Then take mine said the priest. The guard did what he was told. Two-hundred calories a day if you were good. Ceaseless punishing labour, most of it pointless, all of it insane. The ugly ruins of one of the crematoria, untouched since its guilty detonation. The scale model of the gas chambers, mocked-up and put in a cabinet to give a clue of the density, hundreds of white plastic bodies, no larger than grains of rice, packed in to form a single gasping mass. Poland lost 20 per cent of its population in the war – Polish Jews, yes, but also Polish homosexuals and teachers and dissidents and children and parents and siblings and clerks and cleaners. Polish gypsies as well, a million of them. And for what? And for *what*? They should send every schoolchild to the Auschwitz museum, while their morals are responsive, while there's room for new attitudes, while there's time for new kindness. It is a compelling, horrible way to learn. I didn't want to go to Auschwitz because I didn't want to write about it. (I'm barely writing about it now; I'm merely putting down in useless words my fractured, awful experience.) I thought of the lines in *Romeo and Juliet* – 'No words can that woe sound' – and imagined using them as my excuse. I cry outside the bookshop, for the sheer disgusting cruelty of it all. But what good is crying? What good is anything in the shadow of this place? I say nothing for a day after Auschwitz: a pathetic tribute.

19

I don't know the colour of my father's eyes

28 July. Julia is in the kitchen with me. It's unlike a boss to stick their head under the bonnet, so fair play, even if it means I'm unable to casually scoff chips. Julia tells me she's been to the hospital this morning, because her husband found a tick or a flea or a leech on his leg when he woke up. I'm not sure if she's implying I had something to do with it, so I provide an alibi just in case. 'Well I was in Dragon, Julia, so I certainly didn't put it there.' When Julia tells me there'll be some DJs turning up soon, I worry that the guy from Berlin might be making another appearance. In the event, today's DJs are local and elderly. They are graduates of a scheme designed to help people enliven their retirement. They've been training for weeks and today each of them gets half an hour to spin their stuff. The first DJ mostly plays Roy Orbison records, which is fine by me. I enjoy 'I Drove All Night' in particular. I've always loved that song. I like the audacity of the protagonist, who drives all night to the house of the girl he's interested in, enters the house stealthily through the kitchen window, gets into bed with the girl, and only then thinks to ask, 'Is that all right?' A bit of an afterthought, Roy. Better to have called and asked before you set off.[45]

---

[45] I suppose the allegation should be levelled at the protagonist of

After work I go to a restaurant called Modra Kuchnia, where I spend the bulk of my wages on a bowl of beetroot soup, a tower of potato pancakes topped with goulash, and a bottle of old red wine. When I started working at East Coast, I resolved to ignore the few hundred quid I was getting each month from sales of my first book and just live off the Polish minimum wage, in order to better grasp the cost of living here. My resolution may have only lasted a couple of weeks, but it was useful in any case. Knowing what I had to do to get 10 zloty (bone, peel, scrub and stink for an hour), and knowing what I could get for that 10 zloty (a beer, a bowl of soup, a jar of pickled mushrooms) made me look at the Polish economy in a very different way: a cappuccino at Starbucks is an hour and a half in the kitchen, which would be like paying over a tenner for a cappuccino in the UK. Thought about in the same way, it's £15 for a meal at McDonald's in Poland, £4 for a litre of petrol. You get the picture: Poland isn't cheap, contrary to what people say who visit the country for a weekend. It's why the opportunity to earn money in a different currency is so attractive to Poles, it's why Anita said a couple of months ago: 'People leave for money. It's simple. You can go home now.' The reason my resolution only lasted two weeks is because I like being relatively wealthy. I like not having to think twice about going to the cinema to see an old Polish comedy, or taking a train to Gdańsk, or trying out

---

the song rather than Roy Orbison. After all, Robert Louis Stevenson is not Mr Hyde, as Jane Austen is not Mr Darcy. That being said, in the song's music video the protagonist is played by Roy Orbison, which only muddies the waters of responsibility further.

a new restaurant. I am fully aware that your typical migrant (who is 5ft 10, 82 kilos, and a Virgo) is unlikely to enjoy such agency. But I am not a typical migrant. By an accident of birth, and by dint of moving in the wrong direction, I am a privileged one, and I make no bones about it.

29 July. I go shopping for a wedding outfit. Anita comes along to advise. We try the second-hand shops near my flat, where the clothes are sold by the kilo. 'I'll have half-a-kilo of pants, please.' 'Give me a kilo of suspenders – I'm feeling flush.' This is how I like to think the Poles order. I wouldn't know how they really order, because I don't understand them – not enough, anyway. I can't detect their tone. I can't sense their tongue-in-cheek. I can't hear the dry humour and casual affection, the small things that are so meaningful, the small things that can make language and communication rich and precious and poetic. As it stands, I can only recognise odd words. I get by, I muddle through, but that's not enough, not really, because muddling through tells me nothing, because getting by *gives* me nothing. Even the most unseemly of characters – big, bolshie, brash – can be refined and softened by their use of words and their sense of humour, by their short asides and long reminiscences. I miss all that over here, and this account is poorer as a result. When I went around Britain a few years ago, to look at things and listen to things and make a few notes, I was *in tune* with the place. I had my ear in. On the bus I would hear talk of a local councillor who had been caught putting avocados through as bananas. In the pub I would overhear two brothers – thickset, alpha types – struggle to find the words, the right words, any words, to talk about their terminally ill mother. When I go around Poland my impressions are shallow. They are handicapped by my incomprehension. I am locked-out from the poetry, from the small print. Being an outsider here is good for some things – I'm curious, unjaded, on edge – but bad for one thing in particular: I can't hear the people. I can't hear their music, their musings, their day-to-day melancholy, their throwaway joy, their chance remarks, their choice quips, their wit, their manner, and, yes, their poetry.

The second-hand clothes are a different price each day. They are most expensive on Mondays, when the delivery comes in. On Sundays you can buy a kilo of skirts and neckties for 80 pence should you wish. Anita says people skip church to get the best deals on a Sunday. Upon Anita's recommendation, I buy an off-white linen jacket, a pair of black trousers and a black shirt (800 grams). The whole lot costs about a quid. When we leave the shop and I light a cigarette, Anita says: 'You know, you should maybe have a relationship with someone who doesn't tolerate smoking.'

'And do you tolerate smoking, Anita?'

'Yes. But sometimes I feel I shouldn't.'

Well that clears that up then.

4 August. I emerge from someone else's flat exceptionally hungover. I don't know what to do with the daylight. It is just after midday. I'd like to plunge my head into a trough. None being available, I go to Dragon, which offers a comparable experience. I sit outside and drink small bottles of Dutch lager, smoking two cigarettes with each. I say to myself, 'I'll just keep doing this until somebody says something to me.' I drink six beers and smoke twelve cigarettes and slowly read every line of an English newspaper. I write the odd thing down. *Be good to the friends of your mother. I don't know the colour of my father's eyes.* That sort of thing. An English girl called Michelle wonders if she can have the paper after me. Desperate for someone to break my fall, or to accelerate it, I sit with Michelle and her Polish friend Aleksandra. It is evening now. Michelle tells Aleksandra that I'm posh, which annoys me. 'If I was posh,' I say, 'I'd think even less of myself.' I don't know what I mean by this. A cigarette manufacturer – L&M – is giving away packets if you agree to have a polaroid taken. We pose together and say cheese. We look happy in the photo, pleased with our luck, proud of our habit. I go home at dawn, which means I missed all the darkness.[46]

8 August. Without ceremony, without a word in fact, Mariusz moves out. Without ceremony, without a word in fact, I move into his old room (because it's big and has a balcony). In my new room I finish a book called *How to Stop Smoking* and then, as instructed by the book's author, smoke my last cigarette. Aristotle said that people are instinctively extreme, which is bad, and that people who strangle their instincts with

---

[46] That polaroid photo is now on my dad's fridge. I didn't know it at the time, because I couldn't see the wood for the trees, but it captures my lowest moment in Poland.

reason and intellect can achieve a sort of in-between state, which is good. Aristotle called this sort of in-between state the *golden mean*. Well, I mean to achieve it, starting with my last cigarette and the acquisition of some furniture for the balcony, where I plan to be generally fresh and focused and moderate, every morning, for the rest of my life. That this is rather an extreme plan, needn't concern me for now.

20

It won't be an ordinary shift

10 August. My friend Tim isn't known for his moderation. After collecting him from the airport we go to meet my friend Paulina by the river. I'd agreed to teach Paulina's children English for an hour, but obviously got the wrong end of the stick because when she arrives she hasn't brought any children with her. She has brought a dog, however, so maybe she supposes I'll teach that. The three of us walk Andrew south for a bit, towards Krakow and Austria. I throw a stick and encourage Andrew to fetch it, but he doesn't seem interested. Perhaps it's the Polish defiant streak in him. Perhaps if I told Andrew not to fetch the stick he'd be well up for it. Paulina is supposed to be *my* friend but you wouldn't have thought it because she attends exclusively to Tim, which might be because he's unusually pleasant to look at. Tim is explaining to Paulina about being a friend of mine from university, about being unusually pleasant to look at, about being on the telly, about managing to get a week off work at BBC Sport despite being indispensable, an apparent contradiction he doesn't go into. When Andrew has had enough, Paulina takes him home and Tim and I go to East Coast, where I've got a shift. I warned Tim in advance that I'd have to go to work the evening he arrived. He said he didn't mind. He said he'd come with me and just sit in a deckchair and relax.

Julia says it won't be an ordinary shift. The whole place has been booked out by an IT company that's celebrating something, or lamenting something, that they're an IT company for example. Instead of fish and chips there'll be a barbecue, which I will be responsible for. My first task is to prepare vast batches of cumin mayonnaise and tartar sauce, and then distribute each into a hundred disposable ramekins. Then I do a giant salad and then package a hundred blood sausages in baking foil with fresh herbs and onion. By now the first members of the IT crowd have started to arrive, but the barbecue itself is still nowhere to be seen. Kuba has phoned in sick, Philip is on holiday in the southern mountains with the rest of the country, and I haven't even finished prepping. Julia pops her head in. 'The guests will all be here in half an hour and will want to eat straightaway. So maybe stop doing that' – i.e. preparing what they are going to eat straightaway – 'and start making the barbecue work.' Right. Fine. And where is this barbecue? 'At the back of the storeroom. It might need to be cleaned. Maybe your friend would like to help?'

When I ask Tim if he'd like to help, he says, rather snobbishly, 'I would rather depilate my scrotum.' I'm not entirely sure what this means, but we can assume the process is unpleasant. Also unpleasant is the barbecue. It was last cooked on in 1968 to celebrate the Czechoslovakians having a go at the Soviet Union. More to the point, it's not a gas barbecue, as I'd hoped, so it's going to be a bother to get going. I situate the barbecue under a willow tree near the picnic benches and deckchairs. I stare at it for a while.

A hundred people are about to turn up for the social highlight of their lives and I'm to play a key part in it. I continue to stare at the barbecue, willing it to self-immolate. I may look like a man of the outdoors, but my heart and soul are strictly indoors. What did Seamus Heaney write, about his father and grandfather being men of the earth while he was a mere man of the pen?[47] Anyway, I see nothing for it but to get Tim involved.

Tim asks for a quick summary of the situation. I point at the barbecue and then the IT crowd, by now 50 or 60 strong, who are due to eat in five minutes. Tim pours most of the coal into the filthy drum, then makes short twists of paper which he places evenly in the fissures. He lights the ends and we watch the paper twists burn quickly, prettily, but without making much of an impression on the surrounding coal. I am starting to get a bit stressed. As if suddenly aware of the crisis of which he is now an important feature, Tim says, 'What on earth is going on here? Have you had any training? I thought this was a chip shop. Has anyone thought this through? Are these paying customers?' Tim answers his questions by going to the bar, coming back with three large vodkas, taking off his leather jacket, rolling up his sleeves, adjusting his fringe, downing one of the vodkas, and then injecting life into the barbecue with enviable efficiency by tossing another of the vodkas onto it, all the while saying things under his breath like, 'I'm not even getting

---

[47] 'But I've no spade to follow men like them. / Between my finger and my thumb / the squat pen rests. / I'll dig with it.'

paid for this ...' and 'This is a joke – I'm a BBC journalist for God's sake ...' In the vicinity, a queue of hungry people has formed. Its proximity and increasing extent is starting to seriously discompose me. And where is Julia? Where is Anita? The coals have taken at least. They start to smoulder. I go to the kitchen to fetch some of the meat and the salad and some plates and cutlery. Doing so, I curse Anita for offering me this job, Julia for creating it, and myself for accepting it.

We get through it. Just. Kind of. Dinner was served later than scheduled and there was some audible unrest, but for the most part we managed to pacify the hungry line with nonsensical British charm, or something resembling it. It helped that Tim is a natural flirt. He does it instinctively. It is an extension of his friendliness. Case in point: when a member of the IT crowd approached to suggest that some of the meat may have gone out undercooked, Tim put his hand on the man's shoulder and said, 'Has anyone ever said you look like David Beckham?' To be fair to us, it had been hard to tell if the meat was cooked because we had lost daylight by the time we started serving. It also didn't help that the first thing that was ready, or that was apparently ready, was a batch of blood sausages, which look burnt at the best of times. Besides, we didn't have time to be cautious. We were utterly flat out. So flat out that at one point I thought Tim was seriously going to lose his cool. Not only was the workload getting to him, he was also annoyed that none of the executive (Julia, her husband Christopher, Anita) had so much as acknowledged him, which *is* a bit odd to be honest.

Imagine owning a business and returning to it in the midst of a hectic period and discovering that somebody you'd never seen before was single-handedly running the show and then not saying a word and just letting the imposter get on with it. So yeah, I could understand Tim feeling a bit unloved. He didn't want much, a quick thank you and maybe a few drinks on the house. Or so he said. More than once. 'I don't want much, Benny. Just a quick thank you and maybe a few drinks on the house. I mean, do they know I'm almost a celebrity?' To his credit, at the end of the rush Christopher did come over to introduce himself to Tim. It was slightly awkward. Tim's response was a touch sarcastic, even for my taste. 'Oh! Hello there! Good evening! Wonderful to finally meet you. Christopher? The owner, yes? You see I would shake your hand Christopher but a) I don't want to and b) it's covered in grease and soot and blood because I've been slaving behind this barbecue for hours. And to think – I don't even work here! Do let me know when the toilets need cleaning, Christopher, because I've evidently got nothing better to do.'

Tim leaves around midnight with a girl called Mari and her colleague Aga. I join them at Dragon a couple of hours later. I mostly sit quietly in the garden while Tim shows Mari footage of himself introducing a golf tournament on BBC News. Mari hints on several occasions that Aga is keen to know me better. I tell Mari that I'm so exhausted I couldn't desire a sticky toffee pudding, not if my life depended on it. Besides, there is Anita. There is always Anita. She owns the back of my mind.

11 August. It is early afternoon and Tim is still asleep. I get on the floor and shuffle up to his bedside and hope to gently rouse him by whispering in his ear all I know about Poland. I tell him of the king who was kind to Jews because he had fallen for one. I tell him about the various partitions which saw the country portioned like a pie. I speak of 966, of June '56, of 1655 when the Swedes popped over for an ultra-violent session of Supermarket Sweep, and finally the popular pope who got shot in the face but wasn't bothered. I vouch for *golonka* and *bigos* and then disparage Chopin, hoping this last might cause him to stir, it being so unjust. It does the trick. Tim yawns and stretches and then opens his eyes one at a time, which is weird. The first thing he says is: 'Can we go and see *Bridget Jones' Baby* tonight?'[48]

16 August. A slow shift with Kuba in the evening. To pass the time, I am purposefully attentive to small things. The look of paper towel as it slowly takes on oil. The sound of chips and seasoning being thrown about in a slick metal bowl. The gradual softening of frozen cod fillets under a tap. The cling of soles on linoleum. The distant hodgepodge of talk at the bar and at the tables. The wind making music out of the trees. The fit of bubbles as potato lands in boiling oil, and the pursuant drama of a pale limp chip being engulfed and altered in the fryer. Kuba's breathing, louder and heavier when he has headphones on. The slow motion of Lucas

---

[48] The best thing about the film was that we were sat right at the back, as far away from it as possible. Tim left the next morning.

smoking behind the bar. I am attentive for an hour then stop because I cut myself.

17 August. Anita arrives at the flat. The plan was to look at flight options for the wedding. In the event, before the kettle has even boiled, Anita is saying that she can't come because her passport has expired. I let the kettle finish boiling before I reply. That's alright, I say. She doesn't stay long after that. I don't think she even finishes her tea.[49]

---

[49] I remember not being that bothered about Anita not being able to come. If anything, I think I was relieved. For all my daydreaming about red dresses and what-not, I still feared her company, and feared that too much of it would result less in anagnorisis (which is not a type of orgasm) and more in confirmation that we are a poor match, a bad team, at odds, notwithstanding the fondness we have for each other.

21

What do the Polish do at the seaside? (Sopot)

20 August. Sopot is on the north coast of Poland betwixt Gdańsk and Gdynia and its flag depicts a seagull killing a fish. The local tennis courts were put down before the local church was put up. There is an annual Wagner festival that was established by Wagner to celebrate the works of Wagner. The synagogue was burnt down in 1938, the Kaczynski twins (elder died in a plane crash; younger heads the current government) were born and raised here, and, most ominous of all, the town is twinned with Southend-on-Sea.

At the bottom of Monte Cassino (the main shopping street) is a long pier reaching out into the Baltic Sea. I had a Polish teacher for a while, Monika, and she and I once got our wires crossed regarding a pier. For some reason, I was trying to say the word pier in Polish. She leant in, straining to make sense of my effort.

'What are you trying to say?' she said.

'Pier,' I said, in English.

'Ah,' she said – '*gruszka.*' (I now know that *gruszka* means pear, not pier, but I didn't at the time.)

'Fine,' I said, then continued with my story in Polish: 'Yeah, so there isn't much to see in Portsmouth, apart from the big pear.'

'The big pear?' she said.

'Yeah,' I said.

'That's interesting,' she said.

'Well, not really,' I said.

'Not really?' she said.

'Yeah,' I said, 'most coastal towns have got one.'

In any case, I give Sopot's pier a miss because it's 10 zloty to get on the thing. Ten zloty to be 50 metres closer to Sweden? Jog on.[50]

There is a Starbucks on the beach. Not by the beach, *on* the beach. I get changed in the café's disabled toilet. No one from Starbucks seems to mind me doing so. Indeed, the staff seem uncharacteristically friendly. I witness one staff member, a girl in her early twenties and rushed off her feet, give time she plainly can't spare to an old lady who has more than she knows what to do with. I buy an espresso and then tap-dance across the sand to the Baltic Sea – *ouch! ooh! ow! eee!* – wishing all the while, coffee jumping about willy-nilly, that I'd left my socks on.

To speak plainly, it feels odd to be on a Baltic beach, to have one's feet scorched by sand next to a body of water synonymous with frigid conditions. Back in England, to suggest that it's very cold we often say, 'Cor – it's *Baltic*.' I say this a few times a year, which is probably about normal for someone my age, though henceforth I'm going to stop saying it, because it's like the Gobi Desert up here. Half of

---

[50] You would actually be 50 metres closer to Kaliningrad, the Russian enclave that sits between Poland and Lithuania. The term 'jog on', for those over 40, means 'thanks but no thanks'.

the beach dwellers are in their birthday suits or thereabouts. One man is wearing a pair of swimming trunks so small that if he wished to recycle the Lycra he wouldn't have enough for an eyepatch. They call this part of the country the Polish Riviera, if you'll credit that. Polish Riviera doesn't seem to fit, does it? The phrase has an oxymoronic quality, like 'military intelligence' or 'business ethics'. Traditionally, Sopot has been a resort for the well-heeled, and on the face of it continues to be so, though I admit it can be hard to judge the quality of a person's heel when they've nothing on. The sea here is also known for its healing properties. Busloads used to come with fractured ankles and lung cancer to 'take the waters' and be improbably cured. In the event, the only thing that happened when they took the waters was they got wet.

When I call at a bar at the bottom of Monte Cassino and ask for directions to a hostel on the edge of town, I'm given four sets from four punters: my map is massacred with conflicting biro. A long walk follows, through sloping semi-suburbs in search of shelter. The hostel, when I find it, is full. An alternative is suggested via the intercom – Lunatic on Independence Avenue – but that's also full. I don't mind the setbacks: searching for a bed allows for an initial survey, a rough introduction, and it forces me to ask questions, seek advice, off-the-cuff and off-line. Ignorance is fruitful. My slow lap of Sopot concludes at the MOLO Hotel by the train station. It is 50 quid a night. Given that it's 8pm, and given my luck so far, I don't turn my nose up. The hotel is certainly spacious; you could have a cricket match in the lobby; but spaciousness doesn't always add character, if anything it is wont to take it away. The received wisdom has space down as a prize, a reward, a marker of status, something to be strived for, paid through the roof for, and yet in my experience too much space tends to be isolating and stressful, because it takes you away, it removes you. In my hotel room there is room for several others. There is bottled water but no biscuits and no tea and coffee making facilities, which are the only reason the British bother with hotels. I pop down to the spa, hoping to improve myself. I give the sauna a go, but it was hotter in my room to be frank, so give up after five minutes, less relaxed than when I went in. The steam room is on form, however. The mist is impenetrable. I use my hands to find a tiled bench, and then slide into a corner. I close my eyes and deliberately relax.

'*Dzień dobry*,' says a male voice from somewhere in the steam room. I say nothing, thinking it might be coming from a speaker. When the voice sounds again, when it asks me how I'm doing, I know I'm not alone.

'I'm fine,' I say. 'And sir?'

'You should be naked,' the man says, 'I'm naked.' As if to prove his point the man gets up and brings his nakedness towards my nose. He's doing a back stretch, he says, because he can't bear being stiff any more.

I get out and lie down on a heated bench. There are two mirrors directly above me – one reflects my lower body, the other my upper. My midriff is politely avoided. Between the mirrors is a mosaic of Narcissus leaning into a pool of water. I'm not in the habit of looking at myself. Paradoxically, the reason I resist my reflection is vanity – I fear what I'll see, I worry that I'll disappoint myself. It is concern for my appearance that makes me avoid it. If I remain ignorant of my appearance, I reason, I can hold on to the idea that I look like James Dean. I look at my face. It looks tired, there's no doubt about it. It needs a shave. The ears are irregular, curvy, on the large side, which is why I prefer to keep them covered with hair. I've never looked at my eyes. Not really. I quite like them. There's a chip on one of my upper front teeth, which is why I prefer to keep my mouth shut in photos. The teeth aren't white; they speak of bad habits. I move down to my knees. The left is bigger, bloated, damaged. It has been since a bad tackle playing football when I was ten. I don't like the knee, but not sufficiently to hide it away. People don't judge knees. I've got an even coat of body hair, which isn't ideal, but I've never bothered to remove any of it because I don't want people to think I care. It's a blessing my middle isn't reflected, else we'd be here all day. It's a can of worms down there. I close my eyes and count to 50. I get to thirteen then decide that none of it matters.

The main street is swamped with inordinate couples ambling in the late summer twilight. I am not being hyperbolic. There is a very infestation of couples. A plague of conjoined drones, each pairing sun-kissed and senseless. *What do they say to each other?* I return to the bar where I'd been given directions. Sztos it's called, on Generała Józefa Bema Street. (Joseph Bema was a local baker.[51]) One of the girls who gave me

---

[51] He wasn't. That's me guessing. He was in the army – *any army by*

directions is behind the bar. Because we'd had a little chat and a bit of a laugh earlier, she insists I don't have to pay for my drink. I ask where to go next and she tells me to try the oldest pub in Sopot, The Blue Poodle, which has been trading since 1992. I take a table on the terrace, consider the menu. I like its opening boast in English: 'Artistic interior, climatic music, delicious drinks and excellent Polish cuisine mean the already above threshold could fall into the amazing atmosphere.' I'd say that was spot on. The pub's terrace is like the stalls of a theatre, arranged to give diners a view of the street-stage, on which an ensemble of sad clowns and drunk mechanicals perform an unwitting drama: there is a dispute over a spilt drink, and then the man who did the spilling gets up to remonstrate and drops his coins and there is a scrap for the spoils. I feel like a pervert watching; using this unfortunate fish tank for light entertainment. All of us vacationers on the terrace with monkfish and clams, set up to gawp at the resort's Commedia dell'arte.

On a Tuesday there is only one disco open, upstairs in the crooked house across the street. I leave the stalls and cross the stage and climb the stairs to Ego. It is unduly full. Loud, indecipherable music. Couples sit at the bar, while around the dance floor hopeful boys sip their drinks and share agendas. I take a seat to the side and there try in good faith to understand what pleasure is being had by those

---

the sound of it. If there was a fight, Bem was up for it, no matter the combatants. He had a heroic temper, they say, which is a nice way of saying he was a psychopath.

around me. A spirit of enquiry drew me to Ego, but what is everyone else's excuse? The singletons can plead desire, but what about the unspeaking couples nursing drinks they don't appear to want? A girl approaches and tells me to smile. Then she performs the instruction because nothing can be heard. You need to have fun, she shouts. You need to smile. You need to smile because if you don't, I might start to doubt myself. *Smile*, she says. I don't have to, I say. Then go home, she says. I smile when she says that. Because she's got a point. I entered Ego fully aware it wasn't going to do much for me. I entered as a cynic, an ombudsman, a lightweight anthropologist, a jerk. I entered because it intrigues me that at the end of the day this is what we do. People want levity, gaiety – I get that. People want concentration, congestion, traffic, they want to collide – I get that, too. People want an alien-abstract environment at odds with life, where things are on hand to sustain the departure, the displacement, the disappearance. I get it. I understand and relate. I've been here a thousand times, dancing to the tune. But being here alone makes you see more; it makes you see the sorrow.

∼

I go to church after breakfast. It's at the top of Monte Cassino, Southern-German Neo-Gothic allegedly. A few pews in front of me, a Pole's prayer is broken by a phone call. I'm quite sure she takes the Lord's name in vain searching her pockets for the offending mobile. It must be something urgent, because she leaves immediately. The phone call has brought her down to earth. The vignette makes me laugh.

I trundle down the hill then take a left towards the tennis club, where I sit on a modest grandstand and watch four men in their eighties compete fiercely on clay. It is good and sweet to watch this ordinary encounter, to witness the huffing and puffing, the mortal shuffling, the dud volleys that provoke mockery from the other side of the net. Despite autumn being a month away, a leaf falls onto my hand at deuce. I finger it, snap its main vein. It's lost its green and will be mulch before long. Then another falls, and then another, as if the first had encouraged the others. I'm tempted to read the leaves as a symbol or metaphor, but don't in the end. I just brush them off and continue with the game until it's done.

I enter a café called LAS, drawn by its good-looking employee, who tells me her boyfriend has died. All I'd asked was why do you live here? Her name is Alicia and I have nothing to say: I can only look at her and then order something. I take my coffee outside, where a child is busy on a rocking horse. As I chat with the mother, the child keeps rocking and smiling and then asks her mother if the man is speaking English. I point to the horse and say in Polish that it is a cat, a dog, a pig, anything but a horse. She enjoys that, my innocence. She looks to her mother each time I guess wrong, as if to ask, 'Is this guy for real?' I go in to pay, and when I come out they're gone.

I eat a good lunch at a beach café, just fresh cod well cooked and seasoned and served with chips and salad. Customers compete for the sunlit tables. When I took my table it had been undesirable – shady and on the margin – but before long it's the only table in the sun, the apple of all eyes, which says something about the shifting nature of value. It is not unusual for me, I reflect, to be fashionable by chance. When I prolong my visit by ordering coffee and starting to write, I sense stirrings of discontent at neighbouring tables. I imagine the sound of their pain: *The man in the sun is now writing, Kasia – what will he think of next?* Or: *He's gone and ordered coffee, Stan, and I shouldn't be surprised if it's a pint just to spite us.* In the event, by the time my coffee comes I am in the shade again, and where there was lack there is plenty, and so on.

I've an hour before my train. I lie on the beach and read *Status Anxiety*.[52] Perhaps the book is infectious because with each page I grow more envious of the couples around me, of their mutual worship, their rolling about, their coupledom. Yesterday I called them drones. Today I worship them. I watch the best bodies (male and female, mind) with a respectful discretion between pages, paragraphs and sometimes even lines. Basic, I know, to take an easy, low pleasure watching other humans with very little on, but there you are – or there *they* are, rather. When I close my eyes and try to relax, two voluble girls drop towels nearby then proceed to laugh for an hour. I enjoy their friendship though it means nothing to me. What do the Polish do at the seaside? They stroll and play and read and build castles from sand, as others elsewhere.

---

[52] Alain de Botton.

22

It's funny where hearts end up

2 September. I get an email from Richard. He has found out about the spare room and wants to talk about the possibility of filling it. I give him a call and try to discourage the idea as best I can, noting the inclement language, the communist legacy, and the proximity of Germany, but with each warning his enthusiasm for migrating appears inexplicably to increase. We'd be two artists in exile, he says outlandishly. You could keep your diary and I could watch you do it and occasionally take a picture of something sad. But what about your teaching commitments in London, Richard? Don't you have to teach the history of ideas to undergraduates next term? What would happen if you didn't? Ideas might stop. And what about your friends in London, Richard, there must be one or two, and all the nice parks, and the West End shows and double-decker buses, and the nice cheery phone boxes and the Queen? People give their limbs to live in London, how could you be so ungrateful? How could you turn your back on tea with milk, the cross of St George, the toxic political climate? On steak and kidney pudding, on the rule of law and freedom of speech and venerable institutions like the BBC and Primark? We'll see, he says, which means I've won the argument.

7 September. Richard has moved in. Deep down I'm pleased. He is a good friend: wise and candid and blue and wonderful. I do wonder what the British Embassy in Warsaw will make of his arrival though. I can imagine there being some talk on the matter, a junior ambassador having noticed a spike on the graph, a queer jump in the figures. Is this tit-for-tat migration? says the junior ambassador. Does it carry a threat? Are low-status Englishmen coming here to retaliate, to correct a bias, to steal all the jobs and claim all the benefits? The logic behind the wave is certainly abstruse, the junior ambassador goes on. It makes sense for you and me to be here, Jenkins, because we didn't have a choice in the matter and they keep us in mansions with servants, but what explains this pair of dropouts pitching up without an ounce of white-collar between them? I say, Jenkins, put the kettle on, let's get to the bottom of this!

Richard has taken my old room, the small one with two squeaky beds and a pair of motivational posters, which he takes down immediately. He arrived lightly: some socks, pants, a coat and a camera. He's talking about travelling the country and capturing the Polish soul. Good luck to him.

8 September. I am at work with Kuba, the teenage brainbox who sounds like a Dutch prince when he speaks English. While we get on with our tasks, Kuba teaches me words that will impress my housemates – *prysznic* (shower), *ekstrahuje* (extracted), *fart* (a sudden stroke of luck). Then he teaches me some idiomatic phrases: *chodzić na rzęsach*, to walk on eyelashes, said when someone is drunk and can't walk; *rzucać grochem o ścianę*, to throw beans at the wall, said when someone is throwing beans at a wall and/or when a situation is futile;

owijać prawdę w bawełnę, to wrap the truth in cotton, said when someone is being only partly honest; *prosto z mostu,* straight from the bridge, said when someone is being very honest; *narobić bigosu,* to make *bigos,* a meat and cabbage stew, said when someone messes something up; *wypchaj się sianem,* stuff yourself with hay, said when you want someone to leave you alone; *bułka z masłem,* a roll and butter, said when a situation is straightforward; and *czuć miętę do kogoś,* to smell mint on someone, said when you are attracted to someone. They are all nice phrases, so much is admitted, but I don't suppose I'll ever have occasion to use them.

In the evening there is a DJ from Berlin (are they from anywhere else?). Kuba gets to go home at a reasonable hour because he is a child but I'm forced to stay until 2am. When Anita told me I'd have to work late, I said straight from the bridge that she could stuff herself with hay, but I was throwing beans at a wall. In the event, the shift is a roll with butter: I won't wrap the truth in cotton, I'm walking on eyelashes by the end of it. As I'm closing up, a flirtatious customer buys me vodka shots and invites me to a festival in the woods (*not* a Polish idiom), but I don't smell mint on her so go home to generally make *bigos.*

18 September. Asia wrote to me a month ago. She's after English lessons and someone recommended me. We meet at a café. She tells me she used to live in Boston, Lincolnshire, where she worked in a factory. The work was not hard but boring, of course. Enough to scream sometimes. She was treated well, enjoyed the Slavic atmosphere at the factory, didn't make any English friends but didn't experience any hostility either, far from it. She shows me pictures of Boston on her phone. We talk about the European shops on East Street and The Folly and Goldfinger. She is pleased I know the place, that I talk of it fondly, that we have it in common. Her plan is to get sufficiently fluent so she can return to Boston and manage the factory. I ask about her studies in Poznań. She sighs, scratches her throat. 'My heart is in Boston,' she says, and I think: it's funny where hearts end up.

20 September. Anita was hit by a car while cycling. She's on crutches and I'm walking with her to the taxi rank. It might not be the best time to do so, but I say: 'You do realise, Anita, that if I was able to have a relationship with anyone in Poland, then that person would be you.' She stops, asks me to repeat myself, listens to me repeating myself, and then says that she didn't realise that, didn't realise that at all, says that she was under the impression I'd met someone, months ago, or that I simply wasn't interested in her, not like that, not anymore, because after she opened up to me, back in the spring, and said that she was fond of me and wanted more and kissed me – which wasn't easy for her, by the way – I did nothing, *nothing*, and so she closed herself, called in her feelings, and let me go. I say: 'I didn't do *nothing*. I did *something*. I did something several times in fact. I bought you that book by Ian McEwan. I gave you that shell. I kissed you, on 16 June, outside the Sheraton Hotel. I wrote to you, answered you, always said yes. I tried to bring you closer, to encourage intimacy, like that time by the river, when we were waiting for the delivery, when I put my hand on your side and you rejected me.'

'I have no idea what you are talking about,' she says.

'Really?' I say.

'Really,' she says.

I give this some thought, as much as you can in a matter of seconds, and then laugh quietly and say, 'You thought I did nothing. I thought you did nothing. We should have talked more. But what now?' At this she can only sigh, and I know that's it.

'I was open to you but now I'm not. I have met somebody. It's just an ordinary thing but – I don't know – things have changed. Besides, it's hard with me. I've been made hard.' I know what she is referring to, or partly. She sighs again, and it's a nail in a coffin that was ready months ago. 'Benjamin, being in a relationship with me is like being in a war.' A taxi pulls up. She gets in it.

'I'm a good soldier,' I lie.

23

My chip shop swansong

23 September. It is my last shift and I wish Kuba was here. Barely a customer, despite good weather. I drink two beers on the job and once again my tab is outdoing my wage. I have a bit of a spring clean. The rarely-mentioned mushrooms (kept in stock for vegetarians) have taken mould, while the potatoes under the sink are going soft. The fish aren't soft, far from it, they're coming in frozen these days. I let a bunch of fillets defrost slightly and then start removing the bones – the flesh is less vulnerable when it's all but frozen. The floor is in a bad way and the broom has no handle. This place is crying out for autumn.

I lower the shutters at eleven and withdraw into my private trench. I tidy up carefully, savouring the finality. This is my chip shop swansong. I find a new head for the broom, clear my locker of old shirts and forgotten aprons, mark my last hours on the time sheet, then turn the lights off. I drink a nightcap in a deckchair, within earshot of the Warta, with nobody else around. That's it, then.

I go to Dragon, where I make notes for two quiet pints, undisturbed, unthreatened, left alone. Then the customary attention comes, for writing is noticeable, is considered pretentious, especially after dark in a public house. 'I've seen you doing that before. You must need a drink.' I look up and refuse, but the drink comes anyway, and it turns the screw.

My frame of mind lowers an octave, gives an inch. I stop writing, no longer able, and dwell instead in a vague puddle of something – memory, melancholy, bliss. I could do with a new head and a new handle, and I don't care if I become a different broom.[53] I think of leaning on a neighbour and sharing these thoughts, but can't find the chutzpah, the cheek, the brio. I become uncontrollably sentimental and go downstairs to the disco cave and call for 'Enjoy the Silence' by Depeche Mode. The DJ says he'll play it if I get us both a vodka. I get the vodka and then it's four or five in the morning and I'm affecting to dance with a lady who said earlier she couldn't love me because I'm foreign. I said her logic was rubbish. Witching hour has been and gone. It's just the drones left, and a single queen bee.

1 **October.** In the evening Jenny has some friends over, including someone called Mirek, who arrives with homemade rice wine. After four glasses of said, I agree to help edit the abstract of Mirek's PhD thesis (which he's writing in English) the following afternoon. I'd been warned about Mirek. He has a reputation for being thoughtful and awkward, and so it proves. When I show him the cover of a pocket-guide to Poznań, which shows the city's neo-classical opera house, and say that I think it should be something else on the cover because the opera house is an anomaly and doesn't represent

---

[53] As well as Trigger from *Only Fools and Horses,* I guess I am referring to the paradox of Theseus. How different does a thing have to be before it becomes a new thing?

the city at all, that it should be something like the old square or the old tenements or the unpretentious blocks, Mirek thinks quietly on the matter for fifteen minutes before saying with absolute conviction that there oughtn't be anything on the cover. Boy, does that tickle me. It is hard to be sure, but I'd say Mirek is the sort of guy who's excellent once a month.

2 October. When Richard gets back from somewhere, he wonders if I've had a good day.

'It was awful.'

'Oh?'

'Mirek came over.'

'Ah.'

'He wanted me to check the abstract of his thesis.'

'Yeah, I remember.'

'He brought a bag of St Martin Croissants with him.'[54]

'Fair enough.'

'Because he knew damn well it would be tough going.'

'Any left?'

'No, we got it done.'

'Croissants, I mean.'

'In the kitchen.'

'Cool. Carry on.'

'He's writing in English but it might as well be Japanese. It's about a particular legal principle about which I know nothing. The whole thing was impenetrable. Mirek couldn't

---

[54] Local pastries stuffed with poppyseed paste. The recipe is legally protected.

understand why I didn't know my own language. In short, I don't suppose I was much help. And I don't think much of those croissants either. Peculiar density. High mass, low surface area. Like Dhaka in Bangladesh.'

Richard goes to the kitchen, returns with a pastry, takes a bite and then says, 'It's all grist to the mill, mate.'

3 October. The people are in black and the rain is relentless. A thousand have gathered in the square because plans are in the pipeline to illegalise all abortion – plans that I mentioned months ago when crossing a bridge marred with distorted coat hangers. It is a working day, so a good number of those here are effectively on strike. The square is pregnant. A thousand umbrellas against the same rain. There is a stage and speeches are made and chants break out but I don't know the lines. To get through the crowd I must duck under the umbrellas: I enjoy the steady drips on my neck. When I reach the back of the square, I take shelter in an old phone booth. I share the shelter with three others. I ask what they are singing, what they are against, who is speaking, how many women are in government, what the men in their lives think about it all. They ask why I don't know anything. I say I'm in Poland for a stag party, because people reveal more if they think you're innocent, but by playing innocent I can't argue the detail. For example, one lady says the change in abortion law had been proposed by the government, which it hadn't. Rather, the change in law had been proposed by a pro-life citizens coalition. The proposal had gained enough signatures to legally obligate the government to discuss it, which they haven't yet done. That said, there's a chance the citizens coalition is under the influence of the government, who wish to get the motion on the table while seeming not to be its authors. In any case, I can't debate the detail because my opening line had been, 'Pardon me, is this a pop concert?' When I ask a lady if there will be repercussions for her not going to work, she says she has her own company selling wedding stationary and works when she wants. When I ask if business is good she says, 'Yes, because Poland is very Catholic.' As I'm about to point out the irony of Catholicism giving with one hand and taking with the other, I'm handed a tray of soggy biscuits that's being passed around to keep morale up. I take a couple, get them down like oysters, then watch Anita holding hands with a man with a beard. I stay until the end. I cross the emptied square. I watch the stage being put away. I scan the wet ground for banners and slogans. I find one that is torn, not quite down the middle but close enough. It says: 'Humans must have freedom'. The words are John Paul II's, and they are probably being used by both sides of this dispute.

4 October. Because I'm out of work again and have more time on my hands, I make myself available for weddings in the kitchen. Let me explain. Rightly or wrongly, it is considered something of a shame for a Pole to go to a wedding alone. Going alone tells everyone what you haven't been doing with your adult Polish life – namely, getting married and having six Catholic children named after saints. I don't know exactly how much of an embarrassment it is to go alone, of if there's a punishment if you do so; all I know is that it's considered best practice for single people to arrive at weddings with a guest of the opposite sex on their arm and pretend there's a bun in the oven (or a bun about to go in the oven) so that everybody can persist under the illusion that nothing remotely modern is happening in Poland, like the existence of women who are happy to be alone, or the existence of men who don't want to build a house or grow a tree or have a son by the time they're sixteen.[55] Anna told me about a website (weddingbuddy.com/pl) that single Poles use to recruit people to arrive on their arm, partake in a slow dance, and then disappear and never be heard of again. I could do that, I thought. I could disappear and never be heard of again. I get Anna to help me build a profile.

'Height … About 180?' she says.

'About that.'

'Weight …'

'Weight? They want my weight? Why? That's – discrimination. That's fat-shaming.'

'Eighty-five kilos?'

'Seventy-five.'

'Eighty. Physique. Do you have one? There's an option for "not quite fat". Will that do?'

'What else is there?'

'Fat, quite fat, athletic—'

---

[55] It is said that a boy becomes a man in Poland when they've built a house, grown a tree and had a son. Presumably, a girl becomes a woman in Poland when they've seen a boy do these things.

'Athletic.'

Anna stops, turns to me. 'Benny, I'm happy to wrap the truth in cotton, but I don't have that much cotton.'

'Fine.'

'Not quite fat?'

'Not quite fat.'

'Good. Eye colour … G-R-E-Y.'

'Really? Grey?'

She comes close, has a good look. 'You're right. Not grey. They're *beer*.'

'Beer. Great.'

'Religion. *Ca-tho-lic*.'

'Pardon?'

'Non-negotiable. Profession?'

'Writer.'

'You are better off putting nothing. Lifestyle? Urban.'

'Urban? Makes me sound like a fox.'

'Personality …'

'Put modest. And wealthy.'

'You wouldn't be doing this if you were wealthy.'

'A wealthy and modest not-quite-fat 80-kilo fox with beer-coloured eyes.'

'Price?'

'What's the minimum wage?'

'I think it's 12 zloty now. They just changed it.'

'Put that. I don't want anyone undercutting me.'

'Availability?'

'I don't know. Forever?'

'Be serious, Benny.'

'Weekends. October to March.'

'Why March?'

'Because that's when I'm leaving.'

'Why?'

'Because it will be a year and, well, that's when she's going to trigger Article 50.' Anna just looks at me. 'Theresa May, the UK Prime Minister, she's going to press the button that starts Brexit at the end of March.'

'So what?'

'So I guess it's time for me to go home.'

'Who said?'

'Nobody. But, it would be, well, poetic.'

'Poetic? I see. You want me to put poetic on top of modest and wealthy or what? Poetic. *Kurwa.*'

'Are you angry?'

'Angry?'

'Sad, I mean.'

'Sad?'

'That I'm leaving.'

'If you cleaned the shower each week I would be sad. You need a photo and then you're done.'

In each photo I show Anna she sees something in me I'd never seen myself – camp, arrogance, an oily T-zone. In the end she decides the best photo to use is the one in which I feature the least. All in all, it is a sobering hour of my life.

9 October. I am having lunch with Richard at the café on our street. Cucumber soup followed by *pierogi*. Not a mouth-watering prospect on paper but tasty in the event.

I leave Richard to his coffee and pop out to buy some flowers for Anna. You see, I rented out my room while I was away for a few days. It was snapped up by two Portuguese students about to start a term at the university. Anna hadn't enjoyed the experience so I thought I'd make amends with some flowers from the florist up the street – Kwiaty & Miut. I pick a blue variety and am asked for 80 zloty, so I give half the flowers back and pay 40. On my way back to the flat I enter the café to collect Richard. Several of the café's staff are on a cigarette break outside. They watch me enter and approach Richard with the flowers. When I say something banal and heartless to Richard like, 'Do you know how much these bloody things cost?' they think I'm saying something heartfelt and romantic, for I can see them laughing outside and even parodying the scene. They probably think they're onto a choice bit of gossip, i.e. the immigrants are in a relationship. On our way out, I make a point of offering one of the flowers to the antagonist, the waiter who camped me up, explaining in Polish that the flower is for him because both are pretty. He has nothing to say but accepts the flower at any rate.

24

The Manchester of Poland (Łódź)

12 October. I go to Łódź because people say I shouldn't. I take a train. Beyond Poznań the scene opens, or empties, and the frame is full of field and chimney, those laborious opponents, the latter ringed in white and red, the colours of Poland, the colours of England. A cemetery is fully lit with flowers. A farmer is tilling the land with a dog at his side. We pull into a station: two coppers are waiting on the platform. I watch as a passenger is led along the platform and delivered to the coppers, who put him in the back of a van. The whole thing is enjoyed by those on the platform, and by those on the train, who line the corridors to feed off the mellow-drama. It's something to tell the kids about.

Łódź doesn't have a central train station. It gets by with two on the edge – Widzew on the eastern front, Kaliska on the western. I'm told this by a fellow passenger when we emerge at the former. She noticed my uncertainty, offered to demystify, then puts me on a bus into town. It takes the bus an hour to work its way in, to build up the courage. An estate of blocks in green and gold, and then a market teeming with flowers and schoolchildren. A portion of the children board the bus then play up as it plods downtown: a boy's winter hat is plucked and hidden by a coquettish classmate. The boy pretends not to care until his stop is approaching, at which point he grabs the girl by the hair until she relinquishes the hat. The lady who put me on the bus, I remember now, could only laugh when I told her I was here for a holiday.

I get off at the longest street in Poland. Piotrkowska was under repair for ten years but now it's good-looking and fit for purpose. The street is the city's spine, integral and nervous. I enter the Holiday Inn and approach the receptionist for a piece of her mind.

'Do you like Łódź?'

'Yes of course.'

'Why?'

'I'm from here.'

I get that sort of thing a lot, that sort of response, when I issue quick quizzes to clerks and drivers, bouncers and bellboys. People are proud and protective, but they can't tell you why. Being from a place is reason to like it.

I am tempted by Flamingo on the left but opt for Cinnamon on the right. There are no private rooms available, but there's a bed in a dorm at 30 zloty. The dormitory is certainly snug. A quick glance tells me that people live here. On one of the bottom bunks is a long, ghostly Pole, eating toast without spread. On one of the top bunks is a Belarusian, flat on his back, hands behind his head, counting time on the ceiling. I tell both men that I'm going for a beer and they're welcome to join me. The ghost says no, the Belarusian, why not.

It's dark and wet now, drizzling. Sergei is 47, new in town, starts work tomorrow at 5am, first day on the job. He looks at the sky reproachfully: 'typical British weather', he says, then looks at me, as though I'd brought it with me. He smokes as we walk, holding the cigarette in such a way that it's sheltered from the rain. He knows a place near the hostel; we take stools at the bar. Football lends a shared focus. I order vodka while Sergei provides his context: no jobs in Belarus; twice divorced; worked in Norway, during which time his first wife went off with a Pole; worked in Germany during which time his second wife went off with a Slovak. I order another pair of vodkas then turn to my friend and say: 'You know what? You should stay at home more.'

When it comes to settling the bill, I tell Sergei I'm paying, that it's a British custom to shout the drinks on the first date and that I'd be positively offended if he didn't let me honour it. (It's not, of course, but I want him to think I'm being dutiful rather than kind.) But he won't have it, custom or not, duty or otherwise, and practically forces some notes into my pocket. Leaving the bar, he says that he's a bit scared about tomorrow, that he feels like a child starting a new school, only the school is a building site, and the children are men. 'I don't have good Polish,' he says. 'Norwegian, German, yes. Polish, no. It cannot be easy tomorrow.'

I return to Piotrkowska – Long Peter henceforth – and go pointlessly north. It is a mighty, mostly empty avenue, half-lit by identical, elegant lampposts. I see a rickshaw in the offing, coming slowly south. It makes a nice scene in the lamplit mist. I get in its way, stand in its path, play chicken with the pedaller. At 50 metres I gain a crude idea of the passenger: she is broad and made-up and pushing 70, dressed for a lavish ceremony. Her driver is wrapped in black, wears a flat cap and a grimace, is straining for his fare. If I was Richard, who takes pictures as if they were already his, I'd hold my ground and snap as they swerve to avoid me; I'd get their passing faces – his amused, hers haughty – and not think twice about it. I'm not Richard, I'm a hack, so make a note and step nicely aside.

At the north end of Long Peter is the old ghetto, where the city's 200,000 Jews were rounded up to be unmade, to be taken off the books. The heart of the ghetto is the *Stary Rynek*, or old square. It is small and empty and ordinary. It has nothing of the glitz or fizz of Wrocław's or Poznań's. I expected more but am not disappointed: its understatement is suitable. There is one bar on the old square. It is approaching 8.30pm and the barman, I see now, is closing so he might watch the Madrid–Warsaw match in peace. I photograph a hundred pigeons, asleep among the rafters of the arcade, necks drawn in, some alone, others in pairs. I had never seen a sleeping pigeon before, and then a hundred at once.

Across a main road to Manufaktura, once a cotton factory, now a shopping and leisure complex. The original factory was commissioned by Izrael Poznański, who resided in a palace up the road, a stone's throw from harm, a safe distance from the freedom and dignity that came with sixteen-hour back-breaking shifts.[56] Perhaps I'm being presumptuous. Perhaps I'm being unfair on Izrael. Perhaps he was the first to roll up his cotton sleeves and muck in. No matter what, the factory spun its last in 1994. Now the

---

[56] I allude to the Protestant notion that gruelling, often fatal work curries favour with God.

cotton is processed in distant lands – Ceylon, Dhaka, Beirut. So it goes.

For one night only, Poland's best bartender will be concocting drinks at a place called Bawełna (Cotton). I squeeze in at the bar and order an Old Fashioned. Award-winning Mateusz works on my drink in stages over fifteen minutes, displaying a touching confidence in my patience. He moves from customer to customer to rattle and enflame, syphon and explain, while a team of myrmidons carve wedges and salt rims. My drink is worth the wait. It is the best cocktail I have put in my mouth. It is somehow a resolution of conflicts, simple and complex, familiar and foreign, intense and gentle – it is Poland. I want to stay for several more, but my phone has died and I wouldn't be able to photograph my good fortune. If it's not on the record, it's nothing at all.[57]

I head south on Long Peter until I trip on a suitcase. It's bronze and on the pavement because its owner, Władysław Reymont, wrote a famous novel called *The Promised Land*, which shows Łódź in its industrial heyday. The city's boom in the second half of the 19th century owed to plenty of things. The city was usefully squashed between ready markets (Russia to the east, Europe to the west), the chemical composition of the local water was conducive to the processing of textiles, and the city had something of an open-door policy – Germans and Jews and Bohemians and

---

[57] An official Twitter slogan is: 'If you didn't tweet, it didn't happen.' For the love of God, somebody shoot me. And then tweet about it.

Brits were all encouraged to stick a finger in its pie. Łódź was the promised land, the Manchester of Poland. Given what Marx said about Manchester – that it prepared you for hell – one is apt to wonder what Łódź promised exactly.

OFF Piotrkowska is a plot of old warehouses that have been taken over by avant-garde barbers, bakers and brewers. *Tesknie za zydzi toba* has been painted on a wall. I have it translated by a smoking hairdresser. 'We miss you, Jews.' In a Vietnamese canteen, my faltering attempt to order draws the attention of a film student from Palestine called Mohammed, who volunteers to assist. I sit with him and we talk. When I tell him about my arrival at Widzew, Mohammed corrects my pronunciation, repeating the word several times to make sure I've got it. The mention of Widzew alarms a neighbouring diner, who has misconstrued our trivial discussion of the station in Widzew as outspoken support for the region's football team, whom he evidently dislikes. As we pass the man's table on our way out, he gets out of his chair and barks something at us – to do, presumably, with stepping outside and settling this once and for all. The whole thing is fully absurd, but nonetheless real, so I assure the man in toddler Polish that I am from England and won't use that particular train station again, and then we leave, quickly.

In the dormitory, a Bulgarian whose shoes are too small by half shows me his betting slips. Doing so, he tells me in bitty English that he is here to visit his son, that he's only visiting mind you, that he doesn't live in the hostel, not at all, wouldn't if you paid him, isn't looking for work or anything like that, is just here to visit his son, in case I had formed a different opinion. He takes me through to the kitchen, fiddles with the television mounted in one corner. 'They have BBC,' he says, 'I promise they do. I can find it for your consideration. I've seen it – it's good television.' He locates the BBC's international news channel, turns up the volume. 'That's Fiona,' he says, 'she's good, tells the truth.' When Fiona mentions Brexit the Bulgarian looks at me accusingly, as if it were a horse that fell, and I was its trainer.

⊗

I set off for a place called Rudzka Gora (Trash Hill) because I like the name. I take a tram south then get off when I sense a summit. When I reach the bottom, a sign says the hill is closed to climbers. Two women are in conference nearby. Like me, they're unsure what to do. I take matters into my own hands: after quick introductions, we surmount the barrier and I lead them up the hill. At one point the way is blocked by foliage. I'm ready to turn back but one of the girls thinks that with a run up it can be penetrated, and so it proves. It's slippery underfoot, but not dauntingly so. We talk as we go. They are from Taiwan, are studying in Łódź to become teachers of Polish. ('Who are you going to teach?' 'We don't know yet.') The girls find just about everything funny: my nationality, my name, the hill, their career paths, this path. When I say that the hill used to be a pile of rubbish they belly-laugh as if I was Tommy Cooper and had just cracked the joke of my life. We can see nothing from the summit, save for a smattering of treetops and rooftops, and the odd chimney adding to the murk. It is, as warned, a rubbish hill.

I'm at the modern art gallery – MS2. On its threshold, I read the preamble to the current exhibition. I read that 'to appropriate the modernities of yesterday can be at once a critique of the modernities of today and an act of faith in the modernities of tomorrow and the day after tomorrow', and then wonder what that means. I read of the author's uncertainty as to whether 'Poles are real subjects of modernization processes, consciously transforming themselves and the world, or, rather, just objects mindlessly accepting roles written for us in the scenario of modernization', and then wonder what *that* means. I read that the 'incompleteness of this collection and the collage-like arrangement of elements seem to render best a modern view of reality with its fragmentary nature and discontinuity', and then make a note to tell my niece, who's seven, that she might defend her incomplete homework on similar grounds. Finally, I read that the gallery is 'continuously questioning and undermining dominant judgements about what is important in art.' This is fair enough. This I like. I like things to be tested; I like norms defied and perceptions nudged. By extension I like galleries (as this one) that show such art; but for the love of God don't bamboozle me at the front gate with such a cryptic intro, lest my subjectivity be made to feel like a twit and run off.

I'm glad I withstood the prologue because the collection itself is great. A photomontage by Kazimierz Podsadecki shows how unhealthy the urban situation is. A painting by Stanislaw Notarjusz called *Dancing* shows the robotic nature of leisure. Ali Kazma's film *Jean Factory* points at the highly-controlled, highly-constructed nature of identity. Włodzimierz Pawlak's *Diary No. 51* is nothing more than a canvas of tally marks, pointing to the robotic nature not just of leisure but *existence*. There may not be much work here, and it may be chaotically arranged, and I may not understand the curator's stated ambitions, but the collection nonetheless compels, questions and consoles, which is fine by me.

I move to the adjacent shopping mall. There is muzak to stupefy, bright lights to render all things obvious, and uncomfortable furniture to keep shoppers moving. I find a food court and sit on one of a thousand plastic orange chairs. I ponder the garish perimeter of options and the countless uniformed servants and think of Pawlak's diary and Kazma's film. See how art comes with you, leaves its official space and follows you, around the shops, back home, into your dreams? Art is ideas in the end, and ideas can go anywhere.

I can go anywhere but I go to the streets west of Long Peter, which have none of the gloss and sparkle of the city's main artery. Here the buildings only hint at better times; block after block of shell-shocked bunkers that once teemed with overworked hands. For the families that inhabited them, times would have been hard in these tenement buildings, you can be sure of that, but they would have been good and hard, loud and hard, keen and hard, quick and cunning and silly and hard. Now there is nothing, less than nothing, nothing in decline, nothing in reverse. Who owns these streets? Why are they doing nothing? Is ownership disputed? Where is Reymont's promised land? The population of Łódź has fallen by 100,000 since Poland joined the EU, so perhaps it's elsewhere.

I eat a toasted sandwich at Foto Café 102, whose barman remembers a Liverpudlian who came for a drink once and stayed for a year. I can see why they might have done. The pub is comfortable. It has *hygge*, if you're familiar with that bestselling concept. It reminds me of Dragon. It could easily become an extension of one's living space. Mohammed enters. Mohammed from last night. We both say: 'I meant to call you!' He reminds me of Jesse Klein, a Canadian friend, also a filmmaker. Perhaps filmmaking attracts certain types – watchful, shrewd, pithy, as if they're constantly casting and shooting, conceiving and cutting. It can look like anxiety, but it's more a type of vigilance, coupled with an imagination that won't shut up. Mohammed is aware of himself as an auteur, and such a burden restricts levity: when the conversation takes a silly turn, Mohammed instigates a game of Truth or Dare, though soon tires of it because neither the questions nor the dares are sufficiently existential. I am asked to truthfully explain why I came to Poland. It's a harder question than it ought to be. Over the past six months I've given a dozen answers. I was bored. I'm contrary. I got divorced. For the money. Asked for the truth, I give it: I still don't know.[58]

---

[58] I stayed in touch with Mohammed Almughanni. His films tackle issues of identity and conflict, and are worth watching.

I check out from the hostel and then take a tram to the train station. The journey is quicker and more direct than my bus journey into town, and the worse for it. Travel oughtn't be direct, oughtn't be quick. It ought to take a while, the better to see and notice. Then I discover my train is delayed by several hours, and think again.

25

What time are the ambulances?

16 October. I'm going to a Polish wedding. Nobody's paying me: I'll be the guest of flatmate Anna, whose friend Barbara will be marrying a gentleman called Lucas at a registry office near Konin. The service will be followed by an almighty knees-up. In advance of the wedding, Anna insisted I have some work done on my face, the objective of which was to make me seem more winning on her arm, like a fancy watch. In the event, I emerged from the treatment requiring more treatment. Anna had got carried away, believing, like somebody prospecting for oil or gold, that the further she went down the more chance there was of finding something worth looking at. In the wake of my face-job, a crust of dry, flaky skin spread across my face: I was scabbing. Anna told me to grin and bear it, only I couldn't grin, because a side-effect of the work was that I was unable to form expressions. I would simply have to bear it.

It's a civil ceremony, which is a blessing, because the Catholic type can go on for hours. I am dressed as well as possible – I look better than most of those over 50, but worse than anyone under. The ceremony room is small, suitable for maybe 50 people, and yet at least a hundred have squeezed in. Anna and I stand with our backs to the wall. The ceremony's over in about ten minutes: it's more a clash of heads than a solemn conjugation. As the bride and groom take a seat to sign on the dotted line, we're organised into a funnel outside. I suppose we're about to throw confetti.

'Do you want some rice?' asks Anna.

Odd question. 'It's fine. I can wait.'

'Do you want some money then?'

Odd question. Is she all right? 'Sure.'

Anna hands me some coins and tells me to lob them at the happy couple when they emerge.

'They won't be a happy couple if I do that, Anna.'

'Aim for the legs. It will be fine.'

The venue for the reception isn't far, about twenty minutes or so by car. It's a sort of holiday camp, with modest huts by way of accommodation, and a main hall where the festivities will take place. When Barbara and Lucas arrive, a queue forms to give them a present, which is invariably cash, a few hundred zloty per head, says Anna, to cover the costs. When we get to the front of the queue, I explain who I am and that Anna has the money. Anna encourages me to say more, to say something else. To Lucas I say, 'You are beautiful. I am a friend of Anna's. She isn't paying me. I am happy to be here,' while to Barbara I say, 'Thank you for the invitation. You are also beautiful. *Smacznego.* (Enjoy your dinner.)'

I study the table plan. My name stands out like a sore thumb, a queer Anglican arrangement amid a sea of sturdy Polish tongue-twisters. Ten or so long tables, formally set, with a top table for the newly-weds and their special advisers. There's already food on the table: bowls of plain, cold spaghetti. Not being one to look a gift horse in the mouth, I get stuck in.

'What are you doing, Benny?'

'Should I wait?'

'Yes! You must wait for the soup. This is *rosół*.'

There are ice buckets on the table. At first glance, I assume they contain bottles of water but in fact they're loaded with vodka. There appears to be at least one bottle per person. I'm sat next to a man called Adrian Gaszpit. I ask what he does in Poland and he says he works in the field of optic fibres. That is the end of our conversation. One meat course arrives after another. Anna, who is a vegetarian, chews the inside of her mouth and makes do with vodka. After about an hour's eating, DJ Piotr takes up his station and starts us off with 'Hit the Road Jack' by Ray Charles, which might be thought an odd choice for a wedding breakfast. Then the newly-weds are called up for the first dance. The way Lucas and Barbara go at it, you'd be forgiven for thinking it actually was their first dance: Lucas is grinding and twerking like Romeo on ketamine. Children are taking advantage of their parents' turned backs. One youngster has got hold of his mother's smartphone and is snapping his pal pretending to drink champagne, while another is feeding spaghetti to a cat.

I'm outside in the smoking area. I haven't seen Anna for over an hour. She's probably trying to get hold of her vegetable dealer. Adrian Gaszpit comes up to me with a tray of vodka shots. I do one, then he hands me another. 'Steady on, Adrian,' I say. 'It's for the other leg,' he says. I do another, then Adrian tries to force a third on me. 'Just how many legs do you think I've got, Adrian?' I watch the party through the window. Whereas I prefer to move between the dance-floor and the smoking area, the older guests are more inclined to stay at their tables, working on the vodka and picking at the food. They really are spoilt for choice. On top of the various cuts of meat and genres of fish that are doing the rounds, there's a permanent exhibition of cold meats and cheeses to one side of the room. At a British wedding you're lucky to get 500 calories. You might get a bit of pâté to start, then a chicken breast, and then a square of brownie to wind things up. At a Polish wedding, if you approached it as a squirrel, you could take enough on board to see you through winter. There's not much alcohol around, mind you – apart from the bottomless vodka, of course. The Poles know better than to mix their drinks. Lionel Richie comes on, 'Easy Like Sunday Morning.' Easy for you to say, Lionel. You're not the one at a Polish wedding on a Saturday night.

Oczepiny. A customary period of games and frivolity at midnight. The couple sit back to back in the middle of the dance floor and answer questions about each other. I enjoy Anna's translation of the questions. They're not as accurate as they might have been a few hours ago. Example: 'Is it true that Lucas only uses socks for sex?' The next game involves several ladies manoeuvring boiled eggs up and down their partners' trousers. This is done to a very popular Polish song that, according to Anna, is about nothing more than watching legs and wearing mini-skirts. The chorus of the song is sung with such gusto that you'd be forgiven for thinking it was the national anthem. I am quite sure the song must have more historical significance than Anna is letting on. It simply can't be the case that the main substance of such a revered cultural artefact is, 'I want to watch your legs (legs, legs, legs) / I want to put you in a mini (mini, mini, mini).' Barbara's great aunt assures me that it *can* be the case, that it *is* the case, and I'd better get used to it or go home. Then there's a game a bit like Twister only you work in pairs. Anna and I are tethered together and then ordered to put three feet and one hand on the ground and so on. As with any challenge she faces, no matter how small or incidental, Anna approaches this one with the utmost seriousness. Nevertheless, we end up in a heap on several occasions, me happily, Anna incredulously. When the game is done, Anna orders her friend Natalia to delete the photographs immediately, then joins the back of the conga that is now bopping around the room like a giddy queue for scant rations. Lucas, the groom, is at the centre of everything, launching the words, dancing ferociously, hugging anything that moves. Watching him, I learn something of happiness, of ecstasy. Only very rarely during the rest of his life will Lucas reach such levels of joy, such uncomplicated euphoria. I can't help but smile, and love him despite not knowing him.

I return to the table and although it's three in the morning the food keeps coming. I rebuff the soup and the *bigos* but am helpless in the face of a large silver platter of pork knuckles, languishing like flabby monarchs on a king-size mattress of sour cabbage. I permit the platter's delivery, then stare at it with double or triple vision. 'Do you not like *golonka*?' says

Adrian. 'Don't get me wrong, Adrian, it's not that I don't like it, it's that – it's that *I wouldn't like it now.*' Adrian is dubious. 'Were you to smother it with mustard – just like this, with the back of a teaspoon – I promise it will be delicious.' I've experienced this sort of thing before. This sort of Polish problem solving. Poles are quick to present solutions, especially if you suggest you don't like a feature of their cuisine. I tell Adrian I'm not keen on mustard, which is a lie but a nice construction. 'Then you must have horseradish! That'll do it!' I concede to Adrian's fascistic insistence and eat. I manage a few fiery morsels then pretend to pass out until Adrian loses interest in me. Sometime later – an hour? two? – Anna sits down next to me, taps me on the head, puffs her cheeks, and says, 'What time are the ambulances?'

26

I go to Harlow because a Polish man was killed there

22 October. I went on three dates last week. With different people. Same place, same cheese, same wine, same vague agenda. I was feeling low and wanted company, attention, affection. The dates were mostly hard and empty and sad. My behaviour – three dates in a week – was out of line. Out of line according to me. But I've felt out of line for months – debased, ashamed, feckless, perturbed – and so it's little wonder I behaved accordingly. I've lost my way. (I mean, I got so drunk one night I wanted to become a politician.)[59] And when you've lost your way, when you've slipped beneath dignity a notch, it is easy to stay lost, to stay slipped, to mistreat, to be fickle and unfair, to be weak. I am drinking too much and courting three women at once knowing nothing will come of it, wanting nothing to come of it. Does Anita have something to do with it? Do the nicotine and alcohol and their boring, noxious, accumulated effect have something to do with it? Is it being away from home? No. I don't want excuses. I'm just like that sometimes. I'm

---

[59] When I got back from the wedding I topped myself up with whisky then told anyone that would listen how I wanted to become a Member of the European Parliament and single-handedly bring the continent back together. There are several reasons why this is unlikely to happen.

capable of that. I can be basic and indecent and needful and excruciatingly selfish. It's part of me. I know this sounds banal and boorish and self-involved, this confession of sorts, and it is all those things, but it also happens to be true, and an account of my time in Poland without it would be— would be the truth wrapped in cotton.

23 October. I am hungover. I take a tram to Starołęka then eat a miserable plate of food outside a kebab shop. Nearby children stare at me. I drink a beer then go to the convenience store and buy a hotdog and an ice cream. It's that sort of day. When I arrive at the house, at my old school, Tony is putting what we'll need in the back of the car. He looks at me with his customary sceptical grimace.

'I see you're wearing shorts. That's good. You'll be able to see the ticks on you.' The what? 'Ticks. They're tiny but they burrow into your skin and give you brain damage.' I look down at my legs, my shorts. 'It's fine,' says Tony. 'We have some spray. It doesn't work very well but there you are.' He can see I'm worried; he can sense he's scared me. 'What *I* do – right – after we've been picking in the forest – *yes* – is to check Marietta very carefully all over when we return. After supper or something. Isn't that right, Marietta?' Marietta answers from inside.

'It is a nice thing to do – I check Tony, Tony checks me.' I don't want to think about this too much. How do you even get them off? 'Tweezers,' says Marietta. 'They really are very tiny. I have to look everywhere, don't I Tony? Anyway. Are we ready? No. Where's the dog?'

When we get to the forest I want to be left in the car. I am not ready for four hours trudging around woodland looking for mushrooms and getting infested with brain-damaging ticks.

'I think I'll stay in the car.'

'Ha!'

'No seriously.'

'Don't you like mushrooms?'

'I like milk, Marietta, but I don't necessarily want to spend the afternoon milking a cow.'

'Now,' says Tony. 'Let's get serious. Be careful what you pick. Right? Or it will kill you. So: big stem with collar – no. Big stem no collar – maybe. Big stem no collar no spots – maybe, could be a Cossack. Big stem no collar no spots with gills – absolutely not, that's a Fat Head and will kill you in a second. Right? Off you go then. We've sixteen acres to cover. See you!'

And with that Tony is off, on his own, with his crucial knowledge, to scour sixteen acres. Marietta is not much use. She's playing with twigs and pretending to be a fairy. 'It's not really about the mushrooms – it's a social exercise,' she says, to herself, up a tree, stroking its leaves. For Tony it evidently *is* about the mushrooms. He's already out of sight, hell-bent on showing us what a stellar mushroom hunter he is. I catch glimpses of him far off, between trees, beneath bushes, grabbing and prising and pulling at fungi, a fixed, earnest, maniacal grin on his face, like a mythical goblin creature thing, cackling each time he rejects a poisonous specimen – 'He he he, you won't get me!'

'What's that you've got?' says Marietta.

'A mushroom,' I say.

'*Yes*, but which one?'

'This one.'

'*Yes*, but has it got a—'

'It's got a collar and a coat and a backpack, Marietta, so what? I don't care if it's a Cossack or a Fat Head or a Black Head or a Shaggy Umbrella. I just want to fill up my punnet so we can go home.'

After a while, my hangover abates and I'm able to start enjoying myself. I grow conscientious and fastidious about what I'm doing. At first, I was flippant – I didn't care if I got poisoned. Now I'm a pedant, purposeful, boastful. 'Look Tony, you mad old plonker! Look at the size of this Lemon Dangler!' A few hours later we call it a day and return to the car, where Tony carefully checks my mushrooms for anything dodgy. We must have about five bags of mushrooms between us. Despite my earlier misgivings, and despite being hampered by a hangover, I can see why mushroom picking is so popular here. It's not only fun but it makes *sense*. The way the Poles are aware of the seasons and harvest the seasons is a great thing. They go out mushroom picking in October as naturally as they put up a Christmas tree in December. Strawberries appear in June, while apples, beets, asparagus and pumpkin all have their moment in the limelight. There's an attachment to the land and its tides – its calendar, its virtues, its fruit – that is unquestionably good, something to aspire to.

I'm dropped home. Because Anna isn't here, and Jenny and Richard won't mind, I tip the bag of mushrooms onto the kitchen table. I look at them for a bit, then go to my room and watch *Fry and Laurie* for an hour, then return to the kitchen and look at them a bit more. I can't just leave them there, like an ornament – Anna would kill me. Not one of the mushrooms looks up for consumption. I test the most suspicious on passing flatmates – 'Jenny. Hey. How was work? Too bad. Try that. It's a mushroom! It's delicious. Just try it. That's it. Good boy. All the way down. Good. How do you feel?' – and then in the end just throw all the mushrooms in a large pot, add some butter and stock and herbs, let the whole lot bubble for an hour and then blitz it into a soup. It's delicious. Then I invite Jenny into the kitchen.

'Hey, Benny, how's it— ooh, yum. Smells good.'

'Yeah forget about that. Can you check me for ticks?'

27 October. I go to Tandem because a local Pole called Max is giving the second of a series of lectures called *How to Survive in Poland*. Because I could pass as a Pole, I haven't had too much trouble surviving in Poland. Sometimes when I open my mouth it can annoy people, like that time outside the kebab shop months ago, when a bloke told me I was in Poland and should speak Polish, and I said fair enough and started speaking Polish, and we ended up talking about his cousin who lives in Scotland. And then there was the cage fighter in Wrocław, who wasn't especially impressed with me, but these were exceptions: routinely I am treated with respect, with indifference, *equally*. It must be harder for others, for those more obviously from elsewhere – like Mohammed in Łódź, for example. Anyway, when I arrive, the lecture has already started. A group of twenty or so have gathered loosely around the lecturer, who is perched on a low wall in the courtyard with one of his very long legs less crossed and more flung over the other. His very long arms are also crossed, knotted even, and despite these eye-catching contortions the lecturer is able quite comfortably to manoeuvre a bottle of cider with one hand and gesticulate with the other. So pleasing is Max to behold it's hard to pay attention to what he's saying, which is a lot, in short. If this is the second in the series, then the first must have dealt with Poland in the Iron Age, for Max's current musings range in time from Hannibal's crossing of the Alps on an elephant to the Cuban Missile Crisis in 1952. Max speaks more or less without pause – about gentrification (anticipated to commence in 2025), national characteristics (pugnacious, suspicious), the third partition of Poland in 1795 (not as good as the second) – for an hour and a half, at which point he uncrosses everything, mounts his sedan, and is carried off into the night by a team of Ukrainians. No, after delivering his theory of everything what Max actually does is invite questions, of which there are plenty, though they are, in point of fact, less questions and more corrections and complaints. An Indian man thinks it ridiculous to suggest the Alps could be traversed by elephant. A Polish girl says her parents and grandparents are suspicious not by nature but by training, which she considers an important distinction, while a Norwegian dentist takes exception to Max's performance of the Swedish Deluge. As far as I could tell, the problem was that Max had offered his ideas as if they were truths, which got people's backs up. 'If the truth be told' was just about his favourite construction, used to preface most of his instructions. 'If the truth be told, the best way to deal with Poles who want something from you is to run away.' 'If the truth be told, Polish women undress on the nineteenth date, men on the third.' 'If the truth be told, there is no more nationalism or racism here than anywhere else.' For all his peccadilloes, Max is clearly a sweet and bright guy, so I throw him a gentle question about the Polish habit of pickling then buy him another bottle of cider.

4 November. During a trip to England for a family occasion, I go to Harlow, Essex, because a Polish man was killed there.[60] I remember learning of the news back in August. ITV said that a man in Harlow had been murdered for being Polish, and that the killing was evidence of a post-Brexit backlash against immigrants. Any evidence? The deceased's cousin says so. I remember thumping my desk. I couldn't believe how flimsy and irresponsible the reporting was. ITV – and

---

[60] Harlow is a 'New Town' that was knocked-up to deal with homelessness in London post-Second World War. Its master planner was one Fred Gibberd, who invited many of the country's leading post-war architects to design buildings for the town, which is why it's now a bit of an eyesore. It is also an unprecedented town: Harlow can claim to have the first concrete shopping precinct and first residential tower block, should it wish to. Historical high point: losing to Watford in the fourth round of the FA Cup in 1980. Saving grace: it's home to a major collection of public sculptures by artists such as Auguste Rodin, Henry Moore and Barbara Hepworth. Rodin's *Eve* can be found in the Water Gardens just in front of the Five Guys burger restaurant. Like Max the lecturer, Eve is pulling a rum pose: she is recoiling, shielding herself, as if anticipating a pull shot at short-leg.

they were not alone – had readily and baselessly cast Britons as vengeful nationalists ready to kill. The whole thing was confusing. Conventionally, if regrettably, it is the outsider that's scapegoated. On this occasion, it was the native, the local, the *insider*. ITV framed the tragedy as 'British racist kills innocent immigrant', and yet when the bulletin went out there was nothing by way of evidence to confirm the reported motive, but what the heck, said ITV, said the British media, let's run the story, let's push the narrative, let's whip up a fuss, let's accuse Britain of racism, no matter if it puts Poles on edge, no matter if it puts dangerous ideas into impressionable minds, no matter if it's just a hunch. Cause and effect; causality; consequences. These things are real. Yeah, says a teenager in Yeovil, having seen the news, let's rough up the Poles, let's force the point, let's make sure they get the message. Alright, says a Pole in Wrocław, if that's what's going on, let's do something about it, let's rough up the Brits, let them know that Poles don't put up with that sort of thing, that Poles fight back. I remember thumping the desk for a second time and upending my mug. So. Yeah. I wanted to go to Harlow.

I enter a betting shop, speak with the duty manager, hoping to get a sense of the area. I tell Jeanette I'm looking to buy in the area, ask whether she recommends the town. 'Yeah. I suppose. There's a Primark – that's nice. And there's a Wetherspoon if you're looking to eat something. It's not Gordon Ramsay though, not round here.' The betting shop is busy. A rum cast of locals back horses in virtual races. It's a cosmopolitan crowd but the mood is singular: it is sorry. I ask

Jeanette if Harlow has changed for the better in her lifetime. 'Nah. But that's not the people's fault. There's intolerance and stuff but no more than anywhere else. All that was spun by the media, all that stuff about the Polish man. Look at this place – it's the United Nations but there's never an issue. People get upset when they lose, not upset with each other. Don't you think?'

Most of the shops are vacant, but Kebab Land is busy enough. I annoy the owner by going in and asking for a restaurant. 'We don't have those,' he says, 'try the greasy spoon across the street.' Jagoda serves me pie and chips with peas and gravy. The chef pays me a visit. He likes to call at the tables. He's partly Turkish but speaks like a proper Essex boy.

'I gave you a few extra chips,' he smiles. 'It doesn't cost much to be kind.' I tell the chef what I told Jeanette – that I'm looking to buy in the area. He turns into an estate agent. 'I live in Brocklesmead. It's murder central. Bloke got stabbed seven times there walking to work.' I want to suggest that if I got stabbed once walking to work, I'd consider a different route. 'Church Langley's not as posh as it was. And Old Harlow's alright, though you'll be lucky to get a garage.' We get onto the killing. 'Manslaughter,' says the chef. 'It was manslaughter. It was in the paper last week. Trial's just finished. Courts found that the Polish guy and his mate racially abused the young lad that did it. The lad that did it was British-Asian or something, from round 'ere, about fifteen. He punched the Pole in the back of the head, causing him to slip and bang his head on the floor. *Wallop*.

It was that that killed him. Hence the manslaughter. You want any more chips?' No more defensible, this version of events, *the* version of events, no less disappointing, but a very different version to the one reported, to the one broadcast to millions, by the BBC, by ITV, by the *New York Times*, to the one received as wisdom, to the one taken as truth, to the one whose influence went far and wide, certainly as far as Poland. The findings of the local court were not reported on ITV or elsewhere. As far as the mainstream media were concerned, the attention-seeking media, it hardly mattered anymore. After all, if the truth didn't matter then, why should it matter now? Harlow has been misunderstood, says the chef. Britain has been misunderstood, he might have added.[61]

On the train back to London I sit opposite a boy and his mother. It is, I infer, the boy's eighteenth birthday. He's dressed in a suit, doesn't stop talking. There's a surprise waiting for him and his excitement is obvious. His love for his mother is equally obvious. The way he speaks to her suggests a small child recounting a momentous series of events at

---

[61] I checked up on the story, lest the chef had the wrong end of the stick. He didn't. In the *Spectator*, Ross Clark points out that Mr Jozwik's death was not the only reported post-Brexit 'hate crime' which turned out to be nothing of the sort. When a Spanish restaurant in Lewisham had its window broken, it was hastily reported as a result of Brexit-induced hate, but later treated by police as a conventional burglary. 'Then there was the abusive graffiti which appeared on a Polish cultural centre in Hammersmith. This produced understandable horror and a local MP, Greg Hands, underlined that Poles are welcome. Only later did it emerge that the graffiti read "Fuck you OMP" — OMP being a Polish centre-right think-tank which had backed Brexit.' Britain – you're not as heinous as you've been led to believe.

school, when so-and-so ate a crayon, and Mrs Green sneezed during the register. It moves me, *involves me*, as these things will when one is at a certain ebb, in a certain mood. I hope he never stops talking to his mother like that. The back page of an *Evening Standard* on the floor reveals that England are once more struggling abroad.

27

I wake up to snow and President Trump (Lublin)

7 November. When it comes to cities (when *I* come to cities), I've learned not to expect great differences. No two cities are alike, but neither are they essentially unalike. What do you have in a city? Roads. Vehicles. People. Churches. Shops. Homes. Schools. Sure, the look and character of these things will change, but it will remain a chip off the old block: a home, a school, a road, a person. What else is there? The odd bicycle. Suburbs. Estates. Public transport. Pedestrians. A cinema. Opportunities to drink alcohol. Restaurants. Cafés. Supermarkets. Turnings. Junctions. Roundabouts. Bridges. Ups and downs. The odd hotel and maybe a hostel. Police station. Hospital. A park or two. Maybe a river. Usually a river. A square or similar. Benches. Bins. Graffiti. Adverts. Places to go at night, a place with books to borrow. A seat of local authority. Maybe a swimming pool. A place where justice is done (or is meant to be done). Trees. Plants. Dirty air. Buses. Rats, foxes, cats. Dogs on leads. Street names. House numbers. Front gardens. Back gardens. Washing on the line. Postmen. Betting shops. Money lenders. Banks. Monuments. Timetables. Phone boxes. Local heroes. Local heroines. Appointments. Moods. Thoughts. Jobs. Confusion. Effort. Indifference. Desperation. Kindness. Traffic. Sunlight. Lamplight. Shadows.

There's an airport in the city of Lublin and it looks like an alarm clock. It's past midnight. There's no sign of taxis or buses, so I follow some others onto a minibus. We're driven recklessly for twenty minutes then deposited in a deserted parking lot a few miles short of the centre. The other passengers seem to understand what's going on. Some stand about amiably, smoking and chatting, while others walk into the darkness, beyond the edges of the parking lot, pulling suitcases with broken wheels. I join the back of what I believe is a queue for taxis. When I'm the only one left in it, I have five minutes alone in the wilderness.

I estimate that my taxi driver has been driving in Lublin for twenty years – his licence has lost colour, his metre is rickety, his cab is stocked with all manner of distractions, including a television mounted on the dashboard. Despite his obvious pedigree, his experience of driving in the city, my driver keeps on finding dead-ends and diversions he's never previously encountered, forcing him, on every such occasion, to pull over, smoke a cigarette and devise a new plan. He bears it well, bless him, takes it on the chin like the finest of stoics. I think graciously that it must be nice when something so familiar maintains the ability to surprise.

I asked to be dropped at the Hotel Europa because I thought its name would encourage a consideration of its referent, i.e. May and Merkel and Marine Le Pen, freedom of movement (exercised so impressively by my driver), the likelihood of Turkey's accession, what it is to be European, and so on. In the event, Europa is full. I take a room at Vanilla around the corner.

I'm having breakfast downstairs in the restaurant. It's the day of the US election. Trump versus Clinton. A tragicomic battle if ever there was one: the comedy being Trump, the tragedy being that he stands a chance of becoming the most influential person in the world. There should be checks and balances that get in the way of such an eventuality. Surely. You might say the democratic process *is* such a check and balance, in which case the democratic process isn't checking and balancing enough. Blanket 'news' coverage is already rolling. I wonder what the Poles make of all this. I suspect the Polish government wouldn't mind Trump in office. His ideas (if they can be called such) about the nation and immigration chime with their own. Kaczynski would build a wall, if only his bricklayers weren't abroad.

Right out of Vanilla and then right again. On Freedom Square a creamy church sits opposite a mint-green theatre. I wonder which institution tells the better stories, decide that a feather would tip the scales, then enter the theatre's small café, whose owner returned from a motorbiking trip in South America to open it. I ask why he chose to set up shop in Lublin. 'There are opportunities in Lublin but nobody to take them. People go to Warsaw or Krakow or leave the country. Lublin is the biggest city in the east of Poland, but it's still a small pond. I went to Warsaw. To the big pond. I was a small pointless fish there, so I went to South America. In Chile I could see what I couldn't see here. I could see that it's better to be meaningfully small than pointlessly big.' Fair enough.

On the main shopping street, there is music: a gypsy boy is doing wonders with an accordion. His sister, who has heard it all before, appeals hopelessly to passers-by. In a different context, in a different setting, the same passers-by would happily queue and pay for such a performance. If it were in a concert hall, say, and the musician were smartly dressed. The gypsy pair's obvious need makes them invisible, as if their music was muzak, coming from speakers hidden underfoot. I put my back to a sunlit wall and listen to the music. A trumpet sounds. The boy stops his playing and looks west. Everyone looks west. It takes me a while to identify the tune, but it is indisputably the US national anthem. I go after the music, as a rat following the piper, but the unlikely patriot cannot be seen.[62]

For warmth and a chance to write, I enter a café that only does soup on New Fish Street. The scene is heartening: eight wooden tables, softly lit by low winter sun, a dozen lunching figures, lurching over their bowls, bending to their task. Some have their chin on the rim, lest they spill a drop. Others are more cavalier, letting the spoon travel a full yard, their eyes glued to a paper or phone. When it comes the soup is good. Beans and chilli in a thick, dark broth. The chef is an iconoclast: he or she has strayed from *żurek* and *flaki* and *rosół*, the Polish staples, the local celebrities, and towards foreign flavours and unfamiliar broths. Given the seeming

---

[62] It was the town bugler, who goes at it at midday every day. He doesn't usually play the US anthem. It's usually a local tune. An exception was made.

popularity of the café, it would appear the common feeling is that the menu is better for its breadth. When I step out of the café, I notice fish on the walls of New Fish Street. The artful clearance of muck and grime has produced – by reduction – a shoal of innocent mackerel. Odd to think that the act of erasure can be creative.

I am facing a castle that was used as a processing facility by the SS, a sort of antechamber to the concentration camp at Majdanek, three miles south, where half the city's population was erased. The castle is low and broad-shouldered, with a pair of circular front windows that look like eyes. The whole thing looks like a mechanised bug, ready to hop down the road to Warsaw or Lviv. It's a museum these days, and among its artefacts is Jan Matejko's *Union of Lublin*, an epic painting which shows the ceremonial coming together of Poland and Lithuania in 1569. The Polish-Lithuanian Commonwealth was a key player on the world stage until the late 1700s, when it was mistaken for a quiche and divided between Russia, Austria and Prussia. At the back of the museum is the Holy Chapel, whose Russo-Byzantine frescoes are said to be top-notch. When I reach the chapel it's clear you need a ticket to get in. I enter without one, because I'm like that, and have a good look at the frescoes for about five seconds before being ushered out by an usher.

A woman is on her knees at the end of a pedestrian crossing. Her outstretched arm is deflected by shins, as a crossing mob hurry to the market or the bus station. Her appeal has the character of a prayer, a supplication, suggestive of faith rather than belief. I answer her prayer then proceed to the market, where there is no danger of finding eleven types of olive. The goods are strictly run of the mill: knickers, sausage, winter hats. I'm struck by how much each vendor can squash into their section. Often the vendor is lost amid stock, engrossed by jackets and slippers. Perhaps it's a matter of temperature. Five hundred pairs of jeans, suitably arranged, will keep out a chill. In any case, I am more than once surprised to find a person hiding within the womenswear. I buy a pair of orange gloves for five zloty.

I spend the evening at Vanilla, watching the election coverage in my room. The captions are inexplicable, the footage loopy. It's evident the Polish news channel could only afford a certain amount of footage – about fifteen seconds' worth – which it is compelled to repeat indefinitely. The footage shows Trump walking onto a stage followed by his wife, and then cuts to Trump in some other place, feigning interest in a baby, before going back to Trump walking onto a stage followed by his wife, and so on. Hilary isn't getting a look in. The focus is on the rogue underdog, the black sheep with blond hair. I manage a hundred loops – the nonsense is entrancing – and then switch off.

❧

I wake up to snow and President Trump. Both came in the night to reset the known world. I want to open my window and call out to a small boy passing below (as Scrooge on the morning of his revelation) and bid him make a million snowballs and throw them at anything news-bearing until the earth makes sense again. The headlines are in Polish but the message is clear: Trump has been hired, a cartoon has been crowned. The next thing is a pet getting elected. A chihuahua. That eventuality is actually more palatable, because a chihuahua can't talk, or issue executive orders, or antagonise, or impoverish, or build walls, or incite hatred, or promote prejudice. I pick up the phone and share my shock with the receptionist. Would Poland elect Trump? I ask.

'We already have. His name is Kaczynski.'

The receptionist mentions a place called American Corner. She doesn't know what it is exactly, but she knows it exists. That's good enough for me. I take a bus north and then west. We pass a classic façade that bears the inscription '*In Dubio Mitius*', which I repeat until the phrase hardens and sticks.[63] When the bus terminates outside KFC we all bundle off amid a housing estate split by a six-lane highway. I stand on the overpass and look at the tail lights and think of that song by Simon and Garfunkel, wherein everyone's driving around looking for America.

American Corner is not what I expected. I expected a hillbilly in a rocking chair chewing tobacco and singing songs about the ol' river. What I get is a section of the local library. There's an American flag, cardboard statues of Liberty, Pluto and Donald, shelves of *Vogue* and *Time*. I pick up a guide to American slang, commit some phrases to memory – *quit your*

---

[63] Where there's doubt, be lenient. Fine for sentencing, less so when electing representatives.

bitching, plead the fifth, Monday morning quarterback – then return to the main library and go up to the counter.

'Pardon me. Can I speak to an American?'

'There's one coming next week.'

'That's disappointing.'

'Quit your bitching.'

'Sorry?'

'You heard.'

'Who's coming?'

'McKenzie Hightower.'

'Who's that?'

'She's a writer from Kentucky who'll host a fortnightly workshop from next Thursday.'

'Do you have her email address?'

'Sure.'

I send an email from one of the library's computers. 'Dear McKenzie. You don't know me but if you're in Lublin already get in touch. We need to talk about Donald.'

I go to British Corner, a small library sponsored by the British Council about ten minutes away, because the guy at American Corner told me about it. The outfit is winding down, I read. Borrowers are under no obligation to return items. The librarian tells me the slogan of British Corner is 'Be British Sometimes'. To my mind, that's a reasonable slogan. It displays the right amount of ambition, the right amount of zeal. If I were forced to head up a propaganda machine, a national front, that's the sort of thing you'd get from me. *Be British Sometimes*. It leaves room to dabble in other cultures, borrow ideas, go Dutch at the weekend. Leaving British Corner, I spot a poster promoting a forthcoming lecture to do with representations of Polish immigrants in the British Press, to be given by one Professor Irmina Wawrzyczek of UMCS, one of the local universities. I won't be in town for the lecture so decide to go to the university immediately, on the off-chance Professor Wawrzyczek's free to talk. It's a short walk, back towards the centre. I know I've found the campus when I hit upon a statue of Marie Skłodowska-Curie, who lends her name to the institution.

I enter the Humanities Department and ask a couple of ladies talking in the foyer for assistance. It happens that one is a departmental secretary or similar, has keys to every room, is fond of the Professor, has her over for supper once a fortnight, and is prepared to lead me, peremptorily, as if leading a child to detention, via a string of corridors and elevators and cafeterias, to the Professor's office, which my chaperone enters without knocking. It's empty, so we go next door to an admin office, where I'm introduced to all the staff. 'This young man, may God bless his soul, has come all the way from England for a special appointment with Professor Wawrzyczek.' I start to get anxious. I didn't use the word special. I didn't mean to cause such a fuss. I didn't count on the lady being so dramatically helpful. Just as I'm about to burst my own appendix to get off the hook, it's announced the Professor is deputising for a senior faculty member on the floor above. When we reach the floor above my escort enters a room, emerges seconds later with what can only be described as a professor, does a little bow, then disappears. I can sense that Professor Wawrzyczek, Dean of the Faculty of Humanities, esteemed author of several large books and pressed for time, would like to know what this is all about, so I explain as well as I can how I hadn't meant to disturb her, how the lady that delivered me had got carried away when I expressed an interest in locating her, an interest prompted by a poster I'd seen at British Corner that hinted at a forthcoming lecture the nature of which—

'Sorry what?' she says impatiently. 'A lecture at British Corner? I know nothing about it.'

'Ah. Well. Well then. Well then I suppose I … I suppose I'd better—'

'Oh!' she says, the penny dropping, 'I'm afraid that was two years ago.'

'Ah. Well. Well then. Well then I suppose I … I suppose I'd really better—'

As I start to meekly back-pedal, to humbly withdraw, the Professor asks my name, and when I tell her, something happens to her eyes, something magical, something transformative. Almost giddily, almost star-struck, the Professor tells me that her son is also a Benjamin, that she would happily send me a transcript of the lecture and some other relevant articles, that she would be happy to meet me at my earliest convenience to discuss her research, and that I'm welcome to visit the family home at any time to sample her husband's best whisky and cashmere pyjamas. I am quite sure that if my name was Christopher or Robin or Gary or Blake none of this would have been possible. A portion of the unconditional love Irmina holds for her son is, it would appear, involuntarily extended to his namesakes, which is good for me, otherwise I might have got a clip round the ear for perverting the course of higher education. I thank the Professor profusely, then swiftly exit, before she starts to remember the manifold ways her son infuriates her.

I return to the old town and there watch a happy crowd slip out the back of a theatre. They've seen *Twelfth Night*. 'In nature there's no blemish but the mind. None can be called deformed but the unkind.' That's *Twelfth Night*. I think of Trump, the great deformer, as I enter the old square, which is a mere shrub next to Wrocław's or Poznań's, but has charm nonetheless. What makes it charming? It's difficult to say. But let me try: it is the modesty plus the grace. Maybe beauty divided by effort equals charm?

After a nap at Vanilla, I go to a club called Silence, which I spotted while returning from the university. It's 10 zloty to enter and the interior is shocking. So much light. If we must debase ourselves at a disco, let us do it in the dark. The walls and ceilings remind me of the Russo-Byzantine frescoes in the Holy Chapel. I get a beer then sit on a cracked vinyl couch in a corner, over by the pool tables. The music emanating from the DJ zone barely reaches this end of the room; it gives up halfway, which is as well really, because it's Disco Polo.[64] It's taken me months but I've realised that Disco Polo is the only genre of music that is in fact one song.

---

[64] Type of popular music beloved in Poland since the early 90s. Characterised by simple melodies and indecent lyrics.

It's sixteen months, five days, two hours and eleven minutes long. It has all the sophistication of a fart. No, that's not right. That's lazy. To compare anything to a fart is lazy. What else has a profound lack of sophistication? A sock? Peanut butter? The unisex toilet I'm sat close to is probably more sophisticated than Disco Polo. It must be. How else to explain its popularity? There're 50 people in the queue. I've only been here ten minutes but I want to leave. A boy sits next to me. It's one of the bar staff. He might have served me my beer. He says his name's Maciej and asks what I think about Trump. I turn to him. 'Seriously?' He's serious. He wants to know and I've nothing better to do so I tell him.

Trump wasn't born yesterday. He has a billion followers, a trillion subscribers. He's a celebrity, and when celebrities run for office they tend to go well – Reagan, Schwarzenegger. Trump has his own tower. He is the embodiment of the American Dream, which is dreamt, downloaded, pirated, paid for on credit, by millions. Trump is a demi-god and when he started to talk politics he talked it like a regular guy at the bar. People heard the sound of their own voice, their own arguments, their own fears, and they liked it. He was anti-immigration, pro-deportation, pro-life, anti-gun control, counter-terrorist, anti-international, anti-political correctness. He said unequivocal things – build a wall, send them back, the media are the worst people, Obama started ISIS. The primary slogan of his election campaign was Make America Great Again – simple, nostalgic – but when was it great? When everybody was a Red Indian? When it was only the Pilgrim Fathers? When the Pilgrim Fathers were on their way? During the Civil War? During the Great Depression? When racism was State policy? America was never great, and nor was Britain, not fully, not entirely. Great aspects, sure, but plenty of shocking

ones too. To wish for a return to the great days is to wish for a repeat of
something that never happened. It is to fantasise. Trump's was a fantasy
campaign. But it didn't matter. It didn't matter if the campaign was
wrong, bogus or vile. It didn't matter how rich, how unqualified, or how
unpleasant Trump was. It all scored points. He became impervious to
criticism. Punches didn't land. Experts were phonies. Elites were looking
out for themselves. The media were the worst. Trump was more credible
than truth and he spread like wildfire. He got constant media coverage
– major networks got him in the studio for a flogging but only served to
spread his brand. During a televised Brexit debate Boris Johnson used
the phrase 'take back control' 47 times. If you say something enough
it registers. Trump's campaign spent more money on red baseball caps
that said Make America Great Again than on polling, consultants or
advertising. You know about Stanisław Tymiński? Stan was born in
Poland but went to Canada and became a wealthy businessman. He
came back to Poland, utterly unknown and with no qualifications or
experience, to run for president in 1990. Clown, right? A mad man,
yeah? And yet the people lapped him up. They loved him. He was
a maverick. A political virgin. A man of the people. He promised
immediate prosperity for all Poles and in the election he out-performed
the sitting president and forced a run-off with Lech Wałęsa. Politics is
insane because people are insane. Are you insane?

I turn to Maciej. He's not there. He's gone home to order
a hat.

28

Everything is in the east if you keep going long enough

18 November. Mirek (he of the abstract thesis) comes over and says that his colleagues often buy Asian soup for lunch which he thinks is unpatriotic. 'I don't know where to start with that,' says Richard. 'Actually, yes I do, what is Asia, Mirek?'

Mirek looks at me, at Anna. 'Do you not know about Asia, Richard? Have you not heard about it? It is in the east.'

Richard curses. 'Everything is in the east if you keep going long enough. *Jesus Christ.* You're orientalising, Mirek. It's disgusting.' Mirek doesn't flinch. His stance is robust. He is worried for Polish soup in the face of Asian alternatives. He fears that certain recipes will die out, and nobody will notice, because they're on their phones ordering sushi from Warsaw. 'What? What are you talking about?' says Richard. Mirek recalls the time he went to the east of Poland for a bonding weekend and his colleagues ordered sushi from Warsaw, 200 miles away.

'That does seem odd,' I say.

'That does seem absurd,' Jenny says.

'You're all bigots!' says Richard, 'Why the hell shouldn't they order sushi!'

The argument may seem histrionic and trivial, but I think it's important. The underlying struggle, as far as I can see, is between a sort of nationalism and a sort of globalism, between one's country and the world. Where should one's emotional (and thus culinary) affiliation lie? With which community should one primarily identify? Richard is by instinct a humanist, Mirek a patriot. For my part, I don't care where the soup's from: I just eat it.

2 December. I pass a block of flats. In one of the several hundred windows is an Esperanto flag. I've seen the flag before in Poland, several times in fact, because the language of Esperanto was built by a Pole. Ludwig Zamenhof was born in Bialystok in 1859. Not one for football or discos, Ludwig spent his teenage years cultivating a sensitivity to *difference*, and what that difference too often meant: division, confusion, hostility. Ludwig was a Polish Jew living in a town that was culturally and ethically and linguistically and theistically diverse. He valued the diversity, liked the look of it, sensed its *potential*, but at the same time lamented what it too often begot – the hierarchies, the prejudice, the chronic misunderstanding, the scapegoating and gossip. Zamenhof saw that at the root of a lot of conflict is language. From this he extrapolated that the construction of a *shared* language would make it easier for different groups to understand and respect each other, and therefore harder – inestimably harder – to dislike and disrespect each other, to fight and war. Over the next years, Zamenhof got his plans down on paper, swatted up on demonstrative pronouns, studied semantics and sound inventories. He built a language. People cottoned on; the cause was taken up; the Word spread. After the First World War, when a lack of common feeling played out murderously across Europe, the League of Nations very nearly adopted Esperanto as its official operational language. One country vetoed the proposal. Had it not done so, we might have been spared some of the hostilities witnessed around the world over the last century. From what I've gleaned, Zamenhof was a legend, and his language an unsung work of humane genius. He is my new favourite Pole. I will learn Esperanto: *Mi lernos Esperanto.* I'll go to the next international conference (which happens to be somewhere nice and sunny) and chinwag in my auxiliary tongue. It'll be my tribute to the late Polish polyglot who tried to fix the world.[65]

6 December. I go to a place called English Johnny, a café-bar off Saint Martin. Johnny comes over and sits with me. He tells me he's a lorry driver from Newcastle and I think, you know what, you *look* like a lorry driver from Newcastle. Johnny tells me he used to shift pop stars around Europe, including Adele and Engelbert Humperdinck, whose wife had a wonderful pair. 'Big plastic things. Pinky and Perky we called 'em. They kept me going for miles.' What was her name? 'The wife? I haven't a clue.'

'So you're telling me, Johnny, that you remember the names of her breasts but not the name of her?'

'Look, don't judge me – you didn't see these things.'

---

[65] I didn't learn the language or go to the conference, but I did buy a T-shirt with the Esperanto flag on it.

I ask how Johnny wound up in Poland. He tells me that it all started fifteen years ago, when he took a bus load of Geordies to Poland to meet distant relatives they'd never seen before. Johnny's future wife was among the party that greeted the bus in a car park on the outskirts of Poznań. She lit Johnny's cigarette, and they got talking. Years later, after a bit of back and forth, they decided to open a café in Poznań. The café isn't intended for the English. It can't be. There simply aren't enough in town. The idea, I suppose, is less to give ex-pats a taste of home, and more to give Poles a taste of souvenir-Britain: Big Ben posters, HP Sauce and Marmite, Union Jack cushions. Lech Wałęsa, the former Solidarity bigwig and President of Poland, sat on such a cushion. 'He came in with this functionary bloke to order a cheesecake. I didn't recognise him, but the Poles did. I still don't know whether to put it on Facebook.'

'Oh? Why not?'

'Well not everyone likes the guy. That's the problem. I don't want to have him as a patron if he's not liked, do I?'

'Well no, I suppose not, Johnny.'

'You've got to think about these things when you've got a café, Ben. It's about profile. It's about perception. You don't have to worry about perception when you're driving a lorry.'

'Well you say that Johnny but—'

'Brexit doesn't bother me. Before you ask. They're not going to send anyone home, are they? Britain needs the Polish, far more than Poland needs the British. But the campaigns were shocking! All the bullshit and bollocks. It was enough to make you want to leave Europe.' I take a sip of tea. 'You should meet this bloke called Gordon Wilson.' I raise my eyebrows encouragingly. 'He walked here from Oxford. Don't know why. To raise money for something.' The plane fare home, presumably? 'Cancer or cholera or something. He phoned me up, said he was going to walk to English Johnny from Oxford. I asked if he wanted to make a reservation, not really following, like. "Nah, nah," he said. "Just be ready to go on the telly when I get there." And he wasn't an alarmist, he wasn't mucking about – he meant what he said. He turned up two weeks later with the Mayor of Poznań. The three of us were interviewed on national television. I still don't know what about exactly.'

When the waitress comes over to see if I want something, I order a full English breakfast, not thinking that its production requires Johnny to stop extemporising and start cooking. 'Johnny, if I'd known it was you cooking …' He brushes away my concern, then leans in to tell me something. 'I've got an actual Cumberland sausage back there somewhere. Do you want it?' I say it rather depends how long it's been back there. 'It'll be grand,' he says, disappearing into the kitchen, a twinkle in his eye.

29

Skiing is like peeling potatoes (Jelenia Gora)

16 December. Jelenia Gora is in the south-west of Poland, a hundred miles east of Dresden. It is the gateway to the Sudeten Mountains. I'll stay here tonight and then head up to the mountains tomorrow, where I hope to stay with the auntie of Jenny's friend Peter.

At the Hotel Europa (which isn't full), I have trouble conversing with Monika. I'm asking about a room, but she thinks I'm asking about dinner.

'I want a room,' I say in Polish.

'One pork chop?' she says in Polish.

'No, I want a *room*.'

'Two, three, four pork chops?'

'What? No. A *room*. Room. One. Me. Today's evening.'

'Pork chop?'

We get there in the end. I wasn't laying the stresses in their proper place, which meant the word for room was coming out like pork chop. The room's okay. There's a view of a car park and an onion in the wardrobe. It's most definitely a single room: there's one cup, one spoon, one teabag, one chair, one onion. If I had a visitor they'd have to sit on the toilet. After reading about the town for a while – it's the home of Omenaa Mensah, a Polish-Ghanaian weather forecaster – I decide the best thing to do in such a room is vacate it.

The streets are serene, cold, and not without a certain beleaguered charm, while the main square is arresting and pleasing in the way that squares, like sea views, generally are. So used are we to roads and avenues that a square strikes us as curiously bold and generous and interesting. Because a square is designed to stop us in our tracks – to be a talking point, an assembly point, a thinking spot – I can be forgiven when I admit to stopping at this one for dinner.

The walls of Lord Lounge are hung with portraits of anthropomorphised canines, while the décor suggests the first-class waiting room at Manchester Piccadilly station, *circa* 1926. One feels almost compelled to order an Old Fashioned, or, failing that, a bowl of tap water and a dental stick. I order a beer, the spicy beetroot soup, a sort of risotto (pearl barley in place of rice) with mushroom and pumpkin and nuts, and then a sticky toffee pudding. Before any of that appears, I am issued an amuse-bouche – a smidgen of *smalec* on toast – and heaven knows it is delicious. Who'd have thought lard could taste so good? When the soup comes, it is a very firecracker, while the risotto is Virtue herself, and the pudding – why, it contains all of Poland in its humble sponge, and much of Europe in its bittersweet glaze. I am making a meal of my meal – so much is admitted – but hyperbole feels appropriate at Lord Lounge. It is the most delightfully pompous place I've been to in Poland. Waiter! The bill, squire! And a doggy bag besides![66]

---

[66] The dog pictures, by the way, were done by Joanna Burda. They go for about 20,000 zloty apiece.

As plenty of other Polish cities, Jelenia Gora has seen its fair share of drama. The town was Bohemian, then Austro-Hungarian, and then Prussian, with each of those alterations involving a deal of bloodshed. The town saw further upheaval during the Second World War, but not much destruction. Indeed, the main issue facing the town after the end of the war was that it no longer had any inhabitants: its Germans had been expelled, its Jews killed. As per the Potsdam Conference, the town was allocated to Poland.[67] Like in Wrocław, a load of Poles were brought in from the east to set up sticks. The whole ordeal must have wreaked havoc with the town's sense of identity. It must continue to do so. Do the young people feel attached to the place? And what of their parents? And what of their grandparents, who would have arrived carrying their lives on their backs? The local football team plays in the fourth division and draws crowds of a few hundred. As a percentage of population, this is one of the lowest in the country. The local hearts are elsewhere, it would seem.

When I return to the hotel the concierge is in pyjamas. He is busy arranging flowers on the reception desk but doesn't mind doing an internet search for bus times to the mountains. He hands me a note – 9.10am – and then a flower, a white rose. I take the flower to my room and put it in a cup of water, which means I can't have tea.

---

[67] It occurs to me now that some of the cities bequeathed to Poland via the Potsdam agreement would have been bombed to smithereens by Polish squadrons fighting on the side of the Allies. There is probably someone out there who bombed their own house.

Gone is Monika. Gone is the concierge in pyjamas. In their stead is a young, red-headed man called Bolek. Having an hour before my bus, I ask Bolek what he'd do in my shoes. He says that's easy, he'd go to a restaurant called Polish Kitchen, which does an all-day buffet.

'Are you serious?'

'Yes.'

'If it was your only hour in Jelenia Gora?'

'My *only* hour? Well that is different. Altogether different.'

'Okay – so what would you do?'

He gives it some thought. 'In fact, I would still go to Polish Kitchen.'

I ignore Bolek and go to the Church of St Erasmus and St Pancras. Erasmus and Pancras are the city's patron saints. The former certainly deserves the recognition. For a start, he translated the New Testament as a *hobby*. He was also a monk, caretaker-manager of the Catholic Church, a classical scholar, and head coach of the Dutch volleyball team. I first heard of Erasmus when I was studying abroad. The Erasmus exchange program allows thousands of students (and teachers) to skip town for a year to broaden their horizons. Erasmus himself studied at Cambridge, Paris and Turin, and counted himself a global citizen before the term was fashionable. He once wrote to a friend: 'That you are patriotic will be praised by many and easily forgiven by everyone; but in my opinion it is wiser to treat men and things as though we held this world the common fatherland of all.' Erasmus wouldn't get elected these days, I fear.

I've just time to climb the medieval tower at the end of ul. Grodzka. I write down what I can see: rooftop pigeons, the gentle rise and sweep of Bank Street (surely one of the loveliest in Poland), the obscure back alleys beyond the ring road, the sublime contrast of industry and nature, chimney and mountain, all veiled by mist and sun. I watch a *babcia* (grandma) telling off some skateboarders, a spherical gentleman in slippers smoking a cigar, a young couple entwined and grinning, as if this were a month of Sundays. It is a good view to finish on.

On the bus to the mountain town of Karpacz there is a boy and he is alone. I am convinced he's nervous about something, and sure enough a few stops down the line, where the road turns south and begins to climb, a girl gets on and sits next to him. The first thing she does is affectionately count the spots on his face. Then she traces the bumps and vales of his skull. These two don't care where they're going: the journey is the thing. He pulls out a flower and a card. She stows the card deep in her bag for later, then inhales the flower carefully, as if it were something to be read.

I alight in the shadow of a rundown church – a rare site in Poland. This is the town's main road, Maya 3. On each side are souvenir shops and restaurants, convenience stores, grilled smoked-cheese stands, bars and pubs. I continue up the street until I come to Willa Andromeda. Aunt Zofia is peeling potatoes in the kitchen. She has short red hair the colour of her lodging house. Watching her peel, I feel an instant bond, for I have been in her shoes. I will render the following exchange in English, but it happens in Polish, and for the most part I have no clue what Zofia is saying.

'Good day, madam.'

'What?'

'I am the friend of your niece – nephew!'

'Yeah?'

'I am the friend of your nephew from Poznań and I am here to stay.'

'It's my lucky day.'

'I am the friend of Piotr.'

'Never heard of him.'

'Piotr said you are his favourite aunt.'

'Is that right?'

'Piotr said I would be welcome.'

'Piotr says a lot, huh?'

A woman appears at my shoulder. A guest. She is Polish, but fluent in English, and agrees to mediate. Zofia puts her side of the story across, then the lady translates. 'Madam Zofia says there might be a room, at 100 zloty with three meals included, but she is wondering who the hell is Piotr? She says she has never been to Poznań, and never wants to. She says she cannot remember anybody ever calling her *Aunt*. Does she have nephews? Does she have nieces? God above knows. She wants to know what time you want breakfast.'

'Eleven?' I say.

'Madam Zofia says Jesus and Mary, are you serious? She

says she doesn't care if you're English the breakfast will be no later than eight. And she wants to emphasise that the room is for *single* occupancy, no matter the occasion, and you must have a bowl of soup before you do anything else.'

The soup is cabbage-based with bits of redeeming bacon and rib – *kwaśnica* they call it. I eat alone in the dining room, at a table set for two-dozen. There are pictures of the villa on the walls, as well as the Pope and various beach scenes. A slim man – Uncle Anthony? – arrives to take my empty bowl. Only it's not empty. It was a big bowl and I couldn't get through it. He looks flummoxed, scared even, for now he's faced with the prospect of reporting back to Zofia that the soup didn't all go down. He calls over his shoulder. *'Myślę, że pan Anglik nie docenił swojej zupy, moja droga.'* I think that Mr England doesn't fancy the soup, my dear. *'Wylej mu ją na głowę!'* cries Zofia. Put it on his head! Then Uncle Anthony smiles, drops his stern façade and concedes with a wink that he is only playing, before taking the remaining soup to meet its maker.

It has been nearly ten years since I skied. Watching the skiers come down silkily, I am incredulous that I ever managed something similar. They are so at ease they're able to record their competence on smartphones as they descend. I dislike all of them. I enter the rental hut. The outfitters are a jovial bunch who enjoy speaking English. The boss asks if I want boots.

'Just one will do,' I say.

'Very good. Poles?'

'Too many in my opinion.'

'What?'

'Go on then. If only to signal with.'

'Helmet?'

'Nah.'

'Helmet. Now go.'

The worst bit is dismounting the chair lift. After that I'm alright. I fall over once but nothing major. All things considered, it is a generally pointless couple of hours – in that it's perfectly unproductive. This is by no means a bad thing. It is sort of meditational. Skiing at this level, on an intermediate run, requires just enough concentration to prevent you thinking about anything serious or boring – work, debt, erectile dysfunction – but not enough to make the whole thing a strain. In this respect skiing is like peeling potatoes, which is a comparison I never thought I'd make. I'm sure there are some good essays on skiing – plaintive, thoughtful, insightful – but you're not going to get one out of me.

I unclip and shuffle over to a small eatery for a cup of *żurek*. Two men join my table. One asks after the soup, as if it were a relative. I say it's good, but not the best. He shrugs, as if it were ever thus, then says I should have ordered the *pierogi*.

'But I don't like *pierogi*.'

'What was that?'

'I don't like *pierogi*,' I repeat, holding my nerve.

He looks at his friend, then at me, then at his friend, then at me, then at his friend, like a film gangster on hearing bad news. 'Serious?' he says.

'Yup.'

'What filling?'

'All of them.'

'All of them, huh?' He stews on this, chews his toothpick. 'And who, may I ask, if it's not, you know, too impertinent, *made* all these dislikeable dumplings?'

'I bought them from the shop mostly.'

'*To czego sie, do cholery, spodziewałeś?*' He laughs. It's a false alarm. It wasn't real *pierogi*. 'You must try my grandmother's *pierogi* before you say another word.'

'I'd like to.'

'You can't. She's dead.'

I go to a pub called Morskie Oko, where I get talking to a Pole at the bar. We converse in a mash-up of English and Polish. His name is Hubert and is a dairy farmer. I ask about his cows, whether they're good ones etc. Hubert pulls out his phone, scrolls through pictures: cow, cow, cows, tractor, cow, his wife in her wedding dress, cows, milk, tractor, cow. I'm impressed.

'I would like to meet your cows,' I say.

'Yeah? Which one?'

'All of them.'

'I dry them twice every day.'

'Why?'

'I *dry* them. For the milk. Alone. Every day. One hundred cows. You must visit my cows.'

'Okay.'

'Good.'

'Yeah.'

'Fine.'

Hubert's wife comes to retrieve him. We exchange numbers (Hubert and me, not his wife and me), and agree it was wonderful to have met each other.

Opposite the pub is a big hotel. It is twenty times larger than any other building in the town. It is in every sense and aspect an anomaly. *Hotel Gołębiewski*. Upon entering, I am met by the amorphous shriek of children and the smell of chlorine. I take a lift to the eighth floor, the uppermost. I am joined, on the third or fourth, by a woman in a dressing gown carrying a plate of food. I am not sure how one measures such things, but I'm sure she's not pleased to see me. The carpet on the eighth floor is reliably unpleasant, an artist's impression of squashed tiramisu. The corridor is a hundred metres long. There are no windows. You have to reach a wing of the building before there's natural light. At the north-east corner a door gives onto a communal terrace, whence I can see the rear balconies of the rooms I've just passed – identical arrangements of plant and table, with bamboo screens to privatise a shared experience. On three of the balconies women of a similar height look up to the mountain and smoke, more or less in sync. They cannot see each other but I can see each of them. It makes a nice picture. The sixth floor is for conferences. One is ongoing. I wander into the main conference hall, finger some literature, lift some fruit, then proceed to the fifth, where there's a kids' zone. A handful of kids are presently interred. They look bored. One kid, no older than six, is making a phone call. Who's he calling, his lawyer? Around the corner is Tropikana, for swimming and fitness. A vast window lets me experience Tropikana without the inconvenience of entering the place. Adults absorb media on sunbeds. Children travel down chutes like parcels of garbage. I picture the late Theodor Adorno – who wrote about the standardisation of leisure, about leisure time as an extension of factory time – on one of the sunbeds, taking it all in, a scathing review forming on his lips. I return to the main reception and ask if there's a job going.

'Sir can clean?'

'I keep the flat pretty tidy.'

'You've evidence of that?'

'Yeah, I guess I have.'

'Come tomorrow. Between 7am and 3pm.'

'How much is a room, by the way?'

She laughs, enjoys the joke, then realises I'm serious. 'A room is … well … it's quite a lot in fact. Are you sure you want to know?'

A single room is 700 zloty, or 70 hours' work. I take an armchair instead, order a coffee, watch a cleaner buffing the floor. She's got a lot of ground to cover. I watch her steadily for a minute, at one with her trembling machine. Then the machine cuts out. She's reached the limit of her extension. I couldn't work here. I'd freak out on day two, make a run for it, bypass the queue outside Tropikana and jump into one of the pools in my uniform. There's an aquarium by the hotel entrance. I stop to stare at the fish on my way out. The fish look lost and purposeful at once. It would be easy – too easy – to compare the tank to the hotel. Outside, a bank of dark cloud against the fading sky resembles a mountain range. I walk slowly away from the hotel, because the prospect is beautiful.

At dinner there are two Polish families and me. I am ten minutes late. There'd been quite a bit of chat going on before I turned up, but now there is silence. I'd hoped to sort of just blend in, or if not blend in then be ignored, but now all talk has ceased. Because of me. I say a sequence of things in Polish that are either deeply banal, potentially offensive, or so grammatically wrong as to be senseless. *It is my opinion that potatoes have a big meaning; I am happy to be in Poland but not its history; the snow is in the process of being cold.* During the main course – breaded pork cutlet topped with cheese and grated carrot – I opt to perform my ideas rather than enunciate them. I gesture skiing, England, fish and chips, abortion. The adults are unmoved, but the children think I'm a hoot. They laugh at me indulgently. Olga in particular can't stop giggling. I ask her what's funny. She answers in Polish, then her father translates: 'Olga is accustomed to being the most stupid in the room. She is enjoying having the night off.' The children are Olga and Wojciech, who have travelled from Krakow and are well behaved, and Radek, who has arrived independently from another planet. Radek is focused on eating as many potatoes and bread rolls as possible. When Radek starts licking the buttery sauce from his plate, his father, by way of explaining his son's behaviour, says, 'Forgive Radek, he's from Warsaw.' This gets a laugh from everyone. When the pudding arrives and is larger than the main course, I rise from my chair, indicate a bloated stomach, then go out for a pint.

I cross Maya 3, descend Mickiewicza, then enter Paddy's Irish Pub. I sit down and write, my thoughts muffled by the sound of football on the telly – the divisions of Europe are playing out on a split-screen: a duel in Naples, a clash in Munich, a contretemps in London. At half-time, a fiddly trio turn up and start thrashing out tunes. When it all starts to get lively, I leave the pub and continue downhill until I reach Jaśkowa Izba. The barmaid has a sister in Leicester. We talk about her sister and Leicester and her old job at the big hotel. I ask why it's so big. She shrugs. 'Big rooms, I guess.' Then Gregory turns up. Gregory's a cook at the big hotel. Ewa – the barmaid – pours us all vodka then asks if it's true the English don't like the Polish anymore. I drink the vodka then rubbish the notion. 'There were one or two,' I say, 'compared to millions who don't care one way or another, and tens of millions who don't dislike a single human soul. You are welcome anywhere, Ewa. You too, Gregory. Believe me.'

Alcohol inspires candour. When I get home, I am tempted to put a note under the door of room 2. 'Don't let Radek eat so much.'

30

In you come

24 December. The plan is to approach a random house and ask if I can come in for dinner. You see, in Poland there is a tradition of setting an extra place at the table for the Christmas Eve feast in case a stranger turns up. It is meant, I suppose, to reinforce the notion that Christmas is about sharing, kindness, and bearing in mind those who are in need. Everybody I spoke to about it knew and honoured the tradition, though nobody knew of an occasion when someone actually turned up. The doors I plan to knock on later will all be in the vicinity of Jenny's family home, because if I don't have any luck Jenny said I can come to his. With this in mind, Jenny calls to ask if I could come to his parents' house with the chopping board he's made for his sister before I commence my experiment. He left the flat in a hurry and forgot to take it with him. Fine.

It isn't easy to carry the chopping board. It is just a little bit wider than the distance between one's armpit and one's fingertips when the arm is fully extended, meaning I can't carry it as you might a folder or similar. The best way in the end is to use my arms to stabilise it on my head. There aren't many people on the streets to draw odd looks from. They are probably all on their way by automobile to have dinner with people they know. The city feels closed, emptied. It isn't unpleasant, as far as atmospheres go. What is unpleasant is the weather – jolly cold, overcast and windy. Because of my obligation to the chopping board, and a lack of gloves, I'm forced to expose my hands to the elements at all times. By the time I reach the Theatre Bridge, therefore, I have forgotten I have fingers and have largely lost the feeling in my arms. As a result, I've almost lost sight of the fact that I've a chopping board on my head.

When I get to Jenny's house I can see him through the kitchen window. I am worried for a second that he's helping with the cooking, but he's only washing his hands. He spots me and gestures something dramatically, pointing at the chopping board and then at something in the house I can't see. He opens the door before I can ring the bell.

'Benny, hide the frigging chopping board, dude!'

'Jenny, how the frig do you expect me to do that?'

The chopping board is snatched off my head and hid in the garage. Then I'm sat at the kitchen table and told to relax, but I can't. I am feeling increasingly anxious and uneasy. I don't want to be strange. I want to stay here. I want to unwind and put my feet up and chat and be in the company of friends. I don't want to go back outside and wander the streets, knocking on doors to see if I can ruin a family's evening. I don't want to test the sincerity of a tradition. Every culture has empty traditions – so what, big deal. Besides, I'm not exactly in need. I've been invited to eat with Jenny's family. Am I not being insensitive and deceptive by imposing myself on others? Plus it's cold outside and I still can't feel my arms. All things considered, I'm better off where I am.

Which is why I go. I walk up and down the surrounding streets for nearly an hour, trying to identify the most likely house and practising my lines, which I have written down on a Post-it note stuck to the box of chocolates I've got with me in case someone lets me in. '*Dzień dobry. Jestem Benjamin. Jestem z Angli. Słyszałem, że to tradycja* …' Choosing the right house is important. What indicates a kind spirit? What betokens the sort of household that, in order to do a 'good' thing, will risk jeopardising the rest of their evening? I dismiss anywhere too big with flashy vehicles in the drive ('Easier for a camel to pass' etc.) and anywhere with too many Christmas lights ('Methinks the lady doth protest too much' etc.). Then I find the house. It is a modest size, and elegantly decorated with a tasteful number of festive lights. I hesitate at the front gate. I look down at the box of chocolates, look back towards the beckoning warmth of Jenny's living room, take a deep breath, then ring the doorbell. Three people rush to the front window, yank the curtains back and have a good look at me. They are all small – the tallest not much more than a metre – with an average age, I'd say, of about four. They arrived at the window wearing excited smiles. Those smiles have gone. They were expecting someone else. A taller person in a red dress comes to the window, looks at me as though I were an unexpected parcel, then tells the children to withdraw to the back of the house, where it is safe. The lady opens the door the way you might to – well, to a stranger.

'*Wesołych Świąt,*' I say. (Merry Christmas.)

'*Tak* …' (Yes …)

I give my speech. I explain that I am Benjamin from England, that I've heard of a tradition in Poland to prepare for the unexpected arrival of a stranger on Christmas Eve, and that, well, here I am. She says nothing, checks behind me to see if I am concealing somebody else, then reaches out for the chocolates and says, 'You're a bit late, but in you come.'

The children have obviously reported back to the rest of the family in the dining room, because when I'm led through I'm met with seven or eight sceptical expressions. There is an awkward moment – or *another* awkward moment – when Agnieszka, the lady of the house, realises that despite there being a place setting at the table for the unexpected stranger, there isn't a chair for them. She asks her daughter to fetch one from her room. When the chair arrives, it is squeezed in next to Przemek, her husband. While this goes on, I do a lap of the table, introducing myself to each family member, half-kissing the maternal grandmother on the lips by accident. When I tap the maternal grandfather on the shoulder to gain his attention, he almost falls off his chair he's so shocked. A bit hard of hearing, and obviously a keen eater, I don't think he'd realised there was a stranger in his midst. I try to settle him by patting him on the arm, but this only seems to complicate his discomfort.[68] Pleasantries over, I take a seat on the small red plastic chair that has been fetched from Kasia's bedroom, get stuck into the soup, and generally keep a low profile for a bit, giving Agnieszka an opportunity

---

[68] It is said in Poland that a guest in the house is a god in the house. Well, this guy was obviously an atheist.

to justify her actions to her parents and step-parent, who no doubt aren't used to this sort of modern dinner party. Just as my heart rate has started to normalise, Przemek's mother, sat next door-but-one to me, leans across and says, '*Kommst du oft hierher?*'[69] I smile and nod, hoping the utterance doesn't call for a response.

Both parents are unfailingly courteous. If not a god, they treat me as if I might *know* a god. They tell me a bit about themselves. Agnieszka and Przemek met while working at Ernst & Young and now run a herring processing facility. Przemek wants to know about British Christmas traditions. I mention turkey and sprouts and crackers – 'Crackers? You mean for cheese?' – and the Queen's speech, wherein Her Majesty says the previous twelve months were generally overcast with patches of sun and drizzle, and that she's counting on more of the same for next year. Throughout this, Tadeusz, the grandfather, continues to monitor me coolly, as if I was something to figure out. The children, for their part, are equally ambivalent about my arrival. They had thought, when I rung the bell, that I was Father Christmas arriving with a sack of presents, so straight from the word go I was a complete and utter let-down. The boy is too much into his food, and then too often under the table looking for that food, to bother with. An aloof character, if I'm honest, insofar as a three year old can be. The youngest girl is also something of a lost cause socially speaking, but with good reason: she's embroiled in an ongoing psychological battle

---

[69] Do you come here often?

with her mother regarding how much food she must eat before she can get down. The eldest daughter – Natalia – I fancy I can win over. She has a bit of English, which might afford me a way in. Besides, I am sat on her office chair, so we have the experience of sitting on that in common. I ask Natalia what she wants to be when she is bigger. She obviously doesn't think much of the question, for she puts her spoon down bad-temperedly, folds her arms, then says something moodily to her mother, who gives an exasperated sigh then translates. 'She says that she can't possibly say what she wants to do later in life because she doesn't know who she will marry yet.' I tell Natalia that she is very wise – *bardzo mądra* – much wiser than her siblings. She simply shrugs, then throws a dumpling on the floor. I ask her what she enjoys at school. Nothing, she says. I ask what she expects to get for Christmas. Something, she says. I ask if she is enjoying her dinner. I *was*, she says. I ask if there is a carp in the bathtub. She just rolls her eyes.[70] Remembering that my niece, about the same age as Natalia, prefers statements to questions, the weirder the better, I tell her that I ate a lemon last week, a whole one and in one go, and that it still hasn't come out yet. She holds her head in her hands, shakes it from side to side, then turns to me with a massive grin on her face and asks if I want to see her pet rat.

---

[70] Carp is the Polish turkey, and because it tastes best when it's freshest, the carp is traditionally kept in the bath for a week leading up to Christmas and then knocked on the head the day before it's due on stage. Jenny – and this does not surprise me – says that he used to get in the bath with the fish, just for kicks.

As far as rats go, Tomek is a good one. Without consultation, and there not being a place setting for him, Tomek is positioned on my lap, where he does a little dance, finally settles, and then wees a little bit. When I share the news that Tomek has weed a little bit everyone seems very pleased about the fact, if not a touch envious. Przemek explains how they came to have a rat as a pet. 'We reasoned that we already had three disgusting creatures in the house so one more wouldn't hurt.' The explanation reminds me of an idea of my friend Gabriella, a Swedish-Pole, who said that Polish parents will playfully threaten to sell their children to the Russians for the slightest misdemeanour, whereas Swedish parents count even the mildest of admonishments – 'Pardon me, Nils, but would you mind not hiding your vegetables under your reindeer steak?' – as something like bullying. The Poles don't love their children any less, she hastened to add, they just have a different *style*. No matter the style, Polish kids turn out well. For all my complaints and chides, they are a good bunch. Although when it comes to breaking the wafers – another Polish custom – Natalia is unquestionably impolite.[71] Instead of snapping off a corner of mine and making a pleasant wish for me, Natalia snatches the whole thing out of my hand, presses it into her gob, and then wishes I had been Father Christmas and not an immigrant.

---

[71] The wafer tradition was new to me. Before it had been explained that I was meant to break off a bit of somebody else's wafer and then make a wish for them, because the wafer represents the body of Christ, I had tried to use it to scoop up some grated beetroot.

Over the next hour, I eat my body weight in food. I eat herring, carp, 'Greek fish', salmon, two soups, pickled mushrooms, potatoes, *pierogi*, red cabbage and what is left of the kids' fish-fingers. I don't wish to speak ill of the dead, but the carp is perfectly unpleasant – a once in a lifetime experience, if I'm lucky. There is plenty of fat on the fish, which it no doubt put on during its residency in the bathtub, when the children enforced a diet of ice cream and Nutella. Throughout the meal neither of the parents interrogate or scrutinise me. They just let me be, count me as one of the family – which is more of a kindness, I think, than excessive attention. I stay for about an hour and a half – long enough to sample all the dishes, not long enough to overstay my welcome: I'm quite good like that. The family had been astonishingly open and kind, and I didn't want to trespass any further. I also didn't want to be offered any more carp.

As I make to leave, the grandfather rises from his chair, fixes me with a strong look, and then shakes my hand boisterously. '*Nice* to meet you,' he says in English. '*Please* come again.' I tell him I'll see him next year, which takes the smile off his face. Agnieszka sees me out. Putting on my coat by the front door, I apologise again for the surprise.

'It was a lovely one,' she says. I couldn't agree more.

Back at Jenny's house, I am assigned the role of delivering the presents, which is a nice role when you haven't bought anyone anything. Joanna (sister) loves her chopping board. Jenny gets a thermos and a five-kilo sack of walnuts and a one-way ticket to Luton (from me). Andrzej (sister's boyfriend) gets hot chocolate. Ania (mother) gets Joni Mitchell and Czesiu (father) gets a – well, for a long time no one is sure. He unravels his present carefully and mindfully, studies the German description, studies the thing itself, studies the description again, then reaches his conclusion. 'I believe it is a sandwiches maker,' he says proudly, as if he'd just discovered the God Particle. I am very, very touched and grateful to receive a collection of essays by Ryszard Kapuscinski entitled *The Other* and some gingerbread biscuits.[72]

Czesiu's sandwiches maker (which is actually a pancake maker) gets us talking about unlikely presents we have received in the past. Jenny doesn't seem to want to play the game: he brings his knees into himself, shifts back against the wall. 'I know what Jędrzej got that was unlikely …' says Ania. Jenny gives his mum a cross, pleading look, the type a toddler might give during a dispute over building blocks that have been confiscated because they keep being put in the tumble dryer. 'One year,' begins Ania, 'Czesiu was put in charge of buying the presents for the children.' Jenny's face and head slump and sadden. 'They must have been seven and nine, something like that. Jędrzej was desperate for a remote-control car, but Czesiu bought him an encyclopaedia

---

[72] I don't mind saying that it was easier to get through the former than the latter – those biscuits were as hard as nails. I was pleased to read Kapuscinski. I had heard about him – he's something of a Polish legend. He was a foreign correspondent for various Polish media outlets. He would send long, lyrical, fabulous reports from around the world. The essays I received had to do with his experience and understanding of the Other – the person who is not like us. In short, we ought to look out for them, because we're of a kind.

of music, and when Jędrzej opened it and realised what it was, and what it *wasn't*, he cried and cried and screamed and screamed for days and days, *absolutely* traumatised!' Ania starts to laugh and clap; Jenny does not. Twenty years after the traumatic event, he still can't bear to think about it. In Jenny's seven-year-old head, never had the gap between expectation and outcome been bigger. I ask Czesiu how he felt knowing he'd traumatised his son.

'I don't remember! I forgot about that day as soon as I could!'

It's time to go to church. Ania gets serious on me. 'This is not a casual outing, Benjamin. We are not going for a picnic. You are to remember whose house you will be entering. I beg you not to be flippant, and to refuse anything you are offered. If you are offered wine, I want you to refuse. That is not a Shiraz. That is the blood of Christ.'

When we enter the Dominican Church on Independence Street, Ania reminds me to take off my Santa hat. We are a bit late and there is standing room only. I am on my feet for nearly two hours, minus a few minutes when I am on my knees. The kneeling is as much of a problem as the standing. My lack of Polish means that each time the congregation gets to their knees I am the last one standing. Mirek – who met us at the church – thinks I am trying to be blasphemous, to make a point. He grabs my elbow and yanks me down. 'Don't misbehave, Benjamin, or you'll pay for it.' Sometimes I go to mass at Christmas with my dad, but the service is quite short, it's in my language, and we always get a seat because the Church of England couldn't field a cricket team these days. In Poland, the whole thing is a test of faith, to be honest. That said, there is an impressive sense of dignity to it all – the quiet, the reverence, the hymns. As others bow their heads in prayer, I steal sideways glances at tearful grandparents and heedless infants, the latter too young to believe, the former too old not to. I fix my attention on a man nearby whose devotion doesn't suit him. He is on his own, successfully dressed, finely groomed, a worldly CEO with a vast portfolio of material concerns. I saw him outside earlier, doing business on his phone, turning 10 zloty into 100, water into wine. He didn't look like a religious man – I would have put money against the fact. And yet in church his attentiveness and solemnity are awesome. It's as if he knows, or is coming to know, that in the final reckoning all the trappings of his life – money, status, influence – count for nothing. He doesn't require a hymn sheet. He knows the lyrics. Everybody does.

It's 2am when we get back to the house. I ask Ania what her favourite part of the day was. 'I love this,' she says, indicating with a sweep of her hand the wrapping paper and books and chocolates and socks and Czesiu on the floor and Joanna on Andrzej's lap and Jenny on his computer trying to figure out where Luton is. 'I love this mess,' she says.

31

You were never hungry. So be quiet (Konin)

25 December. I'm met by Anna at Konin station. She has a flower for me.

'New coat?' I ask.

'Old. You never pay attention.'

Nietzsche postulated that our best friends are also our best enemies, because they've earned a licence to be honest. Anna doesn't worry about earning the licence, she grants it to herself from day one. 'You need to improve your teeth,' she said in the early days. 'You look pregnant,' she said soon after. 'Shoulders back,' she said once, and then again and again until I got the message. Another time there was a note left on the kitchen table: 'You will not find love if your personality continues like this.' I kept the note as a bookmark.

When we get to Anna's parents' house there is a father in the driveway. He's capped, smoking, moustached, looking very much the sort of man that commanded men in the UB (Communist police service) and then led UN peace-keeping missions in Yugoslavia. His hearing isn't what it was because he's heard too much gunfire. Jacek has a warm greeting for Anna, and a polite one for me. The dog is ridiculous – seemingly shrunk in the wash. Anna's mum takes my coat, stows my bag, then leads me next door to Auntie Danka's.

At Auntie Danka's, I'm presented to a throng of relatives floating around a well-loaded table. I smile and do a series of little bows, like a visiting diplomat. Anna's Auntie Grace – mother of cousins Ola and Dominic, wife of Uncle Wojciech – gets to her feet and says, 'Well, Benjamin, might I say it is a considerable pleasure to meet you,' then doesn't speak to me again.[73] I am pampered from the word go. Would I like tea? Would I like coffee? Would I like my coat taken? My feet rubbed? The newspaper translated? The dog put down? Jacek put away? Wine? Water? I count the clocks (at least ten), and then study the portraits of Anna's great-grandparents, who were forced labourers during the Second World War, among other things. Elsewhere there is a spinning jenny, and mounted daggers and bodkins and various other items of war Jacek took as souvenirs from his peace-keeping jaunts.

We sit down to eat. It is a big spread, at least twelve dishes on the table, some rescued from the night before, most prepared this morning. We are fifteen or so. I'm sat between Anna and her cousin Dominic, who lives in London, where he's completing a PhD about why gay white men like gay black men. Next to Anna, at the head of the table, is Jacek. I'm well within earshot, well within firing range. It's a good place to be. I ask about the pickled mushrooms, about what type they are, but no one seems to know. 'Aristocrat?' asks

---

[73] Anna later explained that Auntie Grace is more or less fluent in English, but is terrified of making mistakes, so holds her tongue. Anna's father Jacek, on the other hand, suffers from a reverse condition. He is more or less influent but is fearless of making mistakes so doesn't hold his tongue for a second.

Jacek, in my direction. I'm taken aback by the question, and a little worried: it used to be Jacek's job to seek out aristocrats and relieve them of their airs and graces, and whatever else came to hand.

'Well, my mother was a nurse and my father a carpenter,' I start. Dominic stops me in my tracks.

'Jacek was referring to the mushrooms. They're called aristocratic mushrooms. That's the best translation.'

The family have heard something about my antics yesterday. They are interested. Anna relays the story – my rehearsing the introduction, choosing the house, the pet rat urinating on me. Jacek is not in two minds about it. 'If he looks like an Arab then he has no chance of entrance!' I am ready to ask Jacek why that would be, why the Arab would struggle, but now he is distracted with his nephew, Marek, who he has in a headlock. 'This man is 100 per cent Tatar! Look at his hair! And his nose! He is a warrior! He fought at the Battle of Grunwald, this boy!'[74]

I ask Dominic about being gay in Poland. He tells me about the time he wrote to the Scouts' National Operations Team (SNOT) to ask if a gay scout would be tolerated. 'The reply was unambiguous: "Anyone can be a scout! Including poofs!"' I ask what it was like telling his family he was gay. 'Everybody was in the living room, or whatever you call it. I was nineteen. I just came out and said it. Dad stopped

---

[74] Battle of Grunwald, 1410. Polish–Lithuanian–Tatar coalition duffed the Teutonic Knights. If you don't believe me, see Aleksander Ford's 1960 film *Knights of the Teutonic Order*.

ironing his trousers, gave it some thought, then said, "Fine by me!" Mum took four or five quick drags on her cigarette then said, "I knew this day would come." My sister, without looking up from the television, said, "Your life is going to be so difficult from now." From now? I thought. Are you kidding me? It had been difficult for years. I was the most feminine thirteen-year-old boy in Poland. You don't get away with stuff like that here.' And is that why you left Poland? Is that why you moved to Northampton when you were 21? 'Partly. But my husband was moving to Northampton, so it kind of made sense.' Husband? 'Yeah. Didn't Anna tell you?'

Dominic is married to a Nigerian guy. They married in London, it not being possible in Poland. They met online, and then dated in Szczecin, a city in the north-west of Poland. Dominic would travel up to visit. He remembers plenty of taunts and name-calling. The verbal abuse wouldn't bother Jermain – who would let it slide over him, choosing not to dignify it with a reaction – but Dominic, honouring a different psychological impulse, would lose his temper and react, and earn one or two bruises in the process. Jermain came to Aunt Danka's house for Christmas a few years ago. How did it go? 'It was fine,' says Dominic, smiling at the memory. 'Everyone loved him. Jacek loved him. Before we arrived, my sister got everyone together and told them not say anything stupid or insensitive, which basically meant that nobody said anything.' I ask how things are in Poland now, alluding to my experience in Gdańsk. 'It's getting better. But to be honest it could hardly have got worse. There are gay characters on TV now. There's even a gay footballer in a popular soap opera, the equivalent of *Coronation Street*. There's a slow normalisation. Or at least there *was*. The government wants a purer Poland, so I don't suppose that will do much for the cause.'

I eat mushroom soup, meatballs in a white sauce, pork steaks, chicken breasts stuffed with tomatoes, duck, salmon in a creamy lemon sauce, four types of potato, pickled plums, poached strawberries and cherries from the garden, and then some Greek fish. While I eat, I keep up a mad dialogue with Jacek, who is determined to share just about every thought process he's ever had. Though more or less deaf, Jacek is the voice of the table, its megaphone, its chief broadcaster. Anna acts as a buffer or cushion, censoring her father as and when, while Dominic on the other side is my analyst, providing footnotes to Jacek's oratory so to contextualise or explicate, to excuse and rebuke. The ladies eat a polite amount then slide off to busy themselves with tea and coffee. The men eat a bit more then leave to take up positions in comfortable chairs. It's an organised retreat from the megaphone. 'This is a psychotic amount of food,' I say loudly.

Jacek sighs ruefully, then says: 'You were never hungry. So be quiet.'

When Jacek leaves the table to smoke, Anna looks at me and shakes her head. She says her father might not be very delicate or politically correct but he is a good man. She tells me that during his time in Yugoslavia, during that country's civil war, Jacek would routinely risk his life by smuggling a Croat across the border in the boot of his car so he could see the Bosnian woman he was in love with. 'When he goes back to Yugoslavia now he has friends in every part of the country. They love him there and I am proud of him but it was hard for me. He was away so much. It was hard for my mum. I was a bad kid. One time I handcuffed my brother to the radiator so I could have sex with my boyfriend upstairs. For three hours!'

When Jacek returns he draws my attention to Anna's new hairstyle. 'She appears to be a German lesbian, right?' Anna looks at me daringly, but I can't defy her father, so I tell him, sure, why not? Anna hits me but what was I to do? Anna has earned the right, or ability, to ignore or rebut her father. I haven't. I have to tread carefully. I may well be a god, but I can be brought down to earth at any moment, and so I humour Jacek, which only encourages him to cast the net of his opinion wider and wider, until his train of thought is practically unstoppable. One doesn't so much talk with Jacek as experience him. All in all, I experience Jacek for seven hours, through dinner and drinks and cake and supper, and then, when it's just the two of us plus Anna and her mum, through most of a film called *Joy* starring Jennifer Lawrence. I don't get a word in. I just listen and watch. It is flipping exhausting. At one point, Jacek halts his marathon address, turns to Anna, and says: 'I like this guy. He's intelligent. He knows what he's talking about. Unlike you two!'[75]

It wouldn't be a fair portrayal of Jacek if I didn't mention that beneath the man's charisma and volume is an obvious

---

[75] 'It's so simple to be wise … just think of something stupid to say and then don't say it.' Homer Simpson.

sadness. During his brief interludes, when he pauses for breath, or stops because his deafness is getting to him, you can sense it. Maybe he can sense it too, which is why it is never long before Jacek rises with fresh vigour and launches into a speech about Margaret Thatcher or the Magna Carta. By now *Joy* has conceded to something darker. The warmth of the fire, plus the evident banality of the new film, encourages Jacek to nap. I follow his example.

⤳

We are due at breakfast at 11am, a special sitting on account of our early departure. Anna gets a phone call as I'm brushing my teeth. It's a minute past eleven. 'Anna! The food is getting cold! *Chodź!*'

We are just four: Auntie Danka and Anna's mum Irena, plus Anna and I. Jacek is in bed with a hangover. In a less crowded atmosphere, the sisters are able to fire some questions at me. Taking it in turns, Danka and Irena use Anna to ask about my age, my job, my prospects; the age, job and prospects of my father and mother; my religion, my thoughts on Brexit, my thoughts on Anna, my thoughts on what Anna did to her brother that time. The latter prompts a question of my own. Was Anna a good child, all things considered? 'There were ten of her!' says Irena. Danka nods enthusiastically in agreement. 'She was everywhere!'

Jacek is playing chess online when we return to collect our things before setting off for Poznań. Anna seems to be taking half the house back with her. She unabashedly loads the boot of the car with a few hundred jars of leftover food, several cooking utensils, whatever bits of furniture she fancies, and the dog. Jacek gives me a parting gift: a book about the Yugoslavian war. He's read it six times, which he thinks is enough.

32

The thing is, I'm not a Catholic (Krakow)

28 December. The days between Christmas and New Year are traditionally odd, so I go and stay with some nuns near Krakow. I'd read in the *Guardian* that the nuns farm carp and let out rooms to make ends meet. That was a sufficient enticement.

I take a train south-east to Krakow, and then another to Staniątki. Lacking a sense of place, I follow the crowd. A spire climbs into view. I cut through a field on a slipshod path until I reach what I consider to be a Benedictine abbey. This is where the nuns live. I head for the adjoining church, it not being obvious where to check in etc. A service is kicking out. A priest is ticking off a pair of boys who left with too much enthusiasm. I ask the priest where I might find the nuns, Mother Stefania in particular.

'Why do you search for them, my child?'

'I've got a booking.'

'Sorry?'

'I've got a reservation.'

'Ah. Is it about the fish?'

'A bit, yes.'

'God only knows what those nuns get up to. Follow me.'

I'm led to a door, told to knock it, then left there. I've never called on a nun before, to say nothing of a nunnery of them. I've a few moments to consider the appropriate way to greet a Sister. Do I offer my hand? Air-kisses like they do in France? Perchance Mother Stefania is colloquial and prefers to fist-bump? The door is partly opened. Part of a sister appears. I take the initiative. 'Excuse me. I'm English. I'm Benjamin. Good evening.' She takes all this on board, then withdraws to get a second opinion. I'm left to consider my performance – was I too much? too stiff? Part of another sister appears. They look similar. They could be sisters. I say the same stuff, but in a lighter, breezier tone. The sister scrutinises me. There's no other verb for it.

'Wait in here,' she says. Here is a sort of porch or ante-chamber. There's not much to do, no magazines or anything, only a picture of Doubting Thomas, so I look at that until the sister returns. 'There's another door, around the corner, I'll meet you there.'

I'm let into a courtyard. Two dogs come up to inspect me. They have contrasting styles. Whereas Reksio barks and barks and barks, John Paul is calm and friendly. And here is Mother Stefania. She looks like she's never had a hangover. I do a little bow then offer my spiel. She cuts me short. 'Yes, yes – I heard from the others. Benjamin. England. Good evening. Is that right?' I'm led inside. We move down a corridor, stop at a map on the wall. She points to Krakow, invites me to point to my home. I point to Poznań. 'England home,' she says. I point to Portsmouth. 'Ports-mouth,' she says, stressing the second syllable. I tell her it's not important or pretty, but she's welcome to visit. She laughs. I make a nun laugh. It feels disproportionately good.

I'm delivered to Room 1. I get the feeling there aren't many guests about. It's a small room, furnished with a single bed, a desk, a crucifix, a reading lamp. There's a view of the top of the church and the wing of the abbey where the nuns lodge.

'Mass is at 7pm,' she says.

'Sorry what?'

'Mass. Seven.'

'Right. Cool. Nice one.'

'Are you Catholic or Protestant?'

'Sorry what?'

'Are you Catholic or Protestant?'

I give this some thought. 'Both,' I say.

She smiles at this, confident I'm being droll, that I must be one or the other, that I'm pulling her leg, then leaves me to it. I partially unpack, flick through the Old Testament, then take a look around my digs. The dining room is set for an army. Apparently, during the spring and summer you can't get a room here for love nor money. I can see the appeal of the place, especially for the converted. I'd sooner patronise the nuns and support the restoration of ancient frescoes than put money in the back-pocket of Ibis. At one end of the dining room is a gift shop. There's quite a spread of merch: fridge magnets, confectionary, fudge, little pope hats, hankies, aprons. These girls are really going for it. They must be proper broke, which is certainly plausible: although God doesn't charge rent, He doesn't exactly pay well.

A dinner has been put out for me in the small kitchen: a plate of liver and onions, with sides of potato and beetroot.

Mother Stefania enters and heats up my dinner in a microwave. Then a man enters. A handyman perhaps. He has an impressive face: it's the facial equivalent of six people sharing an armchair. There's a problem in the garden. That's what I glean. The microwave pings and the handyman exits, pursued by Mother Stefania carrying my liver and onions.

In my dinner's absence, I pick at the beetroot and take in my surroundings. There's a Nespresso coffee machine beneath a picture of a saint, who I assume is Benedict. All I know about Benedict is that back in the day he quit his studies so he could move into a cave on the edge of Rome, where he came to the sort of conclusions that made him a saint. He put down his conclusions in a sort of rule book (*Fifty Shades of Monk*), which remains influential to this day. Mother Stefania returns with my dinner.

'If it's not one thing it's another,' she says in English.

'A problem in the garden?'

'Yes,' she says, 'the *gardener*.'

Mother Stefania talks as I eat. She tells me she's been at the monastery for eighteen years; that she's happy but needs more sisters; that sisters are becoming harder to recruit as the world turns increasingly material and unholy; that tonight she'll be looking for sisters on the internet. I mention that I have a friend called Anthony Russell who has a recruitment agency and might be able to help. I mean it as a joke, but she wants his details. Because we seem to be getting on well, I decide this is the moment to share with Mother Stefania the small matter of my being material and unholy.

'Mother Stefania.'

'I'm listening.'

'I have a question. Maybe serious.' Her smile falters. 'The thing is, I'm not a Catholic.' She waves this away, knew it all along, reckons a feather would tip the scales. 'But I'm also not a Protestant.'

Mother Stefania removes her spectacles, cleans her spectacles, replaces her spectacles, then leans forward with her hands clasped in prayer.

'In which case, Benjamin, what is your question?'

'Do you want me to leave?'

She pretends to give it some serious thought – drums her fingers on her temple, looks around the kitchen for inspiration – then says, 'It is a big church. We have space for you.'

I go to mass. We sing a few songs and then the priest says a few words. I have to guess what they're about – perhaps they've to do with the ostentatious interior of the church, and how much it all cost relative to what the nuns are expected to live off. After mass I do a loop of the village. There's not much going on. The local shop is the big draw. A party of youngsters has gathered outside the shop just to be near its light. I buy a beer then drink it in my room reading the Gospel of John. There's a knock at the door.

'Benjamin?'

It's Mother Stefania. I open the door. Whatever Mother Stefania came to say she doesn't say because she's seen the beer.

'Ah. Heineken. Small problem.'

'Heineken is a problem?'

'Small problem, yes.'

'I should have bought a Polish brand?'

'What?'

'I'm joking. I'll get rid of it. Okay? I'll do it now.'

'No, no. It's okay. Just no party, okay?'

Party? How the hell would I— 'Okay. No party.'

'Do you require more liver?'

'Is that what you were going to ask?'

'Yes.'

'No, Mother Stefania. I'm fine. But thank you.'

When Mother Stefania greets me in the dining room the next morning, she's wearing her Dr. Martens and glasses as usual – plus her habit and gown of course. She invites me to take breakfast, though I soon wish she hadn't. There are lumps in the long-life milk, and the green tea expired in 2000. She asks what time I'll be in for dinner. I'm planning to pop into Krakow, to see what that's all about, so I suggest around midnight. She proposes five and we agree on six. Mother Stefania then attempts to explain that she'll take me in her car – take me where? to Krakow? – but only if I cut my breakfast short and come this instant. I'm more than happy to. The nun-mobile smells of Jean Paul and Reksio. Another of the sisters must take the dogs out, because this is patently Mother Stefania's first time behind the wheel since she passed her test. She fiddles with the radio as we merge onto the motorway, settling on John Lennon's 'Jealous

Guy'. She points at things in the offing – a factory, a farm, a fence – and when she does the car briefly veers the way she's pointing. '*Kurcze*!' she exclaims – chicken! – each time we nearly mount another vehicle. After a while, and after a fashion, we arrive at a place that is patently not Krakow. I've been stitched up. She said she'd take me to Krakow. When she urges me to get out, I give her a piece of my mind.

'This is not Krakow, Mother.'

'*Wiem*.' (I know.)

'So why are we here?'

'It is a good idea.'

'What is?'

'You must go down.'

What on earth are you on about? 'Down?'

'Very tasty attraction.'

'Where?'

'Salt.'

'Salt?'

'You must go down for salt. Quick!'

'Fine.'

'Go!'

It's the Wieliczka Salt Mine. That's what I must go down. Mother Stefania evidently gets a commission every time she drops someone off here. It's 84 zloty as an 'individual tourist'. I'm foisted onto a group of other individual tourists, to be led around the mine by Aga. She's engaging off-the-bat, pithily laying out a few home truths as we descend 350 metres: the mine opened 800 years ago and remained in operation until 1997 when the Poles realised there was salt in the sea;

taken together, the warren of tunnels and corridors measure about 700 kilometres; the salt deposits were discovered when a Hungarian woman told a few Polish boys to start digging and keep digging until they found a gold ring. The lift halts. We step out and onto the moon. It doesn't look like salt. It's grey, for a start, a bit like dirty granite. Aga tells us to lick the walls if we want, then leads us to a pool of water that has formed naturally over thousands of years. Aga says: 'You cannot drown in brine. Would anyone like to try?' I decide it must be satisfying being such a guide. Several times a day you get to deliver a taut and witty monologue that's been heard a thousand times but never twice. Aga's commentary, considered as a piece of literature, is delightfully refined. For Aga, it must be like giving a winning speech at a wedding up to 30 times a week, with each audience as innocent and gay as the last, ready to lap up her salty pearls of cheeky wisdom. I bet Aga's one of the most self-content people in Poland.[76]

We are led into a vast chamber named after Copernicus, who visited the mine when he was a student. There's a statue of Copernicus hewn from salt, and another of Goethe, who came down here in the late 19th century, and another of the statesman Paderewski who came after Poland regained independence in the early 20th, and another of Colin Firth, who came a few months ago having been given no choice by Mother Stefania. Just along from the Copernicus chamber is

---

[76] Months later I sent Aga an email and asked if giving such a fine speech every day made her feel good. Her reply was typical Aga: 'Too much salt will kill you.'

the Adam Mickiewicz chamber, which isn't Aga's favourite spot. 'Mickiewicz didn't even visit the mine,' she says, 'And yet he has a chamber. I don't understand. His poems aren't even very good.'[77]

A series of low twists and turns deliver us to a chapel. A chapel made of salt. I'm impressed. We all are. There are salt chandeliers and salty reliefs of key scenes from the New Testament, including the Last Supper, which has been tinkered with to show Jesus seasoning his soup. Aga says that the miners were very pious and would pray in the chapel for at least an hour a day. (*Dear Lord, is it my destiny to die thusly employed? If so, could you have a look at that. Amen.*) The piety of the miners doesn't surprise me. I would have been in here the whole bleeding shift if I were them. Besides, religion is known to flourish in certain conditions. The more one lacks – wealth, security, direction – the more one has to pray for.

After walking about three kilometres our tour terminates at the lowest canteen in Poland. I have to eat something, if only for the novelty of the arena. I order *bigos*, the national dish. It's not bad. The sourness of the sauerkraut is tempered with a sweet smokiness – lots of meat and paprika – while the gravy is nice and thick and the mushrooms plump. Ironically, if it needs anything it's more salt.

I get a bus into Krakow. It drops me by the river – the Vistula. I cross Most Grunwaldzki, then walk along Starowiślna

---

[77] In Poland, the legacy of nineteenth-century poet Adam Mickiewicz is wildly apparent. He's as ubiquitous as Jesus and John Paul II.

towards the centre. Doing so, I send a text to Mother Stefania saying I won't be in for tea. She replies immediately reminding me that I had agreed to be back at 6pm. I reply to remind her she had agreed to take me to Krakow but didn't. She replies to say that's fair enough.

I continue north until I come to the edge of the old town, which is encased by slim parkland. The name of this popular enveloping space is Planty Park, which can only have been arrived at via a plebiscite or similar, in the way that a new British autonomous underwater vehicle was christened Boaty McBoatface when the Natural Environment Research Council foolishly opted to delegate the naming of their new toy to the British people. Planty Park? *Come on.*

There is no dispute about Krakow being a good-looking city. There are few streets one turns onto and thinks, 'Just what have they gone and done here?' Krakow's market square is the only one in Poland honoured by UNESCO, chiefly because it wasn't destroyed in the war and so chances to be the oldest. The unequal towers of St Mary's Church stand in one corner of the square. You can blame the inequality of the towers on a pair of competitive brothers. Each brother started building a tower, but one brother tired before the other, with the result that his tower ended up being shorter. Struggling to deal maturely with his emotions, the lower brother killed the higher one, before committing suicide by jumping off one of the towers.

I've been told about a good bookshop called Massolit. I nip into a hotel whose receptionist is happy to point out two things: where the bookshop is and my mistake in addressing her as sir rather than madam. (In these fluid times, I consider her remark a bit pedantic.) I follow her direction and locate the bookshop easily enough. It's oddly cosy and restful and ambient. This is odd because Polish bookshops tend to be anything but these things. I buy a collection of Szymborska's poems, Polish on one side, English on the other, then have a bagel in the bookshop's café and read the collection's title poem, 'Moment', which basically tells the reader not to build a tower that's shorter than their brother's.[78]

I step outside. Two nuns pass. My new affiliation prompts me to offer a warm look. It's the mechanics of compassion again – the more you're exposed to, the more there is to value and cherish. I get a cold look back from the nuns, which suggests they could do with being exposed to me a bit more. At the end of Szewska Street, a man is perched on the windowsill of a bank. All his wealth is in a plastic bag. Above him, an advert unkindly screams *0 złoty!*, in reference to an interest rate or similar. It's one of those momentary visual jokes the urban jungle is so good at playing. The man's hands are the hands of an industrialist, a miner even.

I'm back at the abbey at about ten. As I tiptoe across the courtyard, the dogs do their best to wake the nuns, especially John Paul, which isn't like her. I read some poems

---

[78] Wisława Symborska (1923–2012) won the Nobel Prize for Literature in 1996. I had been after a book of her poems since finding one blown up on the side of a building in Poznań.

half-heartedly in bed, then get a phone call. My mother? No. Mother Stefania.

'Where are you, Benjamin?'

'In bed, darling.'

'Really?'

'Yes!'

'Oh.'

'Was there something else?'

'No.'

'Then good night, Mother Stefania.'

I dream about the British Foreign Secretary reading my MA dissertation.

⇌

Again, breakfast is put out for me. I put a finger in the yoghurt playfully (one can hardly do it seriously) and it barely comes out. There's a handwritten note next to some cheese, urging me to try it. I make do with an instant black coffee and a piece of bread then go back to my room to shower and pack. During the shower, there's a knock at the door – the bathroom door, not the bedroom door. Mother Stefania wants to know what my plans are. I put some clothes on then tell her I'm leaving pretty much now. Mother Stefania says this is fine but it's cash only, which makes me wonder what sort of outfit I'm dealing with here. I hand over two 50 zloty notes. She takes them tentatively. 'Spend that on booze and prostitutes,' I say in English, knowing she won't make head nor tail of it. In return for the notes Mother Stefania presents me with a pair of souvenirs: a calendar featuring the abbey and the nuns (fully habited) and a fridge magnet. She won't accept anything for them, which is just as well because I don't have a fridge and the calendar is two years out of date. When the two of us walk through the courtyard to the main gate, it's the first time neither dog barks at me. I have a final look at the abbey, then take a deep and conclusive breath. It's been good. Bloody odd, but good. I should like to hug Mother Stefania but I don't want to get her in trouble. I'm frustrated I don't have the words to truly thank her, to truly sing her praises. I take a few steps towards the gate, then turn. Mother Stefania's smiling at me like a big kid.

33

I suppose it depends how you look at it

4 January 2017. I decide to make the national dish – *bigos*. I've been told it's complicated, so have been putting it off, but tonight I've a pretext: Jenny has some friends coming over to watch a James Dean film. I head to the market at the end of the street – *rynek Jeżycki*. Sour cabbage first, fermented not pickled. An old lady overhears my order and is quick to advise. For six people I'll want double that, she says. Very well, two kilos it is. Then veg: onion, carrot, a fresh cabbage, apple for sweetness instead of prunes. For the meat, I go to the butcher near the flat.

'I will cook *bigos* today,' I say.

'For tomorrow, yes?' says the butcher.

'For today,' I say.

'Are you crazy? Very well, you want smoked bacon, pork shoulder and sausage. Which cabbage have you bought?'

'Fermented.'

'Good.'

From the butcher I move to the convenience store on the corner, where I buy tomatoes, tomato concentrate, the spices and red wine. When I get home, I realise I've forgotten the dried mushrooms. I dash to the shop but it's shut. Jenny insists the dried mushrooms are essential, so he puts out an appeal on social media. He soon gets a tip-off and heads off on his bike to pick up the package. You've got to love Jenny. I put Elton John's greatest hits on and then melt butter in a big pot. I squeeze the fermented cabbage to get the brine out then in it goes. Fresh cabbage: chop, in. Brown the chunks of bacon in a separate pan, in. Brown the chunks of pork shoulder, in. Brown the sliced sausage, in. As it stands, in my pot I've got a blanket of meat on a mattress of cabbage. Chop onions, cook slowly until caramelised, in. Garlic and red wine into the now meaty-caramel pan, deglaze, in. Grate carrot, grate apple, in. Soften mushrooms by soaking, chop, in. Paprika. Caraway seeds. Juniper berries. A bay leaf. A touch of the mushroom stock, touch of tomato concentrate, half a can of tomatoes to lubricate. All in. By now the pot is teeming. Mix, cover, stew for three hours, stirring every half hour. Take off the heat, cool in the fridge until required.

The guests arrive and we watch *Rebel Without a Cause*. When I serve up the stew, I'm pleased with the result. By the end of my second bowl I'm talking about opening a café called *Bigos and Books*. Mirek is supportive of the idea, but the others would rather have another sushi joint. Jenny wonders aloud if there's presently a Polish man of roughly my age serving up a steak and kidney pudding in High Wycombe or someplace to a group of English people. Anna says there's a popular song about *bigos*. Apparently one of the lyrics is: 'Let's make the world a better place, with cabbage as the rule.' I'm in no doubt that if everyone was legally compelled to produce twenty kilos of *bigos* per annum the world would be a more peaceful place. The dish takes so bloody long to make, nobody would have time to squabble.

10 January. I'm about to call a YouTube sensation. Patrick Ney is a friend of Ryan Socash, an American broadcaster I met a few months ago. Ryan said that if I wanted to see an extreme case of assimilation, a fundamental immigrant, I should speak to Patrick Ney. 'Patrick's English, been here since 2010, came over with his Polish partner, makes very popular videos about Polish culture and history, and I'm not kidding when I say he's now more Polish than John Paul II.' In advance of the call I prepare some questions. 1) Despite being from Ipswich, you have stated on camera that you would die for Poland. Are you feeling alright? 2) Why are there 1.2 million Poles in the UK? 3) Can you explain Brexit to me? In the event, I needn't have bothered preparing any questions, because from the word go my conversation with Patrick has a non-linear quality, as if mirroring the commute to work that Patrick is presently undertaking, which involves eleven lefts, six rights and a *volte face*.

'I fell in love with a Polish waitress ten years ago,' he says, 'the economy's doubled in size since.'

'Are you trying to say the two things are linked?'

'I'm saying that Poland is only going one way. I want my daughter to grow up here.' There is a pause while I jot this down and Patrick negotiates a junction. He resumes with a non-sequitur: 'Poland is attractive to foreign investors. Why? You get good workers and low overheads. Bingo.'

'Yeah, but how long will that last?'

'And another thing that lubricates the economy is the fact that Poles don't like to save, they like to spend. For 50 years they couldn't get an orange or a bar of chocolate.

Now they purchase everything they can in case it all disappears.'

There's another lull. In my mind's eye, Patrick is waiting impatiently at a crossing. He goes on: 'Look, being an immigrant isn't easy. When I arrived I had no friends for a year. I knew at that point I needed to learn the language. *Really* learn it.'

And that he did, with the result that Patrick now works in Polish, thinks in Polish, produces children in Polish, and even composes epic poems about the nation in Polish, whereas I'm still struggling to know whether a dog is instrumental or not. It's impressive. Patrick's impressive. If I was a country, I'd want the likes of Patrick falling for me. 'I've got another epic bit of media coming out next week. Have you subscribed to my channel, by the way? You should. This one could be big. I mean, millions. It's about— wait. Give me a sec.' I imagine Patrick picking up the croissant he's just dropped, or quickly taking a call from his mum, who wants to know when he's coming home. 'It's about Witold Pilecki. War hero. Got himself into Auschwitz so he could organise the resistance.'

'Gosh. Rather him them me.'

'His story is incredible and largely unknown. It's an example for us all, really. If I become a Polish citizen I want to apply to join the "WOT" territorial army. A sort of reserve army, so that if the need arises, I can do my bit to defend Poland.' Patrick has arrived at work – I can hear mouse clicks and a coffee machine – so I wrap things up.

'Before you go, Patrick, would you sum up Brexit in a word?'

'No.'

'No. Right. Interesting take.'

'But what I can do is tell you that I find the whole thing frustrating and odd because historically speaking Britain has been exemplary when it comes to diversity and tolerance and race relations. It's sad to see it going the other way. Anyway, cheers for the call. Make sure you subscribe. *Pa*.'[79]

14 January. I go out to eat something at the café on my street. Anita is there. So is her boyfriend or similar, playing on his phone while waiting for her. Then he goes to the shop to buy something gluten-free for Anita to snack on, the sweetheart. I've been invited to live in Hong Kong, she says.

16 January. Richard and I are putting on an exhibition next week. The exhibition will include a selection of Richard's photographs and a selection of my written photographs (imagine describing a photograph to a blind person), all taken from the street we live on. The exhibition will be called *Ulica* (Street) and take place in a small gallery space off St Martin. To make sure Richard and I aren't the only ones there, we actuate the PR machine, which is to say we make an event on Facebook then invite our Friends.

---

[79] The film Patrick made about Witold Pilecki got 10 million views. Patrick now hosts a popular television news programme in Poland. He will one day be President.

21 January. Day of the exhibition. We go to the gallery, remove all the furniture and the Christmas tree, wash the floor, deodorise the whole. I locate a pair of electric radiators, then introduce a few lamps for ambience. Richard has something to say about the lamps. I can tell by his face.

'What?'

'I'm not sure about the lamps, mate.'

'They're for ambience.'

'They'll distract people.'

'What?'

'They'll distract people.'

'You think people will start playing with the lamps? What demographic have we pitched this at?'

'They're distracting, mate.'

'If people are distracted by the lamps that tells us something about the work. Let's keep them.'

I like the moment when, about two hours later, all the frames are hung but still empty. I reckon you could get away with it like this. I imagine the high-brow critics seeing the point of it. 'By maintaining the emptiness of the frames, the artists have put art itself on trial. A triumph! P.S. Lamps a bit distracting.' We come up with an order, carefully fill the frames, and then mount. It is slow, silent work for an hour or so. When it's done, I go outside with Richard's camera and, from the dark street, take a picture of him lining something up, lamp-lit, in the otherwise empty space. Doing so, I have a feeling: something like pride but diluted, and unfocused, and mixed with happiness and anticipation. I want to say something nice to Richard, something honest and nice, about the mix of happiness and pride and anticipation, because it's got so much to do with him. By the time I've got a handle on the feeling, have got some words for it, Richard is on his way to the toilet, and by the time he's back it's gone. How many times a day do we let feelings go like that? How many times a day or week or year do we let good, large, heavy, brief, beautiful feelings like that come and go unsaid, unshared, undelivered?

More people come than expected, maybe a hundred over the course of the evening. Anna arrives with two roses, both for Richard. Jenny is here but doesn't seem to know how it works, while Mirek just walks around forming ideological objections. For most of the evening I am stuck behind the makeshift bar serving wine while Richard gets drunk and mingles. (I'm pleased I didn't share that feeling with him earlier.) We bought a load of booze from Marta, the owner, and are giving the stuff away for nothing, hoping the wine will fill any gaps in talent. As I pour glasses, I can just about hear Richard saying things in a corner of the gallery: 'I wanted to gesture to the fundamental humility of the human condition,' or, 'Ever since I was a baby I've been interested in the contradictions of urbanity,' or, 'Sorry what did you say? I was distracted by the lamp.' Now and again, when a series of bodies all move at the right moment and in the right way, Richard accidentally finds himself staring at me across the busy room with a delighted, half-cut grin on his face. On each occasion, he's good enough to raise his glass in my direction. Most of the people I pour wine for have no idea I'm one of the exhibited artists; they assume I've been hired on minimum wage to pull the short straw. Some, intuiting from my appearance that I hold artistic aspirations myself, touch my arm and tell me to keep believing. I try and amuse myself by making small talk as I go, but each time I ask what frame they like the most it is always Richard's photograph of the women and the dog. One time I'm brave enough to ask what sir or madam thought of the texts. 'They're to be read, are they? I simply didn't realise …'

Tony is my best customer. He's been to see me at least five times. I put this down to the fact he's a teacher. He refuses to ask for a refill directly. That would be too uncouth, too undignified. Instead, Tony prefers to stand somewhere near the bar, put his glass down in my vicinity, pretend to be interested in something else entirely, then whisper over his shoulder, 'I've *heard* the wine is quite good,' which I rightly understand to mean he wouldn't mind seeing for himself, again.

On one occasion, when I was new to this routine, Marietta approached Tony just as I was sliding a full glass across to him. In something of a fluster, Tony pretended he didn't know anything about the glass of wine, didn't know anything about the person sliding it in his direction, didn't even know where he was, which only prompted Marietta to say, 'Well I'll have the wine then!' and knock it back in one. I don't like to think which of them is driving home. Anita comes, does a slow lap, and then leaves. We haven't spoken for weeks, not really.

I've just called last orders when Richard wanders over for a top-up. I'm about to say something heartfelt about his pictures when Tony approaches and says, 'I'm afraid you lost, Richard.' (The white wine Tony's heard so much about has plainly made him candid.)

Richard doesn't know what to say. Then he does. He says, 'Well I suppose it depends how you look at it.'

Tony doesn't think much of this. 'No. I've looked at it every way and you lost.' I fill all our glasses and propose a toast to there having been a contest in the first place.

12 February. Tony calls.

'You mentioned a native English speaker – is it still around?'

'You mean Richard?'

'No, a girl from Essex.'

'I don't know what you're talking about, Tony.'

'What? Wait. Marietta's saying— Ah. It was Jędrzej. Jędrzej said a girl from Essex is moving into your room. Given that you're leaving. Know anything about that?'

'No.'

'Fine. I'll give him a call.'

When Jenny gets back from work, I ask about what Tony said.

'Tony said a girl from Essex is moving into my room?'

'Looks like it. Got a problem with that?'

'It just feels a bit sudden.'

'Dude, you're leaving.'

'And you're comfortable with the idea of me being replaced?'

'Yeah.'

34

And to think I almost died getting here

13 February. I'm going to the mountains again. I've been told about a hut where gregarious ramblers sit around the fire and cook sausages on sticks and sing songs and feel cosy. Richard met a pair of musicians in a bar who said they'd done a concert there. They told him to go; he sent me instead.

I take a train south and then another east to Piwniczna-Zdrój. I seek instruction in the tourist information office. '*Chatka pod Niemcowa?*' I say. The info team say it takes two hours and a torch. I barely have one of those things, I admit.

'Then you can take the bus to Kosarzyska and then walk the shorter, steeper route from there. That way you'll have a chance of arriving before sunset. Maybe I can mark the route on your map?'

I don't have a map.

'So you don't have a map, or a torch, or much time. Are you certain this is your intention?'

The bus driver is jolly. The jolliest in Poland. He greets me with a beatific smile and a high five. I ask for Kosarzyska. '*Prosto, prosto!*' he says, simple, simple. I take a seat. Fellow passengers touch me on the shoulder to confirm the driver's prognosis. '*Prosto, prosto!*' they say. After a few simple minutes the driver stops and points vaguely into the forest. 'Up!' he says. Up. Right. Got it. I thank him, go for another high five but he can't because he has to hold the handbrake else the bus will recede. I turn to the passengers. They nod, point. 'Up!' they say.

The ladies at tourist info quoted 45 minutes from the bus stop. I've got about an hour's light and only a smidgen of battery on my phone.[80] It's a gentle incline at first. Front yard dogs announce my passing to their keepers. Most are securely tethered and mild enough, just going through the motions really, but there's always a jobsworth: a Patterdale Terrier, not content to issue a few barks, jumps onto the garden wall, which is level with my neck, then puts its teeth through the wire mesh fence the better to scare me. It doesn't work. I'm unawed. I'm buoyant. I'm on an adventure and some mutt with ADHD isn't going to ruin my mood. I whistle a tune as the houses thin out. The road thins out as well: it's more of a track now, icy in patches, but nothing bothersome. For twenty minutes there's nothing doing, just a relatively easy incline flanked by forest, and the odd detached property, but then the going gets harder, undulant and increasingly steep. Before long I'm using my hands as much as my feet. After what feels like an hour I finally sense a summit, which is as well because it's almost twilight. I can make out four properties, the size of cereal boxes, each box solid black and pitched on the snowy mountainside. One property has lights on. A ten-minute march through snow gets me to a path that leads up to the property. It's impossible underfoot, an ice rink in the dark. By now I'm panting, straining, and less buoyant

---

[80] You know things are going to go wrong, right?

by half. The back of the property is occupied by animals. I happen upon chickens. It's patently not the *chatka* (hut) I'm after, but at this point I just want to tell someone I'm lost. There's no obvious front door, so I knock on a window. There's no answer. No movement. I retrace my steps (if they can be called steps), using my 1997 Nokia to lend a splash of light. The light falls on a stream. That wasn't here before. I think of hurdling, start to fantasise about falling in and drowning in freezing water, then choose not to. As I follow the stream, the snow is mostly knee-high but occasionally I fall through into waist-high stuff. It's the idea of drowning in snow that really gets under my skin. There aren't many advantages to dying in plain sight, but at least you'd get hoovered up pretty quickly. If I drown in the snow I won't be found till spring. And then, because I'll look fresh and ruddy like I've just got out the shower after a game of squash, people will think I just fell over, or had a heart attack because I eat too much butter. I don't want to overstate the degree of jeopardy. I'm not panicking. Danger of this sort – clumsy, incremental – is actually rather prosaic. I'm not stood at the edge of a precipice. No one's holding a knife to my throat. I am just slowly and steadily being a twat. When I'm still, I can hear a low symphony of vague noises. I think about animals. Hunting is popular in rural Poland. It wouldn't be so if there was nothing to hunt. Many animals that have died out in other parts of Europe survive in Poland. There's the bison, the brown bear, the grey wolf, the Eurasian lynx and the beaver. I could hold my own against a beaver, but I don't fancy running into a lynx. Some people like danger. They get a buzz. You know the type. They drive with unnecessary speed. They climb trees. They marry Italians. They need to risk their life to feel fully alive. I don't. I feel fully alive when I play golf well, or cook something that tastes nicer than expected, or receive a handwritten letter. If I met Bear Grylls we'd have nothing to say to each other. There'd be a prolonged awkward silence. I'd order the soup, he'd order the stingray. The next closest building is about 100 metres away. I start to climb towards it but it's hopeless: the approach is too steep, the way too icy. God knows how the inhabitants commute to work.

A car approaches from below and then parks. Nobody gets out. It's a youngish couple. I know because I'm at the driver's window. The poor things have come out to the middle of nowhere for some peace and quiet only to run into me. The driver lowers her window and confirms I'm off course. She shows me on her phone where we are and where I should be. Four kilometres separate the two. I should have turned right about an hour ago. She tells me to get in. The young man next to her is plainly not impressed by this development. I sense they were about to have a meaningful conversation. We descend gingerly. They've chains on the wheels. I try to break the ice – *you two from here? Doing something this evening?* – but my efforts only add to the chill. I'm told to get out. Sorry? 'Here,' she says. 'Here you say goodbye.' We're down by the Patterdale Terrier. She points out where the track splits. I was too busy eyeballing the dog to notice. I hesitate. If I'm honest I thought she was going to drive me to the hut. '*Idź!*' says the man – go! I offer money to be driven all the way. '*Idź!*' he says again. I get out, they drive off, and I'm back to square one. I plod judiciously in the right direction for ten minutes, but it's no good, I'm on a sodding treadmill. I'll have to swallow my pride and ask for a lift. I call the hut.

'Who are you?'

'Benjamin.'

'Where are you for the love of God?'

'By the bus stop on the main road.'

'Wait.'

I wait until a jeep pulls up. I apologise repeatedly but Jerzy doesn't want to hear it. With some people you get an immediate sense of their character. I've not been in the car a minute before I've decided the man next to me is deep. Visually – slight, sixties, unkempt – he reminds me of Walt, the guy in my neighbourhood who can't ever rub two nickels together. It's not a quick ride, and nor is it an easy one. I wouldn't have stood a chance: the way is barely passable in a jeep. Several times we get caught up and are forced to slide backwards momentarily as Jerzy tries to find some traction by shifting gears and doubling the revs. He is impassive throughout, showing no outward sign of consternation or unease. For him, this is hanging washing on the line. There's a pocket bible on the dashboard, for reading at red lights.

There are two main buildings, each built from logs and sealed in places with flattened beer cans. One is for Jerzy, the other for guests. No electricity, no running water, no signs of life. I'm shown to my dormitory. Double bunkbeds, and a couple of singles. He tells me to sleep on top because it's warmer, and that I should start a fire in the oven for the same reason. He shows me the small kitchen space – tea and mugs and leftover mustards – and a larger dormitory which sleeps up to 50 in season. *In season.* I'm his first guest since the end of summer. There's a reason: although charming and rustic, this place is a fridge. A long-held suspicion that I'm a wally is confirmed. He lights a few candles, gets together a couple of blankets, reminds me where the water is – out there, in the darkness. The blankets don't seem enough. Good night, he says. When I look at him, I hope he can see the moisture in my eyes.

I think about leaving. If I'm already cold, then what is to come? I weigh up my options: they weigh nothing, because I don't have any. I thought there'd be a restaurant, and a warm communal space where a group of us would watch *Good Will Hunting* and drink red wine. In the event, I've checked in to an unheated shed for the night and been handed a table cloth for warmth. And to think I almost died getting here. I try to light the fire. I arrange the smaller logs into a pyramid in the chamber of the oven. I twist and light newspaper and nurse it into gaps, willing its flame to spread. But it's no good. I've said it before: I'm not a practical person. I make jogging look difficult. It ought to be otherwise. My dad was a shipwright and a carpenter. He can put things together in his sleep. And my mum was a nurse. She had to inject and repair. So where the hell is *my* nous, *my* dexterity? Jerzy's back with another blanket, thank goodness. He sees me struggling, tuts, shakes his head, then does it himself in less than a minute.

The round hole in the roof of the oven is covered with a big kettle, which is constantly heated, constantly whistling, constantly topped up. He gestures food, eating, have I eaten? I shake my head, communicate with sad eyes that I thought there'd be a restaurant, or sausages on sticks. He looks at the ground, takes off his cap, scratches the crown of his head. He hadn't anticipated this. He's accustomed to guests being resourceful, self-sufficient, especially those travelling alone in winter. I'm like a cack-handed nephew that's come to stay. Only he doesn't love me, and he doesn't have to pretend to. '*Chodź,*' he says. Come.

He takes me through to his place. There's electricity. There's a radio. The fire is big and blazing. Without saying a word, he sits me down, gives me an apple, some coffee with milk, then heats up a stew of beans and sausage and garlic, which he serves with bread and butter, and a single gherkin. I have never seen such tender and comprehensive hospitality so reluctantly bestowed. I savour it. Boy, do I savour it. The coffee, the stew, the fire, the warmth of each. Simple things, suddenly precious. Value is circumstantial, I think, cradling the mug, beholding the apple, mopping up the stew with bread. As I sit and eat, Jerzy transcribes every detail he can find in my passport into his ledger. My mother's maiden name goes in, as does the fact that I was in Russia a few years ago. Jerzy has learnt the value of information.

'Are your mother and father still married?'

'No.'

'Do you go to church?'

'No.'

'Wife?'

'No.'

'Employment?'

'No.'

'So why are you here?'

When I admit that I'm not entirely sure, Jerzy is forced to conclude that there isn't much to me, that I'm remarkable by dint of doing and believing nothing, that my life is characterised by a lack of faith and a lack of meaningful action. He leaves the room and returns with more food. Not one to serve breakfast in bed, he's serving it now: a jar of gherkins, a tin of *gulasz angielski* (spam), bread and butter. I cradle the largesse in my arms. On top of the picnic he puts a sleeping bag and a key. 'Better to lock,' he says.

I write by candlelight for an hour, drinking cups of hot water to keep my hands warm. I keep the oven full of wood, and the kettle topped up. I start to warm to its whistle and what it means. Coldness reassembles around my bones, notwithstanding the fire. I go outside to piss. The wind – coming up from Slovakia – howls. There's a bounty of stars. One is shooting. I've never been curious about the firmament. I spend my curiosity elsewhere, on more down-to-earth stuff, like cricket and party politics. How we allocate our curiosity says a lot about our character. Note to self: wonder about the stars more. The darkness scares me less and less. I load the fire, put on all my clothes, ignore the sight of my breath and try to dream.

❧

The Pope is at the end of the room. Beside him, two guitars, each missing a string. A chest of drawers is spilling left-behind shoes and hats and T-shirts. No whistle from the kettle, sunlight at the edges of the curtains. I stretch like a cat, drag myself outside. The jeep is gone. Jerzy's out. I see everything by daylight – the huts, the outside toilet, the mountains, the Poprad Valley. Five cats are snoozing in a basket in the sun: the youngest are the friendliest. I sit on a swing and count twenty peaks, not including our own. I look at Slovakia to the south, at its shape and palette, and decide it could be Poland. The grass is as green, the peaks as tall, the air as clear. I listen to snow or ice melting or breaking. You can hear it pop, crack, snap. There's a barbecue area, a campfire, a shower drawn from a natural spring – in this light, at this temperature, this place is idyllic, a brief Eden.

I return to my room, rip pages from my diary and try to make a fire, but it doesn't take to me, I don't catch on. I hear Jerzy return. Some minutes later he brings me coffee and shows me how to do it. He signals for me to watch and learn, to note what he does with the wood, how he scrapes candlewax onto the pyre, where he attempts ignition. His tutorial is – to an extent – self-interested. He thinks I'm here for a few days, so he'd better teach me lest I remain in his care, a prospect that scares him. The coffee is unusually enjoyable. I take it to the outside toilet, where I think about satisfaction. My coffee was unusually enjoyable because of the context – it was unexpected, I was touched by Jerzy's tuition. Now I'm on the loo it isn't the same. In pursuit of happiness, my habit – and I don't think I'm alone – is to consider the thing too much, and the context too little. The trouble is you can't buy a context at the shop. You can't order a batch online, or have one heated up for you. A context can't be summoned; it can only happen. When you ask someone what satisfies them they'll probably give a list of things – badminton, Spain, Naomi. Our conception of pleasure is habitually limited to one ingredient, one constituent – the thing, the place, the person. Closer to the truth is that pleasure is a composite of many small things, some of them invisible, intangible, contextual – mood, temperature, company. One crucial element in any pleasurable context is a *lack* of pain. The stew and fire and apple were all pleasurable because they were preceded by cold, frustration, anxiety and confusion. At the end of the day – and at the start of it – pleasure may be little more than the absence of discomfort, or the presence of relief. Schopenhauer said something along these lines, if I'm not mistaken, on the toilet or otherwise.[81]

I've decided to move on. For all I've said about the site's virtues, I simply can't do another night like that, in that cold. It won't kill me, I'm sure, but I won't enjoy it for a second, and a night made up of seconds is a long one. I'm glad I came, glad I got here, glad I met Jerzy and was prompted

---

[81] Although Schopenhauer's take on pleasure looks downbeat it is arguably the opposite, because it implies that happiness isn't about acquisition but avoidance, and generally speaking, it is much more affordable to avoid something than acquire something. We don't need to fly to Miami, we simply need to *not* be in Walsall. We don't need a personal cinema in our basement, we simply need to *not* be thinking about work. We don't need popularity as measured by likes or followers or accolades, we simply need to *not* be so hard on ourselves.

to think about his character and what he needs from life, and so doing what I need from life. What I don't need from life is any more *gulasz angielski*. It's disgusting, no matter the context. I eat what I can then take my diary and pocket dictionary outside and write. Coincidentally, Jerzy emerges with a cup of tea and a newspaper. He sits elsewhere, reads silently for some minutes – twelve, thirteen, something like that – then laughs of a sudden, fully and throatily. It makes me smile. I don't turn to ask him about the source of his laughter, though I should like to. Something dry, I would have thought, dry as a bone. Then another laugh, though this one's not Jerzy's. I turn to see a man reading the *regulamin* (regulations) posted to the door of the guest hut. He's a hiker, that much is apparent. Maybe he wants a bed? Jerzy continues with his newspaper, as if the hiker weren't there. 'We have a friend,' I say to Jerzy.

'I don't know,' he says, without lifting his head.

I go to the hiker. He is well-built and affable; his sweat smells of white wine. He wants tea with lemon, isn't interested in a bed, wouldn't mind knowing what an Englishman is up to in this neck of the woods. I tell him to speak to the governor if he wants tea, that it's as well he isn't interested in a bed for it's like a fridge in there, and that I'm just passing through. His English is copious but irregular. 'Passing through, huh? Then I must ask God for a copy of your route!' He reads the *regulamin* once more, shakes his head, disbelieving. 'You have to be the Pope to stay here!' he laughs. 'Or Saint Paul at least. I'm religious but I don't like this severity, no-no, not this way. I'm surprised he permits respiration.' He turns to me abruptly, has a point to make. 'Religion is like your penis,' he says. 'You have one, I have one. You don't show me yours, I don't show you mine.' I agree this is probably for the best. He gets out his crucifix. 'See? I wear it under my blouse. That is the difference. It is personal and not on the outside. All this' – he waves a hand at the rules and the icons – 'is too much on the outside. This guy is showing everyone his penis. I will ask him for some tea with lemon.'

I pack my things and tidy the hut. I return the key to Jerzy and he gives me an apple for my journey. For the amusement of the hiker, Jerzy says, 'I feed this boy. He came with nothing and now I feed him, like a cat.' They both laugh.

The hiker asks me if I think Jerzy is a sad man. I say it's hard for me to judge, knowing him so little. The hiker throws away my response, says I'm being polite. 'Be *honest*,' he says. 'Listen to your *soul*. What do you *feel*?' I notice a bottle of vodka on the table, mostly gone. It's clear the pair moved on from tea with lemon.

'He has been good and kind to me,' I say, 'but unhappily so.' The hiker wills me on – yes, yes, he says with his hands, give me more, that's more like it. 'He is certainly sad,' I say, 'but he is impressive and dignified, which must console him.' This satisfies the hiker. He nods solemnly: that will do, that will do.

'We spoke about you,' says the hiker. 'We decided, somewhere near the top of this bottle of vodka' – he points to such a spot – 'that you are *in between*, sometimes happy, sometimes sad. Also, we want to know about your little red book. Jerzy thinks it must be a bible, but I am not convinced.'

'It's a dictionary,' I say.

He translates for Jerzy, who groans playfully, conceding defeat. The hiker says: 'Okay, it is a dictionary, but this still fits our analysis. We decided you are searching for something, perhaps in your little red book, perhaps up here in the Polish mountains, perhaps everywhere.' I ask Jerzy how best to return to the town. He gives a set of instructions that I half understand. The hiker senses my uncertainty and says to follow my nose. The two men lead me out of the hut and watch me go.

35

It's okay because you can live with me and become a farmer

23 February. Ełk. North-east Poland. Home to Hubert's cows. (Hubert whom I met skiing.) The cows are not at the station. No one is. I go to a milk bar down the street to see if the cows are propping it up. Milk bars are cheap canteens that were ubiquitous during the communist period. They were subsidised by the state and in the early days all the products were loosely milk-based, hence the name. There are significantly fewer of them now, because people won't stop experimenting with Asian soup. From my experience, the décor of a milk bar tends to be effortless, the food straightforward, and the aroma starchy. So it is today. A vase of plastic flowers and a display of Pepsi and Fanta cans represent the only efforts to win me over. I have *gołąbki* – mince wrapped in cabbage leaves and topped with a tomato sauce – and a side of warm shredded beetroot.

On the road north, I ask Hubert about Russia, which is only 30 kilometres away. I wish I hadn't because Hubert's answer involves taking his hands off the steering wheel. Basically, Hubert thinks I needn't trouble myself to go there. The idea of my going somewhere – or not going somewhere – gets Hubert thinking. I've not seen this before. He doesn't make it look easy. Before a kilometre has been added to the clock, Hubert is offering me a permanent job on the farm 'drying' the cows, four hours a day in perpetuity, 1,500 zloty a month. I say nothing. He assumes my hesitancy has to do with the terms, rather than the life he is offering. 'I can't pay more than 1,500,' he says. 'But it's okay because you can live with me and become a farmer.'

Hubert's house is being built twenty yards from his parents'. Two men are on the roof, not doing a good enough job apparently. I am introduced to the dogs and Hubert's mother, Joanna. I'm told to take my shoes and hat off and go downstairs for soup. Downstairs is the workers' quarters. A few of the men working on Hubert's house sleep here, because they live a long way away – Ukraine, for example. Two such men are presently enjoying Joanna's soup sat round a table. Hubert tells me to sit there and eat that. (I rather like Hubert's rough brand of hospitality. You are rarely left in doubt regarding what's expected of you. The lack of independence is liberating. Instead of making decisions I can look at things and daydream.) The fiddlers on the roof come in for their lunch and the five men talk shop as they eat. It is slightly unnerving being among them. I take my time with the soup so I can appear at ease. (I know how to eat soup, don't know how to be with a basement full of working men from behind the Iron Curtain.) Sensing a spare part, Hubert tells me to go upstairs and watch television in the lounge with his younger brother and his girlfriend. We soon stop watching television because Magda and Jacob both speak excellent English and have a keen interest in Britishness. If I had to put a figure on it, I'd say the two of them are three times more interested in Britishness than I am. They bombard me with questions.

'Is it true you have afternoon tea every day?'

'Twice a day in fact: once in the afternoon and once in the evening.'

'Is divorce really as common as I've read?'

'Thankfully, yes.'

'Does the Queen really have those little dogs?'

'No. They're holograms.'[82]

'Are there any nice cities apart from London?'

'Sorry?'

'My uncle is in Peterborough and apparently that's not an oil painting, and his uncle is in Basingstoke and apparently that's even less of one.'

'I've heard Coventry is nice.'

'What's a scone?'

'No idea.'

'Why are the buses red?'

'So the blood of cyclists doesn't show.'

'Is it true the Earl of Sandwich invented bread?'

'Er …'

'Is it the case that animals are cared for better than children?'

'In my experience, yes.'

---

[82] The Queen stopped breeding corgis in 2015. Her final corgi, Willow, died in a car crash in April 2018. The Queen also likes cocker spaniels. She has previously owned cocker spaniels called Bisto, Oxo, Spick and Span. It's such quirkiness that keeps her in favour with the British public, and thus in a job.

'Are the Poles going to be sent home?'

'No. But there'll be no more arrivals.'

'That's sad.'

'I'll send you a scone in the post.'

It is time to dry the cows. I'm given a suitable outfit. There's quite a lot to it. Dungarees and wellington boots and goggles. What eventualities is Hubert allowing for? The wellington boots are too small by half, but I don't make a fuss. While Hubert's dungarees warm up in the tumble dryer, he makes a few phone calls in his Y-fronts and wellies, every inch the modern European farmer. When we get down to the cowshed, Hubert gives me a comprehensive tour, probably so he doesn't have to do it again when I start working full-time. It becomes apparent during our site inspection that the cows prefer to toilet without warning, and at unlikely angles. You need eyes in the back of your head. I thought my milking outfit was a bit excessive, a case of belt and braces, but in the event the outfit isn't sufficient – I take a strain of urine on the neck, and a flick of crap in the ear. Hubert has developed a sort of sixth sense; he's able to anticipate where the shrapnel will come from: on more than one occasion he pulls me out of the firing line just in time.

Hubert hurdles a fence and gets among his herd. He slaps the odd bum to get it moving in the right direction, then invites me to do likewise. His invitation having no appreciable effect, he orders me to do likewise. Hubert funnels a batch of fourteen into the milking zone. It's clear they know the drill. They respond to Hubert's instructions as privates to an officer. Once in the milking zone, each cow is allotted a station, given a quick udder wash by Hubert's sister-in-law, then hooked up to the grid. The craziest cows – whose parents had grass problems – are restrained with brackets. Were this precaution not taken, Hubert says, I wouldn't be going home with many teeth. As if to support Hubert's claim, Camilla starts lashing out and very nearly knocks Hubert's nose off. Each drying bay is worth a fortune. The tech is impressive: it registers the cow's identity – 'Welcome back, Santiago!' – and then displays their vital statistics on a screen. A red light starts flashing above one of the bays. I look to Hubert for an explanation. 'She wants sex,' he says. I'm disconcerted: surely that doesn't fall within a farmer's remit? I'm all for improving the welfare of animals, but they oughtn't take the biscuit. 'She needs to visit the bull,' says Hubert, by way of explanation. Hubert then applies the extractors, a nozzle on each nipple, which draws out the milk and conveys it to a huge tank in a neighbouring room, where it is turned and cooled. These nozzles (to say nothing of the nipples) are clever little things. When the nipple is spent, the nozzle recognises the fact and simply falls off. When all the nozzles are off, the udder is cleaned and disinfected, and the cow is given a magazine to read. When all udders are empty and shining, the fourteen cows are ushered off stage and down a corridor that feeds them back into the main shed. All the while this is going on, the cows that are next in line clamber to get a peek of the action. I don't mean to blow my own trumpet, but one cow in particular has been looking at me more or less constantly since the moment I turned up.

Here she is now, straining for a close up, desperate to figure out what my arrival portends, and whether I'm free after work. While I'm considering the cow that's been considering me, another cow starts lugubriously licking her ears and face. When I think the picture couldn't get more amusing, a ginger cat enters the frame, clambers onto the licking cow's head and settles there. All things considered, it's one of the unlikeliest compositions I've ever seen. If Henri Cartier-Bresson were here, he'd say this was the decisive moment.

When the second batch have been admitted and hooked up, I'm sufficiently at ease to get up close and study their appearance. They are so *angular*, so irregularly bony, each frame a geometric puzzle, the work of Picasso. Moreover, each hide and udder is uniquely flecked, infinitely various like fingerprints, or butterfly wings. I'm convinced that various personality traits can be detected in the cows' eyes. Take Camilla, the one whose alarm went off. There was naked ambition in those eyes. Take Janet, whose legs had to be bracketed. It was obvious from her eyes that the world makes less sense to her than to her peers. Take Megan, the one who can't keep her eyes off me. She's obviously an aesthete, born with refined taste, a superior critical faculty. Indeed, had Megan been born human – which, when you think about it, was as probable as her being born a cow – I've no doubt she would have become theatre critic for *The Times*.

When the milking is done Hubert takes me through to his office, which is decorated with pictures of half-naked women (not *more* nipples) and trophies for outstanding yields. Hubert pulls up some milking data on his computer then leans back proudly in his chair and gestures for me to take a closer look, as if showing off his children's exceptional exam results. Most of the cows are knocking out 50 litres a day. Gosia has given 146,000 litres over her working life, God bless her. Hubert leaves me in the office while he helps his sister-in-law finish up. The office has a side door. Naturally, I open it to see what lies beyond, only I can't, not fully, because a stream of cows is on the other side. It's like the M25 out there. Quite why this is the case (the case being Hubert's office having a door that gives onto a cow highway) is anyone's guess. Perhaps every so often one of the herd is invited into Hubert's office for a random drugs test, or to go over their stats. My boots are hurting now. They've been hurting all the time but now they're *really* hurting. When Hubert returns to the office he can see I'm in pain. He probably thinks I'm deeply unsure about whether to take the job.

'What's wrong?'

'My boots.'

'What?'

'Too small.'

'Since when?'

'Always.'

'Why didn't you say?'

'Not polite to say.'

Jezus Maria, Benji. Can you be a farmer like this?'

'I don't know, Hubert.'

'We need to clean.'

'Can I stay here?'

'*Nie, kurwa!*'

Cleaning is evidently (and odorously) the worst part of the gig. Basically, we have to move everything that has emerged since yesterday into a central latrine. Hubert hands me a shovel and allots me a zone of interest. To take my mind off the task in hand, I ask Hubert whether the EU has been good for him and his girls. Hubert's reaction is pleasingly dramatic. It's like I've mentioned Russia again. He drops his shovel, sticks out his chest, regards me stonily for a few seconds, then spits on the floor. And that's just him getting started, that's just Hubert's way of easing himself into the subject, the subject being the chronic mistreatment he suffers at the hands of the EU, who are nothing but an albatross about his neck, a thorn in his side, a faceless plutocracy designed to slowly smother his will to live. When he's done, I mention the little plaque in his office that acknowledges receipt of a handsome amount of EU cash. Hubert tells me to shut up because I don't know what I'm talking about. And he's right. Knowing next to nothing about EU agricultural economics, I shouldn't automatically take Hubert's anti-EU sentiments with a pinch of salt. Sensing my thoughts, Hubert says: 'Benji. Listen. They bought me things to modernise and grow. For this I am happy. But the tax they take gets me crazy.' He lets his shovel fall to the ground despondently. He feels trapped, tied to the land, *in debt*. Worse still, he feels there's no way out of it, that this cowshed is the rest of his life. I think: *poor Hubert*. And then: *there's no way I'm taking this job*.

I am sent to my room to shower and change. I say 'my room' but of course it's not mine, it's Jacob's. I have a nose around.

Jacob is a dancer, that much is plain. The room is full of ballroom dancing trophies and certificates, and countless framed pictures of Jacob in competition. The only indication that ballroom dancing isn't the only thing Jacob does or thinks about is a crucifix and a Pope figurine, probably installed by his parents to remind their son that Catholicism can be every bit as thrilling as throwing his girlfriend around a dancefloor. I find a board game under the bed called *Unia Europejska*. Who would have thought the EU could be transformed into fun for all the family? I suppose it's like Monopoly, only instead of travelling around London buying things one travels around Europe investing in them – in a dairy farm, say, or a new fleet of trams – and I suppose instead of being sent to jail arbitrarily (which is pretty messed up when you think about it), players are interred for ignoring their constitutions, for refusing refugees, for working more than 35 hours a week, for letting straight bananas through the net and so on. If Sweden is Mayfair then what would Poland be? Trafalgar Square, I'd say. Not a bad part of town. Well-loved, historic, arty, a bit stressful at times. As for Britain? It would have to be Leicester Square. Overpriced and overrated. In any case, I'll see if we can play tonight. I'm sure Hubert would love a game.

I'm called down for dinner. Hubert's dad is home. More specifically, he is sat at the head of the table. The first thing that strikes me about Mirosław is that he is drinking from a mug that depicts a cow in sunglasses relaxing in a deckchair while being milked. The second thing that strikes me is that he's wearing a gun. He's a hunter. Much of the food on the table was once gambolling around in the form of a wild boar, which was subsequently reworked into paté, steaks, salami and ribs. A lot of the meat is smoked, which Mirosław does in a smoking hut at the bottom of the garden. The apple juice is also homemade – and so is the vodka, says Hubert, filling my shot glass. It really is a terrific spread: as well as boar six ways, there's pickled mushrooms, pickled cucumbers, and eggs from the farm's chickens, which have been boiled and minced and mixed with butter and mayonnaise and seasoning. I gesture to all the food and then suggest as a joke that Mirosław probably fashioned the table himself, the chairs, the house. 'Yes,' he says matter-of-factly, 'I did all those things.' Gosh. I begin to suspect that Mirosław drives a chariot, assembled with his own hands, pulled by homemade horses. Part of me is impressed with how Mirosław engages with the natural world, while another part wishes he'd just leave it alone. I don't know whether to admire Mirosław's evident and rampant capacity to husband nature, or to question his willingness to take life and be proud of the fact. In the end, I resolve to do both. I raise a glass and tell the table I'm grateful – to be here, to eat, to Poland, to Hubert and his family. Mirosław raises his glass, higher than mine. *Nie*, he says, *we are grateful*. I'm given no choice but to drink to that. Doing so, I feel a belated twinge of homesickness. It's taken another's home to remind me of my own. Hubert tells his dad what he told me about the EU. Mirosław nods knowingly, familiar with the arguments, then turns to me and whispers: 'The EU is six of one and half-a-dozen of the other. Is that correct?' I admit that it is.

Hubert insists I take a packed-lunch with me for the train. He watches me make a roll but isn't satisfied. More! he demands. Keep going! he shouts. He puts the rolls in a bag then half-a-dozen ribs in another. I am told to come back any time, that all I need to do is call.

I share a train compartment with a young man who tells me that Poland is better off without the millions who have left the country because they are mostly pathological. At Olsztyn, the young man is replaced by an old lady. She wants her seat by the window, so I move to the opposite one. At the next stop, another old lady enters and wants *her* seat by the window. I take my packed-lunch out to the corridor. I see a wind turbine catching its breath, a man in a tent, a scarecrow, mistletoe. Everything added by man looks like an injury. But then where would we be without man's additions? I shouldn't be on this train for a start. Now here's a picture. Four boys are in conference in the middle of a snow-covered football pitch. I say they are in conference but what am I getting at? I mean they are stood around the centre spot, close to one another, interlinked, their outward breaths commingling. One has the ball under his arm. Another wears the captain's armband. All are wearing scarves – blue, green, black, beige. What is discussed at their summit? What is at stake? (Who shoots which way, I bet.) Do they notice the passing of a train? Could they have guessed that someone was peering down at them and wondering what they were about? I'll never see those boys again, to say nothing of know them.

One will live to 100, another will make films, and the smallest will rise like a star and then burn out at 50. Or perchance they will all stay as they are now, as they were then, young and earnest, stood in the centre circle of a snow-covered pitch, talking about nothing and everything at once, at the edge of Neverland. I return to the compartment: the two women won't take their eyes off the world.

'Madam likes the window?' I ask.

'Yes,' she says, 'Why not?'

36

A thirteen-mile souvenir

14 March. It is two days before the Poznań half marathon. I've been training extensively since last Thursday, and unconsciously carb-loading for years. I entered because I thought it would be a nice way to say goodbye to the city – a sort of lap of honour, without the honour. I go to the World Trade Centre to register. I'm given fudge, beer, a sponge and a bin-liner. A video of the route is played on loop on a big screen: it promises to be a bleak few hours. Anything mildly diverting or usefully distracting – the old town, the zoo, the river – has been avoided. Special running vests and supportive underwear are for sale, but it's too late for any of that: it's going to be unpleasant and there's no two ways about it. My lifestyle the past year has been abysmal. I deserve to suffer.

Some friends and family from England will also be doing the run. The first batch are due to land any minute. I take a bus to the airport to collect them. Tom has been to Poland before. It was he who threw fast-food at a statue in Krakow. (See Chapter 1.) The others aren't equipped with Tom's experience. They're fresh. As far as I'm aware Merle has never been outside Scotland, while Jimbo works in marketing so doesn't get out of the office much. The airport makes a good first impression on Merle; I think she expected to land in a wheat field. We take a bus towards town then get off at the Mercure Hotel on Roosevelt Street. After everyone has checked in at the hotel and registered for the run, we eat at Oskoma on Mickiewicza. Merle is impressed with the food: 'I thought it would be just bread and stuff.' Merle is an unusually smart woman, and yet her preconceptions of Poland are somewhat lacking. I don't mean to poke fun at Merle or the Scottish education system, rather to show how limited and negative the general understanding, or the common sense, of Poland is.

We go to the flat. Batch number two arrives in a cab from the airport. Cheesy runs an unsuccessful recruitment agency and is so called because he's lactose intolerant, while Dinita is an actor, a bit Indian, and in her spare time Tom's wife. We get a few bottles of red wine in. Talk turns to the 'race'. (That the run is being referred to as a race instantly tightens my hamstring.) Merle has learnt a particular breathing technique. Cheesy has invested in some Hugo Boss cycling shorts. Tom can't be sure what shape his marriage will be in after thirteen miles in tandem with Dinita. Chafing comes up and Vaseline is enthusiastically prescribed, apart from by Jenny, who thinks lubrication is for wimps and snowflakes. He says that if he starts chafing, he'll just run with his legs farther apart.

We take a tram into town, dismounting outside Hotel Rzymski. 'I spent my first night in Poland there,' I say. 'Imagine trying to say that when you're drunk.' I hope the mention of my debut in Poland will prompt a series of questions about the early days and my awkward attempts to assimilate – pushing when I should have been pulling, waiting when I should have been going, expecting customer service when I shouldn't have been expecting customer service – but it doesn't. Instead, Merle continues to point amazedly at things she didn't think they had in Poland, like pavements and electricity and disposable income. We go to Dragon for a single beer, but don't quite manage it.

～

To Drukarnia for breakfast. There's confusion among the group about what should and should not be eaten on the eve of a big run. Merle ate so much pasta leading up to the London Marathon that she couldn't sleep all night and was absolutely knackered before she'd even started. Tom says too many bananas will block you up. Cheesy has been eating protein more or less exclusively for months, while Charlie, who arrived late last night (being married to Merle, he prefers to travel independently), hasn't given the matter any thought whatsoever, although he has cut his hair to reduce drag. Talk turns to what people plan to consume *during* the race. Jimbo relies on boiled sweets. Richard will be taking his tobacco along. Merle says she'll snack on a haggis she plans to keep down her pants. Anna says nothing because she is not with us. She is working, like she always is.

After breakfast we go to the old square to watch the diurnal goats do their clunky dance in the tower of the townhall. It's the first time I've seen the spectacle. I've been meaning to take a look for ages but could never quite raise the requisite curiosity to actually do so. A ceremonious trumpeter warns of the goats' imminent appearance, and then out they trundle, into the public domain, where they proceed to butt heads for a while before withdrawing back into their tower. I think of a photograph Richard took of people watching the goats, with each member of the gobsmacked mob staring up at the entertainment except one man who's looking at Richard instead, bored as hell.[83] Merle wants to know why the goats do it, so I tell the story, which involves a medieval cook who burnt the king's venison and couldn't find a replacement so went after a pair of goats who legged it up the tower and did a little dance, then enjoy how the story changes as it goes round the group: by the time it's reached Cheesy, it was the cook's first day and the goats jumped off the tower to avoid capture.

We go to Cocoa Republic, just across from Dragon, where we drink thick hot chocolate on low sofas upstairs. There's a general will to reminisce. The weekend when Tom and Dinita first locked horns is remembered. We were all in Buxton, at a campsite, because I had a play on there, an obscure two-hander that went nowhere in one act. It happened that Tom had a company car at the time. It was a chintzy Audi M6 or something. It is Charlie's opinion that if Tom hadn't had that company car there's no way he would have ended up marrying a successful actor. 'Tom's a handsome man,' explains Charlie, 'but you have to admit

---

[83] Richard won £10,000 with that picture. Apparently, Richard is now Urban Photographer of the Year, at least according to CBRE, a construction conglomerate that likes to champion goat-related material.

A THIRTEEN-MILE SOUVENIR

he's far more eligible sat behind the wheel of the latest Audi than stood at a bus stop.' More stuff is dragged up from the archive.

Jimbo says, 'Do you remember the pickle factory?'

Tom says, 'What about that time Ben and Davy planned to rob Domino's?'

Charlie says, 'What about that time we went hunting with a crossbow, Tommy!'

Merle says, 'Bearing in mind I didn't study with yous [sic], would you mind changing the subject?'

At 1pm the group splits along gender lines, the men to watch Warta Poznań play football and the women to be beautified by Anna. (I wish as a group we were more progressive and gender fluid, but there you are.) Warta Poznań are not to be confused with Lech Poznań, who I saw last year, a couple of weeks after I arrived. Lech are in the *Ekstraklasa*, the top division, while Warta aren't. Lech's stadium can accommodate 40,000 people, Warta's can't. Because it's chilly and the first half is a bit of a damp squib (Warta are a goal down), morale is dropping. I try to gee up the boys by pointing out that if Warta can turn it around they'll move up to thirteenth in the table. When that fails, I resort to a platitude: 'Come on boys. When in Rome!' Charlie, who is on the pedantic spectrum, points out that 99.9 per cent of Romans are elsewhere in Rome, doubtless doing something warm and lively and genial. Richard has been to a couple of Warta games before. On each occasion, he came home raving about Warta's number nine, who he reckons has bags of talent. I keep my eyes on number nine for ten minutes: if he has bags of talent, then he's struggling to open them.

'Richie? What about your number nine then? He's crap.'

'Give him time, mate. He'll turn up. He was in Dragon last night.'

'And what about the left-back? He won't shut up.'

'Never seen him before.'

'He looks a bit like … Blow me – is that Mirek?'

'It can't be. Mirek's in Asia.'

'Are you actually joking?'

'Nah. You see number seventeen?'

'I do. He's handy but he can't get on the ball.'

'That's the thing. I'm given to understand Legia Warsaw are after him. The other players are jealous. They won't pass to him.'

'Bloody hell. It's like that joke I told you.'

'About the pots of oil?'

'That's the one: three pots of boiling oil. 'Ere, Charlie, Tommy, listen to this. And you Jimbo. A joke vis-à-vis why no one's passing to number seventeen. Three pots of boiling oil. The devil, right, for want of anything better to do, has flung the French in the first, the Germans in the second, and the Poles in the third. Following?'

'What type of oil?' asks Charlie.

'Doesn't matter. Devil goes off for a while, for lunch or whatever, then comes back to check on the pots.'

'I suppose it wouldn't have been olive oil – bit expensive.'

'The French and the Germans are helping each other get out of their pots. But nothing's coming out of the Polish pot.

The devil pops his head in for a look, sees that every time a Pole begins to advance up the side of the pot a compatriot pulls him back down.'

'Him or her,' says Charlie.

'What?'

'Really you should have said him or her, in today's climate.'

'Fine. There were women as well as men being burnt to death by the devil.'

'Good. And how does the joke relate to number seventeen?'

'Don't worry about it.'[84]

The Warta manager is a short man with thick white hair and a moustache. He patrols his technical area non-stop. You'd think this was the European Cup final and he'd staked his grandchildren on the result. Periodically, he calls over his young assistant for an intense tactical discussion. ('Hey. Przemek. Is that Mirek playing left-back?') They're like a pair of field marshals at the Battle of Grunwald. I could do with a bit of their passion. So could most of the Warta players. As if privy to my thoughts, the home side finally start to push for an equaliser. And they get one: a powerful half-volley from number seventeen. Just when it looks like the home team might seize the initiative and sneak all three points, the Warta left-back allows his man to cut inside and somehow plant a

---

[84] Naturally, Charlie isn't quite as pedantic and bothersome as this, but it's the prerogative of the non-fiction writer to exaggerate as much as he wants.

low shot into the roof of the net. Two–one. Full-time. I turn to pundit with my friends, but they're already halfway back to the hotel.

As far as I'm aware, my Auntie Jo has never run more than a mile in her life. When I told her about the half marathon in Poznań I didn't think she would even register the idea, let alone pounce upon it.

'Got anything coming up then?'

'Meh. Might stay with some nuns for a bit. Half marathon in Poznań.'

'A what where? Say that again.'

'Meh. Might stay with some nuns— '

'The last bit.'

'Half marathon in Poznań.'

'What's that then?'

'It's when you run for a long time.'

'Not that bit, the other bit.'

'Poznań?'

'Yeah. What's that?'

'That's a place, Jo. That's where I live.'

'Really?'

'Yeah.'

'I think I'd like to do that.'

'Yeah?'

'Yeah.'

'Do you run?'

'No.'

'Do you have an interest in Poznań?'

'Not really.'

'Fair enough.'

She booked a flight the next day, and then another for her ten-year-old son, and then, remembering she couldn't leave her son unattended for six hours during the run, another for her son's father. I go to meet them at their hotel. The receptionist can't tell me which room they're in but can invite me to search the hotel as comprehensively as I wish. I fancy they might be in the pool. When I was Oliver's age, if there was a pool to be in, I was in it. To enter the pool area, I'm obliged to put blue plastic covers over my shoes. I must look rather odd, dressed for winter with blue plastic bags on my feet, snooping round the spa facilities of a decent hotel. A small party in the jacuzzi eyes me coolly, trying to decide whether to alert security. It's them. It's Jo and Oliver and Kev. They've definitely spotted me but they're pretending not to have. I'm tempted to get in the jacuzzi without even acknowledging them, just climb straight in as I am. At the very least, it would make Oliver laugh.

Jo takes me to her room because she wants to show me all her energy products. She has bought a small suitcase full of the stuff. It can't all be for personal use – she must be dealing. It's clear Jo's race philosophy is thus: if I eat an energy paste every hundred metres, I won't actually have to run. She shows me what she'll be running in. It's a T-shirt dedicated to her late rabbit. When I see the picture of Ralph, I can't help but laugh. It stirs a memory. Last Christmas I sent Jo and my cousins a card, but decided to address it to Ralph, who unbeknownst to me had been run over and killed the Tuesday before. When they got the card they didn't know what to think. Jo thought that it was something to do with Ralph's will or life insurance. So yeah, when I see Ralph I can't help but giggle.

We meet the others at the café on my street for dinner. I try not to notice Anita floating about. I drink beer and eat beef and order a pudding. I guess my thinking is that the more of me there is, the sooner I'll cross the finish line. By now we are a full contingent. We take up most of the café. It's nice to have everyone bunched together like this, tight-knit and fraternal. I make the most of it while I can. No doubt tomorrow will be a different story entirely.

❦

I try on Anna's leggings. They were bought for her when she was thirteen. They fit nicely. I match them with yellow socks, a red sweater and a turquoise headband. Jenny has one thing to say to me this morning: 'Do you wanna have a bet cos I reckon I'm gonna beat ya?' Jenny is ferociously competitive. To his credit, he tries to keep a lid on it, sensing that it's undignified to care so much. He's probably been awake half the night debating whether to make a bet with me: *I know I shouldn't care … but I think I'm going to beat him … so why not be rewarded?* I've known Jenny a year and he remains a beautiful enigma. I can sincerely say I love him. But I can sincerely say I haven't a clue why. He would have made a wonderful subject for Freud. We put a bottle of vodka on it.

Richard and I were up at 6.30am to start digesting. Richard was quite adamant on this point. 'Ben. Listen. The last thing you want is porridge running down your leg halfway round.' I couldn't argue with this assertion. It was as true as anything he'd ever said. After about three hours sat at the kitchen table digesting, we stretch-walk to the Mercure to round up the others. They're gathered in the foyer.

'What the hell do you look like, Bonza?' says Charlie.[85] 'Actually, I know what you look like: you look like one of the very first recorded joggers known to man.' Merle's sensibly dressed, which is surprising. She's known for her outlandish fancy-dress outfits, and I thought she might whip out one of her classics today, like her inflatable obese ginger Scottish highlander. Cheesy looks reliably ridiculous: he's wearing a turtleneck and eating a guinea-fowl. Everybody starts to stretch and talk about target times. Jimbo is a veteran of such races, is in decent shape, is going for a PB – around one hour 40 minutes. Despite his rock star lifestyle, Richard has a good engine and means to keep up with Jimbo. Charlie has his sights set on the two-hour mark. Merle is carrying a knock and might take the bus. Dinita and Tom are running as a couple holding hands, so they don't count. Anna keeps quiet but I know she's a dark horse. Contrary to appearances, she's got stamina. When we go for a run together, she may well be stooping and wheezing by the time we get to the end of the street, but can carry on in this fashion for hours.

---

[85] Bonza was my nickname at university because for the first six weeks I pretended to be Australian.

When pressed, I admit I'll be following a two-stop strategy: a stop for a coffee at kilometre seven, and then a cheese roll or similar at kilometre fourteen. I explain that such a strategy will render the whole experience more satisfying, which is the point of life. Auntie Jo is nowhere to be seen. Maybe she's still in her room marinating herself in energy paste.

It's chaos around the start line. We soon start to lose one another. I cling on to Richard and Jimbo, meaning to stick with them as long as possible. We wiggle forwards through the crowd, so that we're going off with runners aiming to run a 1:50 pace. It's a party atmosphere: model athletes on lofty pedestals encourage runners to dance to the music, to put their hands in the air, to wave to the camera, to choose life. Last-minute selfies are taken and swiftly shared. I can see Jenny ahead, arrogantly bobbing about with the 1:40 crew. He drops out of sight. He must be tying his laces. No doubt he'll tie some others while he's down there. Tom and Dinita are farther back, around the 2:10 mark, along with Charlie and Merle. Still no sign of Jo. I wouldn't be surprised if she was up the front with the pros, adjusting the vest of energy bars that's wrapped around her torso like a bomb. I feel nervous. My legs are wobbly. I think I need the toilet. I should have worn a nappy. (Maybe that's what the sponge was for?) The siren sounds. The front runners set off. It will be a few minutes before our tranche will be on the move. It's the calm before the storm. I wonder what the storm will bring. Cramps of nostalgia, I hope. Pangs of sentiment. I want to dwell on memorable spots. The park where I went on my first evening to search for a sculpture in the dark.

The train tracks that go south to Starołęka, where the school is, where I was given a chance. The section of riverbank where Anita slept in the sun while I looked at her fearfully, lovingly, stupidly, vainly. Others are loading their cars but I don't want music. I want to listen to the city. I want to absorb the environment and its associations. I want to go back on myself, one stride at a time. I want to feel wistful, introspective, sad and happy at once. I want a two-hour rehearsal of my time in Poland, a thirteen-mile souvenir. There'll be a lot to remember, a lot to cherish. I shall want the race extended. I shall want to do it again.

I shall not want to do it again. By kilometre three I'm about as reflective and nostalgic as the late rabbit Ralph. The first section of the run, along Grunwald Street and then left on Roosevelt, saw a lot of jostling, as runners found their feet, fiddled with watches, called out for comrades lost among the 20,000 heads rising as one and turning onto Poznań Army Street, where I was caught from behind and sent tumbling. I was a jockey down at the first fence, foetal and defenceless, ready to be galloped on. In my darkest hour, Richard was there. He pulled me to my feet like a war hero and said, 'For heaven's sake, Aitken.' That was then, this is now: we turn onto Garbary, head south along the old town's east flank, past the old slaughterhouse where I bought my bike last spring. How I could do with it now. Every kilometre, Jimbo turns to Richard and points to his watch and gives a thumbs-up signal, to indicate, I presume, that it's a good watch. He doesn't turn to me to show me his watch. He doesn't know I'm here. He hasn't seen me since kilometre zero, when I went down like a shot swan. I decide I'm wasting energy pretending not to be in pain: I lower my head and pant. Buckets of water have been put out on trestle tables. So that's what the sponge was for. It was meant to be dunked in these buckets. As well as buckets, there are cups of water. I snatch one and try to drink, but the water jumps all over my face. I try again, this time just shoving the cup in my face, hoping some of its content finds my tongue. I'm sweating generously. I thank God for my eyebrows. Richard, increasingly distant, turns around periodically to check on me. Over the past years he has become like a brother (or step-brother, rather; I don't want those genes), and brothers look back by instinct, whether they want to or not. It's still early days; we've completed but a third of the course; and yet I'm seriously tempted to call it a day before my pancreas blows up. I do the math. The run I sometimes do around the lake is six kilometres. It takes me 35 minutes. That's closer to six minutes a kilometre than five. It exhausts me. So just what do I think I'm up to, eight kilometres into the 21, trying to run five-minute kilometres? I try to think of equivalents and analogies but can't, my mind won't let me, it's too shagged to be imaginative. There are sweets and bananas being bandied about but the idea of consumption repels me: simply put, if I eat something I won't be able to breathe. At the bottom of Wilda we come to a hairpin. I spot Rimbo (that is, Richard + Jimbo) on the other arm of the pin, about 30 metres ahead but only two or three as the crow flies. The paradox – so close yet so far – enlivens me, gives me the courage to chase, despite a chase requiring me to step up the pace, to run faster than they are, faster, that is, than the rate that's already killing me. I bow my head, sublimate the pain, draw on previous displays of personal heroic endurance – the drawer's empty. I hit an uphill stretch, three or four miles along Hetmanska. Just what I need. There's a band playing on a stage at the side of the road. So inappropriate. Would you get a band in for a hanging? I see a woman on a balcony, grinning and smoking. I hate her, as I hate all things that aren't similarly in pain. It's a dark lesson to learn on a sunny day: that suffering breeds aggression and cancels sympathy. Richard's shiny pate is now my beacon; it surfaces now and again like a lollipop and gives me hope, a target, a dream. Had Richard's DNA been otherwise, had he hair like Hagrid, I might have given up all hope twenty minutes ago. I'm 100 metres back. I keep pushing. I'm determined to chase down the vanguard, to reclaim my seat in the royal box, where I belong. Because that *is* where I belong. If I believe anything else at this stage, I'm done for. I reckon it will take 2,000 metres to reclaim the lost hundred, a retrieval rate of one metre per twenty. For inspiration, I entertain fantastic ultimatums – for example, that if I don't catch these men every member of their family will contract prostate cancer within a week. It does the trick. Within ten minutes, I'm up on Rimbo's bumper. It feels like I don't have any lungs. When we cross the fifteen kilometre mark, I am pretty much dying in Richard's ear. The fact isn't lost on him. He turns to see who's making all the fuss. He's never been more surprised to see me. He stares at me the way people stared at Christ on Easter Monday. When we pass the Lech Poznań stadium I say, 'Rich. The stadium. Still a long way to go.' A fellow runner interprets my breathless observation as an invitation to chat.

'Where are you from?' he asks cheerfully.

I give it a minute then answer the question. 'Europe. But let's not talk about it.'

Rimbo are pulling away again. I don't mean to keep up. Not this time. I couldn't if I wanted to. As we hit kilometre eighteen, they are out of sight and my battle is privatised. Up to this point I have only overtaken. That changes. Everything changes. Blisters announce themselves. Organs clock off. Even my elbows start to hurt. I desperately want to stop and walk the final two miles. I blaspheme liberally but my outbursts, designed to propel me, only eat into my meagre rations and upset spectators. People are passing me by the dozen. Bystanders shout distances to go. 'In English!' I scream. 'How far in English?!' We turn onto Grunwald, the home stretch, and I think of the battle of 1410. If I fall on Grunwald, I tell myself, then so be it, for there would be poetry in my collapse. I channel the spirit of Forrest Gump. I hold my breath. The finish line keeps receding, like a mirage in the offing, a half-truth on the horizon. I enter the Trade Centre, lit like Hades, still galloping like Gump. The noise is echoey and surreal. I don't know where I am. It's not an unpleasant feeling. End.

There is no pleasure in completion. Just a new type of pain. Jimbo is here, and so is Jenny. If the latter brags I'm going to chin him. We file out, receiving medals as we go. I lie in the sun, euphoric and bleeding. I eat some bananas conferred from above by an angel, but I don't wrap myself in baking foil as do others, not convinced of the point. I find a spot about 50 metres from the finish line to encourage others. I see Merle come through and then, about an hour and a half later, just as the organisers are starting to pack everything away, Jo. She's on the bloody phone.

I go back to the Mercure to find the others. They're lounging in the sun with cold beers. Our times have already been listed online. Cheesy went sub 1:40. Dinita went sub two hours, beating Tom by a head having dipped at the line. Richard got the better of Jimbo by a matter of seconds. I was a couple of minutes back, on the 1:45 mark, which gains general approval. Anna is just pleased to see me on two feet. 'I saw an ambulance, and a guy on the floor with leggings and a beard. I thought it was you.' We all head down to the hotel's spa to drink beer in the sauna. We compare sweaty notes, measure up our complaints, trade vignettes. 'Jenny went off like a house on fire …', 'I saw Charlie at one point and he just looked confused …', 'I hear this panting in my ear and I think: that's nice, that's what Ben used to do …', 'I couldn't stop farting …' A Polish businessman (you can just tell) enters and immediately wishes he hadn't. He wasn't expecting a pack of noisy foreigners. I don't think he's ever seen the likes of Dinita, to say nothing of Cheesy. He squeezes in. Merle asks, 'Did you run, pal?' He puts up a hand in refusal, not wanting any of it.

We eat at a traditional Polish restaurant off the old square. The mood is good, which is to be expected given how many happy hormones we have collectively liberated.

Despite feeling fresh and jubilant, when I go to the counter to order the girl says I look hungover. Fancy that. You do all that sodding exercise and you still look hungover. I eat tomato soup in a bread bowl, then salmon with spinach and groats, then a platter of dumplings. Charlie braves the carp, while Cheesy has three pork knuckles and a bucket of cabbage. Cherry vodka shots all round, to chase the wine and beer. It's a veritable feast but we owe it to ourselves. That's the evening's logic. We've spent 7,000 calories a head and are keen to repay the debt.

We go to Dragon. Merle insists on ordering in Polish, despite only being able to say hello and thank you. The mood shifts from buoyant to ludic. Anna kisses a stranger at the bar. Merle eats some tulips. Cheesy stands on the table and roars. We move downstairs to start a disco. Anna dances the tango with Jimbo, and it's like watching my dad play golf with Fred Couples. (I know that simile won't mean much to a lot of people, but I won't apologise for it because it is the perfect approximation.) We do the conga, for heaven's sake. I request 'Modern Love' by Bowie and nearly burst. There is a complete lack of restraint, a flagrant shirking of etiquette, a perfect absence of care. It's like we've survived a war, or won a long-winded court case and been awarded damages up to a million pounds but on the condition that it's spent by tomorrow. Everyone feels like Warta Poznań's number seventeen – on the brink of a big move, tipped for success, better than the others. I whisper to myself: 'I love these people, as I love this city.' Jenny's the only one not on top of the world. Turns out I beat him by seven seconds.

37

The thing is to go, really, is to have gone, is to have been elsewhere

29 March. Theresa May sends a letter to Brussels that says, 'Hi there. We would like to say goodbye now.' By sending the letter, the UK now has two years to organise its divorce. In other words, we've all got 700 days of breaking up to look forward to. May doesn't send the letter via Royal Mail or anything modern like that. She goes for a more pedestrian approach. She gives the letter to a friend to deliver. Sir Timothy Something will go by foot from Westminster to Brussels, stopping only to say platitudinal things to the media in Dunkirk about getting the job done. Today's newspapers, I speculate, are full of interesting conjecture as to the suitability of Sir Timothy, who last ran an errand in 1967, as messenger. Either way, it's also time for me to get on my bike. I'm not legally compelled to leave (yet), it just feels right. There's a bleak neatness to it. I arrived just after Cameron came to Warsaw to get the Poles to cut some slack, and I will leave with the sound of the triggered article still ringing in the air. What more could you want?

2 April. Jenny does duck in a bag with *pyzy*, which are little doughy bun things. I tell the table it's my last Sunday, that I'd like to remember the flat in broad strokes. Jenny coming home – *hey there!* – then washing his nuts in the bathroom sink. Anna coming home – *siema!* – to find her favourite things in my room being used as ashtrays. That sort of thing. That sort of stroke. But nobody wants to play. They just want to eat the duck. I guess it makes sense. After all, they're not leaving, they're not about to lose something. It's hard to be nostalgic for things that will happen tomorrow, and the next day, and the day after. It's only me who's feeling at the end of something and keen to hang on.

5 April. I should fly home. That would be the reasonable thing to do. Two hours and twenty quid. Yes, that would be the reasonable thing to do but it would also be … insufficient. You see, this is a final journey, and to fly would be too simple and too swift. It would feel – it would *be* – too abrupt. I'd like the sense of an ending to linger. I'd like to drag out my leaving, drag it across the continent, the better to understand both. To this end, I use a car-sharing website to sign up for a lift to west Germany with a 35-year-old Russian called Andrew. Andrew wants me to be at the Polish–German border at 9.30am on Thursday. I'm quite sure the Polish–German border isn't a conventional meeting point on account of its length, so I call Andrew for more detail. A woman half his age answers the phone. Andrew's daughter perhaps.

'Can I ask about the journey next Thursday?'
'Yes.'
'Would you mind being more specific?'
'What is your meaning?'
'Where *exactly* on the border?'

'Does it not say in the advert?'

'No. It says Polish–German border. That's it.'

'Are you sure?'

'Very.'

'So I wonder why you've already agreed to come with us?'

It's a fair point. I'd fallen for the idea of setting off from the border, from a cusp, a historic threshold etc. 'I like borders,' I say.

'Weird, but fine. Frankfurt-Oder. There is a train from Poznań, I believe. We can collect you from the station, but my mother says you will have to pay more.'

'Fine. And what about Andrew?'

'Who?'

'Andrew.'

'Oh. Andrew is not real.'

'What?'

'If the advert says two Russian women, it attracts too much attention, if you understand me. We want somebody who is happy to travel with Andrew.'

'Well, I am happy to travel with Andrew.'

'Good.'

'I look forward to meeting him.'

'Very good, Benjamin. Just don't be late or Andrew will be pissed.'

8 April. I'm leaving so much behind – people, possessions, commitments – that although they may end up being so, the days don't feel final. They feel *almost* final. Perhaps that's the best atmosphere in which to depart, sensing a return, sensing the story isn't done, with socks still in the drawer, and butter in the fridge. I've decided I'll live in Portsmouth. When I get back. It's not much but it's home. My dad has just retired and is due for a hernia operation and cooks a lot of nice dinners and doesn't charge much rent and does the cryptic crossword at the kitchen table every day and I could do with his company if I'm honest, more than he could do with mine, I'm sure. I'll get a job in the Polish shop at the end of the road. I'll go up to my mum's for tea, see my grandparents and my dog, help my sister with her first-year university exams, and in the gaps I'll try to come up with something, try to put *down* something, regarding Poland, I mean. Whatever I produce won't count for much in the end. I know that. It won't change minds or alter moods. It won't bother the course of history or the nature of ideas. It will give a few hundred people something to do for a few hours, that's all. Which is fine, because the thing is to go, really, is to have gone, is to have been elsewhere.

38

We must be coming to the end of Poland (Cologne)

15 April. I've a bag and a sandwich. I walk to the train station. I get on a train going west and slightly south, towards the Polish–German border at Frankfurt-Oder. It is early. Early enough for frost on the fields. I have a hot chocolate on me. I bought it at the train station. I don't really like hot chocolate but I was in a hurry and needed something sugary. I wasn't meant to be in a hurry. I had meant to allow plenty of time, so the walk to the station could be slow and observant, self-consciously final, and the richer for it. I wanted to mark the bullet holes and the Indian restaurant, the stagnant old zoo and the green and yellow trams, Jenny's old school and the World Trade Centre, with the imperial castle in the offing, and the university's economics building. As it was, I was in a hurry and saw nothing. So it goes.

It could be any season outside. A bad day for summer, a good one for winter: quality owes much to timing. A woman in a window keeping an eye on the crossing. Retired carriages in railway sidings. Tracts of plain flat land that millions died over. A football pitch. A church. A factory. Fundamental things. Basic things. The stuff of life. Cloud cover is total and yet the land is lit. How is the light getting through? We must be coming to the end of Poland. At Rzepin, a group of men in orange stand between tracks and discuss the mess they've made. It shouldn't concern me really, what these men are up to, it's none of my business. But in a way it is. I like what they do, even if I sometimes wish they'd do it quicker. I'd sooner have a memory of people mending the way than a prize cathedral or a landscape at sunset. We've a very narrow understanding of the picturesque. At the River Oder, I watch the lorries heavily cross, to and fro between old foes, going as bidden. Mutual flogging keeps us in line, I think.

I arrive at Frankfurt-Oder and enter the white Volkswagen. We are a quartet. There is Alicia and Valeria, mother and daughter, whose journey this is, and there is Marco, who responded to Andrew's invitation as I had. Marco wears a bandanna and muddied boots. Like me, he will be put down in Cologne. The Russians will go no farther west than that. It's convenient for me. Clara S, who owes me a favour, lives in Cologne. I met Clara in Slovenia a few years ago. I offered her and her boyfriend a free ride to Croatia in my campervan. I shouldn't have. We were stopped at the Slovenian–Croatian border that evening, introduced to a pair of sniffer dogs, then invited to pay a €700 fine or have the campervan confiscated, the dogs having reached the conclusion, accurate as it happened but news to me, that there were drugs in Clara's bra. There were seven of us in the van. We pooled our resources and just about managed to pay the fine. Hence: Clara S owes me a favour.

Valeria goes to an international school in Brandenburg. She likes it there. 'Everyone gets on. Poles, Germans, Ukrainians, Chinese. But everybody has money and maybe it's easier to get on when you have money.' Alicia steers the car with her knees, watches video clips of elephants swimming on her phone. I felt safer with Mother Stefania. We pass under Potsdam, where the big boys met to shift Poland to the left, where Stalin said, 'Don't worry about Poland – I'll sort it out.'

Signs for Berlin: I think of the Wall, and what it stood for. Compared to the one Trump wants to put up, it was a peanut. Just a hundred kilometres long. That's all that was needed to contain West Berlin, to quarantine its thoughts. The wall's official name in East Germany was the Anti-Fascist Protection Rampart. It's got a ring to it. Who wouldn't want one of those in their town? In truth the wall was put up to trap East Berliners, who had shown a bothersome inclination to sneak across the border and get on a train to Amsterdam or Antwerp and never come back. Three-and-a-half million East Germans jumped ship before 1961, representing 20 per cent of the population. Socialism was clearly not everyone's cup of tea. Something had to be done about the westward traffic: the wall was erected and defection made a crime. The wall proved an effective barrier until a series of events weakened its foundations. In June 1989, Hungary – another member of the Eastern Bloc – took down the electric fence along its border with Austria. Thirteen-thousand East Germans who happened to be on holiday in Budapest made a dash for it there and then. Then East Germans started escaping through Czechoslovakia. The will to leave East Germany grew too significant and conspicuous to be ignored or controlled. The East German government's stance began to falter. On New Year's Eve

1989, ex-lifeguard David Hasselhoff climbed onto the wall and sang of liberty to 500,000 on both sides. The song he sang was called 'Looking for Freedom', which sounds appropriate enough, but in fact the song tells the story of a boy born into a rich liberal family who flees his home to find freedom working on a farm in the middle of nowhere. The song was number one in the German charts for eight weeks. It was the soundtrack of reunification, of Communism's demise. It has to count as one of history's greatest ironies that David Hasselhoff's neo-liberal anthem, his hymn to the West, could have been written by Chairman Mao or Joseph Stalin. Despite the demolition of the Berlin Wall in 1991, Marco says that the East Germans are still *apart* somehow: in their way of thinking, in the nature of their concerns. *Mauer im kopf*, they call it. The wall in the head. Of all walls, this might be the hardest to level.[86]

We push on towards Hannover, where King George I of Great Britain and Ireland was born and raised and lived happily until being forced onto the British throne because he was Protestant and second-cousins with Queen Anne. On the face of it, George didn't take the job very seriously. He had Robert Walpole run the country and spent most of his time back in Germany, which is fair enough: if a second-cousin of mine died in a distant land and I was invited to assume their manifold responsibilities for the rest of my days, I wouldn't think much of the proposal either.

---

[86] Margaret Thatcher didn't want a unified Germany, by the way. She felt a unified Germany posed a threat, especially at World Cups.

Just as history is one thing after another, so is Europe. We enter the Rhineland, a part of the world which made headlines in the 1930s, when an increasingly pugnacious Nazi Party put a load of tanks in the area, and so doing defied the Treaty of Versailles, that disarming slap on the wrists meant to punish-pacify Germany after the First World War. Other than the militarisation of the Rhineland, the other big news story to come out of the area was the Peace of Westphalia. Remember that from school? (Remember school?) The Peace of Westphalia (1648) was a collection of treaties that sought to put an end to the theological disagreement that was then rampant in Western Europe, which had started in earnest when the Catholic monk Martin Luther stopped being monkish and started being a radical big mouth. Luther's nonconformity caused Christendom to fracture into loads of conflicting bits, or denominations. For the next century or so, these denominations fought among themselves (and with the Catholics) over such things as whether Jesus had a middle name. Eight million people died. By 1648 it was generally agreed that enough was enough and the key people needed to meet in Westphalia and talk peace. The outcome of their chat was, more or less, 'each to their own'. And thank God it was.

Marco and I are put down in Longerich. We take a train into central Cologne, where we hug and say goodbye and it was nice knowing you. The station is situated next to the cathedral. A couple of years ago, on New Year's Eve, some men attacked and harassed about a hundred women in separate incidents in the vicinity of this cathedral. Because the men were found to be mostly immigrants or asylum seekers, the story was astonishingly popular. Plenty used the incident to argue that Europe should close its doors, that diversity doesn't work, that people can't be trusted to mix well. News is too popular for my liking, if you don't mind me saying. I find the extent of its influence disagreeable. It steers our instincts and hunches, our sentiments and inclinations, to an undue degree. It stands to reason that if the news we consume is bad and unkind and unnuanced and erroneous and reactionary, our instincts will follow suit. It stands to reason that if we are fed stories of extremism and violence and criminality, and fed them in a hysterical manner, we will emerge from the banquet believing hysterically that the world is thus. As big a problem as bad or hysterical news reporting is misreporting – or fake news. Fake news is an old problem. In 1213 BC, Rameses the Great told his mates he'd had a blinder out on the battlefield, going so far as to commission murals and artworks to illustrate his heroics, when in fact the battle had been a stalemate and Rameses the Great had spent most of it eating grapes. These days Rameses would have taken to social media, which is a propaganda tool *par excellence*, because it is unpoliced and seemingly has no standards whatsoever. Traditional media at least have to pay some attention to the credibility and potential ramifications of the content they put out. The stuff that turns up on social media can be as fanciful and inflammatory as its authors want it to be. The quality of information entering the public sphere – and thus shaping opinion, arousing emotion, determining the results of elections – is getting monumentally worse. Tim Berners-Lee, who invented the web, said that misinformation is stopping the internet from serving humanity.[87] In light of the above – that we are bombarded with bad news, skewed news, bogus news – I try not to listen much these days. I try not to be led to the 'truth' but to find my own way to something approximating it. I trust my own data and I ask you to trust yours. How many times in your life have you been wronged or injured or abused or victimised or swindled? Take that figure and compare it to the number of times you weren't treated this way. The discrepancy is gorgeous, because people are overwhelmingly gentle and cooperative. People that do terrible things – like the men in Cologne – only represent themselves. 'Sun destroys the interest of what's happening in the shade,' wrote Philip Larkin. Bad news gets too much sunlight, I'd say.

When I try to buy a ticket for the tram or bus, it's clear I'm an alien again. '*Ein, er, ein klein ticket, bitte.*' I change, as instructed, at Barbarossastraße. A treacherous address. Operation Barbarossa was when the Germans turned on the Soviet Union, broke a pinky-promise and launched an eastward attack on their former ally. Unlike the Germans, I stick to the plan: I board the second tram towards Clara's flat. We pass Frau Wong's, Baghdad Shisha, Hollywood Bar and Schmuck. The range is promising: a city that can

---

[87] I just made that up. No I didn't. He said it in *USA Today*, 11 March 2017.

accommodate such scope is unlikely to work up an appetite for war, if only because its constituents wouldn't be able to agree on a *casus belli*. Clara meets me off the tram, takes me up to her flat: a bedside lamp built from old cassettes, tobacco pouches, heaps of clothes. Clara is doing an internship at an advertising agency. She doesn't like it. I'm not surprised. 'Ads are pollution,' I say. 'Let's go,' she says.

We walk to a dinner party. Clara asks what I thought of Poland, all things considered. I decide to start with something trivial, and then go from there: 'I like the food but then again I like the food everywhere. The people? It's hard to say. When I travelled Britain, I learnt so much by eavesdropping. Small things, chance remarks, at the bar or on the bus. In Poland I was deaf. Therefore, I can't say the Poles are this or that because I haven't heard them, haven't *overheard* them. I could *see* people, of course. I could see how they treated guests, how they came together for national holidays, how they went to church, how they gathered to protest or remember. What of Poland's artists? Again, I'm hardly in a position to judge. And even if I had dedicated myself to Polish art, reading two books a week, watching a film a night, listening to an album each morning, I still wouldn't be in a position to. I can say that I like the poems of Zbigniew Herbert. I can say that I like the essays of Miłosz. I can say that I like Kieslowski's short film about love, but not his short film about killing. I can say I like Chopin's quiet stuff but wouldn't get out of bed for his dance music. If, for the hell of it, I was to take all of what I've seen and heard and attach an epithet to the sum, a label to the lot, I would call the art *painful*. I like the old market squares. I like the lakes and the mountains. I like the dogs that look out the window. I like sitting on the balcony, listening to the people, to the trees, to the traffic. But I would like these things anywhere. And maybe that's the thing. Maybe that's what's crucial: that I was as happy in Poland as I might have been anywhere else. Edmund Burke said that for all it's worth Poland might as well be a country in the moon. Well, not for me. For me, Poland is very much of this world, a chip off the old block. When I'm in Poland, I could be anywhere. If that doesn't sound much like a compliment, then the fault is mine, not Poland's. Would I go back? Try and stop me.'

We reach the dinner party. I'm introduced to a pair of DJs who are making a name for themselves. They are playing tonight at a popular bar up the road and Clara means to take me there. Because tomorrow is Good Friday, there can be no music after midnight, which is a small blessing as far as I'm concerned, though the DJs are livid. I attempt a bit of small talk by asking one of the DJs – Lauritz – about Angela Merkel's position on the migration crisis. He says: 'Her father was a preacher. She has a strong moral compass. She knows about history, about German history, and maybe this openness to migrants is a kind of atonement? In any case, she might pay for it.' I want to know why he said that. 'Because integration has been hard. The benefits aren't always obvious. And then you have incidents like the attacks on New Year's Eve and then what happened yesterday.' What happened yesterday? 'Islamic terrorists bombed the Dortmund football team bus.' He shakes his head, exasperated. 'And you can imagine the shitstorm that has created.'[88]

I am fed well – pasta with rocket and cherry tomatoes and parmesan and oil and vinegar. I'm not made a fuss of – 'Oh wow, a stranger!' – just taken easily in. After the meal, we go to the bar where the boys are DJing. I buy a drink then find a place to sit out of the way. It is avant-garde disco music: abstract yet accessible. I love it. A pair of Israelis sit next to me. The boyfriend says he photographs food for a living, snaps salad for bread, meat for lolly, pudding for salt, and so on. 'I couldn't cope with the emotional detachment,' I say. He shrugs then goes to the bar to photograph the lemon wedges. The girlfriend lives in London and I tell her that Richard will have an exhibition there soon and she really ought to come.

'I might come,' she says.

---

[88] The Dortmund bus was on its way to the first of two matches against Monaco. When reading up on the incident, I enjoyed the ambiguity in this report: 'Spanish footballer and Dortmund's team member Marc Bartra was wounded by shards of glass from the shattered bus window; he was taken to a nearby hospital where he was immediately operated on, and was forced to miss both legs.' Incidentally, the attack was initially blamed on Islamic terrorism. Police found letters at the crime scene saying the attack was revenge for German intervention in Syria. You can imagine the narrative that dominated the media. It was discovered months later that the letter was a fake, that it was planted by the German-Russian guy who also planted the bombs. His motivation was to attack Borussia Dortmund so the club's share price would plummet, in the event of which he stood to make lots of money. The bomber believed, accurately as it turned out, that the public would blame the Muslims.

'You're invited,' I say.

She holds my eye, not for the first time, and I don't mind, she can do what she wants. I go onto the dance floor and dance, after a fashion. Unrelatedly, Clara says it's time to go. She says she's going to walk me home and then return to the fray, because there's going to be a lock-in between midnight and six. In short, I'm being put to bed.

Back at her flat, Clara forces a grapefruit on me. She says she's on a liver and kidney detox, which involves eating food that helps those organs, not refraining from eating those organs. Her flatmates are pretty square, she says, pretty German. I enjoy hearing a German recycle lazy stereotypes about Germans. They study physics and maths, she says out of the side of her mouth, as if the subjects were wildly taboo. She asks if I like what I write. I say, 'I like it when I've forgotten it.' She insists that I sleep in her bed, since the collapsible bed is rubbish.

'Yes, but then you'll be in the rubbish bed.'

'No I won't,' she says. 'With any luck, you'll be gone by the time I'm back.'

39

I want to see the European Union

16 April. I'm up at seven, or just after. I eat another grapefruit, pinch a German's coffee, put on the same clothes, borrow a squeeze of toothpaste. My tram is at 7.50am. I should leave the flat at 7.40am. Clara was quite clear about it. I leave the flat at 7.45am. I miss the tram. The service is irregular and infrequent because Jesus was crucified today. If I wait for the next tram I'll miss my train. I have to walk, and quickly. The streets are quiet: barely breathing, still stirring, putting the kettle on. I'm the only thing moving. My footsteps wake up the birds. How rare to walk through the middle of a city and hear birds singing. I arrive at the station with just a few minutes to spare. People are running for the Brussels train. A tall official says to buy a ticket on board.

The guard wants €70 for the 90-minute journey. It was advertised at half the price online. The guard is Belgian but sounds like someone from Birmingham. His grandfather was English, he says. My grandfather was Irish, I say, but I don't sound like someone from Galway. Then maybe you didn't listen to your grandfather as I did, he says. I say: 'Look, seeing as we're getting on so well, how about we take a look at that price you quoted. It's a bit steep, isn't it?' He agrees that it is, but insists I cough up.

The landscape is nice as we approach Liege. I'm at an advantage: the railway is raised here, expanding the scene, pushing back the horizon. The city is done in brick around a river, set among low hills. If it had a cricket pitch it could pass for Durham. Continental goods go by in freight containers – croissants, sprouts, bratwurst, vodka, fresh copies of *Le Monde*. The green and yellow fields bring the trams of Poznań to mind – that wouldn't have happened a year ago. A young man gets on with a cheeseburger. He doesn't want to buy a ticket, and I don't blame him. He tells the guard he hasn't got money or identification, says in French that he lives in Rome, near the Colosseum. Fair play to him.

Brussels. I have four hours before I need to move on towards the coast. I want to visit the European Union. I want to meet a bureaucrat. I've heard so much about them. I'm anticipating somebody broad-shouldered – you'd have to be to get in the way of so much. I want to tell them they're famous, that their tape is legend. I want to see the infamous law-making machine in action, fat on stolen power, swollen with ill-gotten sovereignty. I want to see where the undemocratic EU Council meets (the Council is the 28 elected Heads of State). I want to see where the undemocratic EU Commission meets (the Commission is the 28 representatives appointed by the elected Heads of State). I want to see where the undemocratic EU Parliament meets (the Parliament is the elected MEPs). I want to see where Tusk and Juncker and all the other members of the EU brass band lounge on beds stolen from NHS hospitals, where they rejoice on thrones made of pure regulation, wiping their ever closer bottoms with sheets of unearned cash, and laughing, laughing that they get away with it, get away with pumping out the thick bureaucratic fog that has settled over the continent of Europe, from Stettin on the Baltic to Trieste on the Adriatic, the better to obscure its institutional evil. If I reach the EU and see a thousand humble souls pretending to toil so Europe might tick over smoothly, fairly, peacefully, boringly, I will call them out. I will tell them what they really are, which is mean, spendthrift, socialist, capitalist, fat-cat, paper-pushing, bone-idle jobsworths bent on ever closer union, when what we all really want is ever more distant disunity, to be a continent of lone rangers, lone strangers, because there is safety in isolation (everyone knows that), and joy in solitude. I want to go up there and have a chat with a low-ranking Europhile so I can put a face – just one – to the headlines. And then I want to stamp on that face, like Big Brother, forever, because I want Britain to be great again, and the only way that will happen is if it trades with New Zealand.

I study a map outside the station. I can't find the EU: maybe it's in hiding. Across the street is The Museum of Absence. Britain will be in there soon, a headline exhibit, the great absent nation of Britain, last seen getting its knickers in a twist *circa* 2016. I enter Twin's Bar for advice.

'*Parlez-vous l'anglais?*' I say.

'*Oui!* I mean yes.'

'Where is the European Union?'

'I don't know.'

'Oh.'

'But wait. Wait here. Okay? Somebody must know.'

I am on the metro, because somebody did know. We pull into a station; the doors open; a person pops their head in and asks in Dutch where the train is going. I panic and just point, which isn't especially useful, but they get on anyway. Detail doesn't seem to matter to this traveller: I like his style.

I know a bit about the European Union. It wasn't easy to acquire the knowledge, and nor was it a terrific amount of fun. I bought *A Very Short Introduction to the EU*, hoping for a page-turner. The book begins with a four-page glossary of acronyms – EDC, CJHA, BRIC, EAGGF, QMV, ERM, TSCG – which the reader is encouraged to learn before going any further. After the glossary there's a few pages of charts, then some maps, and then a list of numbers to call in an emergency, if you suddenly feel suicidal for example. Only then do we get to the first chapter, 'What the EU is for.' The authors might have done well to put that at the front. In any case, I got through it. Here are my top eight things about the EU.

1) It won the Nobel Peace Prize in 2012.
2) Britain couldn't join until Charles de Gaulle died: De Gaulle wasn't keen on Britain joining, but his successor Georges Pompidou was more relaxed about the whole thing.
3) As well as its 28 Commissioners, the EU Commission has 25,000 staff, which is 375,000 less than the UK's Civil Service.
4) In 1984, Margaret Thatcher felt the UK was paying more than its share. An opportunity presented itself. The EU needed unanimity before it could raise the membership fee to deal with an agricultural crisis. In return for her

endorsement, Thatcher got a 60 per cent discount. Go, Maggie.

5) Half of the EU budget is spent subsidising farmers.

6) Courtesy of the European Regional Development Fund, the residents of Cornwall stand to net €1,000 per head over the five years up to 2020, because apparently they could do with it. The fund is there to help develop poorer areas. That it was poorer areas of the UK that voted to leave the EU, needn't detain us here.

7) Thanks to the Treaty of Rome (1957) men and women must be paid equally for the same job.

8) Captain Euro is the official mascot of the EU. He/she is androgynous, has an arch-enemy called D. Vider, and looks like a young Nigel Farage.

I emerge from the underground. It's oddly quiet, given that I'm in the thick of the EU Quarter. I try the information point but it's closed. Through the window I can see a pile of souvenir tea-towels patterned with the heads of 50 key bureaucrats, a sort of Who's Who of the EU's top brass that you can wipe your hands with. I wander over to the entrance of the Commission building. It's as dead as a doornail. Sod's law that the one day I choose to visit the EU the damn thing is shut. There's a beggar sat outside the building, probably thinking the same thing. He's bearing a cardboard plea in four languages. He could appeal in ten for all the good it would do him. 'Fuck TTIP' has been scrawled on a lamppost. That's the sort of graffiti you get around here: attacks on acronyms.

I go to a pub across the road called Kitty O'Shea's. The pub is empty but for an old man having a quiet pint. I take a seat at the bar and finger a newspaper. It appears Manchester United couldn't get past Anderlecht last night in the European Cup: not the only British outfit struggling to break a deadlock in Brussels. Also on the front page is a security warning in light of the Dortmund bus bombing, and a discount voucher for a jar of bolognese sauce. The barman is Hungarian. He supports Viktor Orban, the Hungarian Prime Minister. 'Orban is very hard. He will call a spade a spade to its face. He is like this. He has delivered economic growth and social improvement, but the media only shows what he says to the spade, you know?' Reading between the lines, I'd say the spade the barman's referring to is the number of migrants and asylum seekers entering Hungary. I point to the solitary suit in the corner. 'He used to work at the Commission,' says the barman. 'He resigned years ago. Now he just hangs around.'

I'm on the train to Blankenberge, a small coastal town close to the ferry port at Zeebrugge. When I look out the window the land reminds me increasingly of England. I suppose they were of a piece once, before water came between them. The bright sky adds life to the ongoing scene: it burnishes, enlivens, adds lustre to what is lugubrious. Can a landscape be lugubrious?

Seaside air smells of the gas given off by ocean-dwelling bacteria feeding on dead seaweed. Unrelatedly, the first thing I hear in Blankenberge is: 'Her bucket list is so damn long I think it might kill me.' There's philosophy in that complaint,

I'm sure. I call at tourist information. I ask about the local mood regarding Britain's departure.

'We all know the EU's not perfect but you carry on. Like in a marriage. Countries are less intelligent on their own and more dramatic. Britain has always been less committed. It is naturally detached. That might explain its decision, but it doesn't excuse it. If a country is naturally detached, it has more use for bridges.' I can't argue with that.

The main street is a pedestrianised affair, which is fine if you like pedestrians. It runs from the railway station to the sea. It hosts an odd demographic: tourists on the one hand, fumbling about as per the terms of their bucket list, and beggars on the other, wishing they had a list, or a bucket even. The beach is nice and sandy. There are some bars and a bank of naval-gazing hotels, stretched out in uniform, a mile either side of the pier. This is the end of continental Europe. I should probably get on a knee and contemplate – about end points, thresholds, and their relation to my story and so on – but am keen to eat something, so do that instead. I eat a waffle and it reminds me of the Paris metro, where you can get waffles from the platform vending machines for a euro a piece. The server is Italian. I ask him a question, for the heck of it.

'Why did you move here?'

'I don't know.'

'How long will you stay?'

'A long time.'

Although unlikely to win any literary awards, the exchange pleases me. I recognise the casual mixture of ignorance and certainty in the face of a large existential question, but I can't say where from.

I hop on the tram that runs along the front to the ferry port. I speak to a pair of Canadians. They're on a cruise, like most folks in town. The boat sailed out of Florida, heads for Porto this evening, before rounding the corner and entering the Mediterranean, where it will call at Malta and Nice and Naples. Telling me this, they don't seem too enthused about it all. I suggest as much. She yawns, then shrugs. 'I just wish Europe were closer.' I know the feeling.

It's not easy to walk to a ferry. There's no apparent footpath, and I don't want to get squashed by lorries, so I drop into a wine bar for instruction. The bar is empty but for its tall handsome barman and a glamorous woman perched beneath his hungry eyes on the other side of the counter. The conversation I have just interrupted did not, I fancy, have to do with what a nice guy the woman's husband is. It more likely had to do with what flavour ice-cream they most want to lick off each other. I ask the barman in Dutch if he speaks English. He replies in French that he doesn't but she does. She looks at me, removes an olive stone from her mouth, hands it to the barman, and says, 'What's up?' I tell her that I want to get on the boat. She says, drily, 'That's interesting, because you don't *look* like a refugee?' She enjoys her joke – which is quite a good one, seeing as it was off the cuff – then says there's nothing for it but to follow the traffic.

Before making my way to the ferry, I take a quick walk on the seawall. Back in the good old days, when the countries of Europe had a gorgeous amount of sovereignty and borders were delightfully stiff, thousands died hereabouts during the Zeebrugge Raid. The First World War operation was meant to block the canal that led inland to the German U-boat facility at Bruges, and thereby hinder the German war effort. The idea was to sink a couple of obsolete Royal Navy warships in the entrance to the canal so they got in the way. I don't think the operation went entirely to plan. I'd love to elaborate on the detail but I can't, because I don't know it, so we'll have to assume that it was six of one and half-a-dozen of the other and that if either side claimed a victory, it was almost certainly a pyrrhic one: nobody wins in war, it's just a matter of how much you lose.[89]

---

[89] For your information, the British plan was to wait until the wind was right and then set up a smokescreen. The next job was to park HMS *Vindictive* – a massive warship – next to the heavily-armed seawall that protected the harbour (the mole), not easy to do discreetly and without incident. Once parked, some Royal Marines would get on the wall and fight the Germans and hopefully take the position. During the fighting on the mole, three old cruisers (blockships) would stealthily tiptoe around the back, get themselves into the mouth of the canal, and then sink themselves, but not before their crews had sodded off on smaller accompanying vessels. That was the plan. In the event, a few things went wrong. First, *Vindictive* struggled to park close to the mole, which made it difficult for her men to get onto the mole and encounter the Germans. Second, there was a fully-loaded German ship on the other side of the mole that wasn't supposed to be there. Third, the wind changed and the smokescreen lifted, meaning the old cruisers trying to sneak round the back got a lot more attention than was ideal, with the result that they weren't scuttled in the perfect spots and therefore didn't do a great job of blocking the canal. All in all, 600 people lost their lives.

From the seawall there's no obvious way of joining the dual-carriageway that leads to the ferry. In the end, I have to hop over a fence then scramble down a dusty hill, before proceeding in the cycle lane. I come to a sign that says: 'HULL THIS WAY'. Normally such a sign would deter me, but not today. I continue for five minutes until I reach the terminal. I approach a counter to check in. I say *bonjour*. She says, 'No need for that, pet.'

All the crew speak with Yorkshire accents, which is to their advantage. It's a disarming accent. It's the sound of Alan Bennett and Geoffrey Boycott. I can't imagine anyone with a Yorkshire accent doing something unkind or criminal, though I'm sure plenty do, including Bennett and Boycott. It's an unmistakable feeling, boarding a big passenger ferry. So different to boarding a train or plane. There's just so much *space*. Apart from in my cabin, that is. In short, it's small – the size of a big cupboard. No sea view, which is a bit of a shock. You don't mind if you don't get one at a hotel but you do rather expect to get one on a boat.

I buy a coffee then take it onto the viewing deck, where a Mancunian bloke is explaining the history of Dunkirk to his hungover mates. They've been to the football, to the Anderlecht match that finished in a draw. Calais is further along the coast, I suppose. Is that 'jungle' still there? (How did they ever get away with calling it a jungle, by the way?) The last I heard it had been destroyed, and its inhabitants transported to start new lives somewhere else. The existence of the camp on the North French coast suggests that England was the migrants' destination of choice. Having made it that far – to Europe, to France, to North France – you'd think they'd be exhausted and unwilling to go further, and would just claim asylum there, as is their right. And yet they are willing to push on. I wonder why? What have they been told? Why go after the island off the coast of continental Europe, when it's no more amenable to unexpected arrivals than anywhere else, if not less so? Is there a sort of British Dream doing the rounds? A set of notions and fantasies that Britain is soft and warm and doughy? That dream – if it exists – is a lie. Britain just voted to leave the EU because it wants to control its borders. The British government wants to cut legal immigration numbers by over 200 per cent, to say nothing of what it wants to do to 'illegal' immigration. I suppose the migrants might have family and friends already in the UK, with whom they desire to be reunited. At all events, their desperation is plain, no matter its motivation. To be so desperate that you will sleep rough and risk your life is categorically a pitiable situation, deserving of remedy, not that I've done anything about it.

I go to one of the lounges, take a seat near the window. A man with thick, grey, shoulder-length hair makes rough notes in his broadsheet as he gulps prosecco, circling cabinet ministers he'd like to hit, shares he might dabble in. There's a small stage at the end of the lounge. A man gets on it to announce there'll be bingo later followed by a disco. Blow me, I think. Bingo and a disco. I wasn't counting on that. I quite like the idea of bingo. It's a decent amusement. Plus I could do with a windfall, given that I'm just about skint. I look out the window. The water is brown. Seagulls tail the boat – for fun, I fancy – doing loops and dives. A singer with a guitar takes to the stage. He's in his forties, has a soft, high voice. You might get him in for a funeral, or a wake, or both if his rates are reasonable. When he sings 'To Love Somebody' by The Bee Gees my eyes warm up, get heavy. That song is emotive for me. Something about the strain in their voices, the sincerity, the way the song rises and falls is reliably upsetting, but not in an unpleasant way.

I go through to the cheaper restaurant and have a bowl of soup. The restaurant is managed by João, who is two weeks on, two weeks off. João is from Portugal, now lives in Hull. 'It's alright two weeks a month,' he says, 'but I don't think I could do it full time.' I don't know if he's talking about working on the boat or living in Hull. My waiter is Bruno, also Portuguese. Bruno looks like a young George Michael, which is good for him.

'Mr Benjamin! Is the soup going well?' I assure him it is. 'And the tap water also?' Equally, Bruno. It is announced over the public-address system that the ship's balls are ready to drop. Interested parties are invited to the main lounge. I'll be damned if I miss the bingo, so I hastily finish and settle the bill.

I go up to the guy selling the coupons.

'Just the one?' he says.

'Five, please.'

'Five? Does your mother know about this?'

I hand over the cash, he hands over the coupons.

'How do you do it again?' I say.

'You are kidding?'

'Well I've got an idea, but—'

'Flippin' 'eck, son. I've been doing this for reet ten year and you're the first to ask how to play bingo. Where yer from, flower?'

'Portsmouth.'

'Pompey? That'll explain it. That'll be why there's nowt in that 'ead of yours. Look, I call the number and if you see it on your ticket you cross it off. Nowt to it. First to cross out all the numbers in a box shouts bingo. Naw then, go and sit down yonder, and see if you get jammy. Okay, flower? Off you go.'

I play anxiously, intently, alone. When someone wins the line, which offers a smaller cash prize, I'm nowhere near. All of my crosses are evenly spread over the lines and boxes, when what you want, I sense, is for a concentration of the buggers. Several balls in a row land in the top of my five boxes, and I'm back in the running. Then the bingo caller says that he really must visit the bathroom. There are a few tuts and moans but mostly people are sympathetic. When the caller returns he reels off half-a-dozen balls without fuss or decoration. 56, 72, 74, 25, 6, 8, 88. One of the Manchester lads feeds pound coins into an unhealthy fruit machine. The sound of his bad luck is the only noise in the room save the caller. 24, 26, 13. I need 1 and that's it. What if I win? Make yourself known, the caller had said. But how? 12, 2, 1. When I jump to my feet I knock my knee on the table and upset my drink. '*Mam to!*' I shriek instinctively in Polish, *I have it!*

'We have a claim!' says the caller. 'Or at least I think we do.'

The caller checks my ticket. The other players hope I've made a mistake. But I haven't. The numbers add up. I've won. The caller gives me 50 quid in a little brown envelope. I'm ready to give a small speech. Returning to my seat, I say to the Dutch couple next to me, 'That's the first time I've won a bloody thing in my whole life,' but they merely nod indulgently. The caller withdraws backstage and then returns moments later as DJ Yorkie. I love the man. He starts with Paul Young's 'Wherever I Lay My Hat' – which I *love* – then moves on to Bob Marley, Jerry Rafferty, Blondie. I enjoy it all, softly basking in my hard-earned victory. I know bingo is far from a meritocratic competition, and that I shouldn't read too much into my success, but still, I can't help but experience a significant self-esteem boost. Reflecting on my departure from Belgium and my immediate windfall, I decide that maybe leaving Europe isn't such a bad idea after all.

40

And where are you going now?

17 April. The captain comes through the public-address system to say something about breakfast and disembarkation. Whatever he's saying, it doesn't sound official. Nothing sounds official in the local East Riding accent, only advisory, a wee bit of encouragement.

I go up on deck to watch Albion inch nearer. The Humber Bridge is quite something. Boy, is it big. All that effort and ingenuity just to make it easier to get to Scunthorpe. There's plenty of dirty energy being made yonder, judging by the amount of high-rise chimneys letting off steam. I suppose a town has to do something for a living. Not everyone can be a bingo caller. It used to be fishing that kept the locals busy. They used to go after whales back in the day, until people started complaining they couldn't finish their chips. Then it was cod. Thousands of trawlers would go out for weeks at a time, right up to the North Atlantic, up near Iceland. For the Icelanders, the British boats were overstepping their mark, sticking their nose in where it wasn't welcome. Cue the Cod Wars of the 70s, which Britain lost. Within a decade Hull's fishing industry was all but gone.

I'm not the last off. A few of the Manchester lads are, because one of their number was bringing something up in the loo, and it wasn't a topic of conversation. 'UK BORDER' it says. A popular threshold. Too popular for some: the people of Britain have spoken and they've said they want it to be harder to get over this line, because there's no room on the other side, no vacancies, no left overs. A light interview to figure out my movement.

'How long have you been away, Mr Aitken?'

'About a year. I've been living in Poland.'

'But you sailed from Belgium.'

'Yes. I got a lift to Cologne with two Russians and then a train to Zeebrugge.'

'That's odd.'

'It was fun.'

'Why did you avoid flying?'

'I wanted to consider the state of Europe.'

'And?'

'Relatively speaking, it's doing wonderfully.'

'Do you have anything on you? Cash? Food items?'

'I've got some cash in a brown envelope.'

'And where are you going now?'

'Not sure. Might try Philip Larkin's house.'

'That's a friend of yours?'

'No, he's dead.'

I wait for a bus outside the terminal. 'Hull and Proud!' it says on a billboard, as if the city was generally considered to be an affliction, something to be borne with a brave face. We pass Sausage Meat Suppliers, Discount Hunters, a franchise of Her Majesty's Prison, before being set down outside the main train station. I ask a florist where Philip used to live.

'Around Pearson Park wasn't it?'

'And how do I get there?'

'Down Spring Bank then up Princes Avenue.'

Half way down Spring Bank, I enter a Polish butcher shop. I don't want anything. Just a chat really. The proprietors are from Katowice. I tell them about watching the tennis there. They seem delighted I know where they're from. I feel bad for bothering them so point to a bucket of gherkins and say in Polish, 'Please, that one.' I try to give the lady a pound from my bingo money, but she won't let me pay, shoos me out the door, like a kind neighbour sending somebody else's child back outside to play with the others, having given them a biscuit and told them not to tell their mother.

Just before Spring Bank meets Princes Avenue, I enter a greasy spoon for breakfast. The table top is a glossy Union Jack coming away at the edges. I order chips, cheese and gravy for two quid. A food hygiene certificate on the wall (1997) tells me that John Green is in charge. I assume it's John Green at the helm today. Only a boss could be so chipper.

'You're happy today.'

'I'm always like this. I've only had three hours sleep. I'm a professional entertainer. I'm flipping nuts, to tell the truth.'

'How do you entertain exactly?'

'Bit of comedy, bit of karaoke. It doesn't take much round 'ere.'

'And do you like Hull?'

'Of course.'

'Why?'

'I'm from 'ere!'

I head north on Princes Avenue until I reach Pearson Park. I know Larkin lived on the south side of the park but which house? I fancy it's the one at the end of the terrace. (I saw a documentary last week which contained footage of Mr Miserable coming home from work.) Despite his miserable reputation, there's something strangely buoyant and cheering about a lot of Larkin's poems. 'Aubade', for instance, is about death for the most part but makes me want to live. And there's a couple of others about working life, about the drudgery of it, the slow, long routine. The toad life, he called it. I can't say the toad poems made me want to go to work, but they did make me smile at life, and how we tend to live it. A few years ago, on the 30th anniversary of Larkin's death, the city commissioned 40 toad sculptures to be scattered around the city. There was a toad that looked like Larkin sat outside the library. There was a toad that had a Mohican, and another that was gender-neutral. The toads were obviously very popular because half of them were stolen. I stick my head over the front gate for a better look. My hunch is correct: a small blue plaque confirms that Larkin lived upstairs. It's a bit ramshackle: the garden needs tending, and there's a sizeable hole in the front room window, through which a small girl watches my clumsy attempt to open her gate. I wonder if she's a little Larkin, a wee toad. She rushes off to tell someone that a man is trying to break into the garden. Seconds later, a woman comes out to deal with me.

'I like his poetry, madam, and I was wondering if I could take a picture.'

'Fine.'

'Sorry to bother you.'

'Used to it by now.'

'Get a few do you?'

'In the summer, a coach-load of Chinese pulls up once a week.'

'I didn't know he was translated into Chinese.'

'He's not.' She turns and looks up at the house. 'He had the top floor flat. It's all one house now. My son-in-law had Larkin's room done up like it used to be. The university did some filming.'

'Yes, I think I saw that.'

'Of course, my grandson wasn't best pleased because it was his bedroom and it looked Edwardian. He had a few ladies up there.'

'Your grandson?'

'Gi' o'er. Larkin. Not that it did him much good. His main inspiration was the park,' she says smiling and closing the door, giving me a clue it's time to move on.

I go to the park. A man on a bench is drinking beer and watching the ducks, while a father and daughter sit cross-legged on the grass and share an ice cream. A Polish family – I can tell by the cries of *'kurwa!'* and *'nie!'* – are playing football, using a statue of another immigrant – Prince Albert – for one of the goalposts. A woman in a headscarf and leggings is using the outdoor gym equipment, while a young girl in neither rides on the back of her granddad's mobility scooter, pointing the way. They alight at the pond to feed the ducks bread, which they shouldn't really, because an easy diet of bread makes them lazy and can even prevent them from flying. People think they're doing a good thing but in fact they're screwing things up. It's a pity, really.

I'm outside the train station with ten minutes left. A wedding party is put down in the taxi rank. I watch the ladies correct their dresses and hats, each grinning and squalling after early champagne. I go through to the station concourse. There's a statue of Larkin done in bronze with spectacles and a suit and a folder under his arm, as if he were on his way somewhere. Here and there, excerpts from Larkin's poems have been added to the floor. Scanning the departure boards for news of the delayed Skegness service, the locals get to stand on sentiments, bide their time on lines that are both sad and not sad. I peer between my feet. *Struck, I leant more promptly out next time, more curiously, and saw it all again in different terms.* I like that one, as I like all these lowly scraps that have been taken from their harbouring wholes and settled beneath us, to be stood on mostly but sometimes seen and taken on board, as we wait, as we all wait, for that delayed Skegness train, or the 1.20 to London. I take a few paces forward, homeward that is, then look down once more. *Always it is by bridges that we live.* Hmm. Nothing wrong with ending on the words of another.

Acknowledgements

Giulia Spinicci for sorting out your nan's flat for me. Mike Lamont for the cheese factory. Erin Trummer-Lamont for feedback on the cover. My dad for low rent and hot dinners. Charlotte Horton and Alexander Greene for giving me the afternoons off. Sylvia Whitman and Shakespeare & Company for ongoing support. Kim and Stephan Menzies for two stints in Majorca. Tony Moult and Marietta Milewska for hiring me despite my lack of qualification or motivation. Julia Klorek for doing similar. My friends and family for their sustained and sincere interest in what I've been up to the last couple of years. Megan Menzies for lending both ears and much of your heart. Jenny Suska for reading the third draft to make it Pole-proof ('Benny, if you publish that you'll be arrested'). Anna J for taking me to a wedding, for improving my face, for being wonderful. Patrick Ney for answering my call. Mother Stefania for not kicking me out. Jerzy up in the mountains for starting my fire. Hubert for granting me an audience with a hundred cows. Christian Davies for watching the England–Belgium game with me in Warsaw. Ellen Conlon and everyone else at Icon for making the book better. Ed Wilson for doing the deal. The European Union for making such a migration possible in the first place. All the Poles in the UK for giving me something to bounce off. Anita Anioł for being kind to a stranger. Richard Morgan for plenty of things. Auntie Jo for coming over to run the Poznań half marathon against all common sense. Oliver and

Kev for carrying her home. My friends that also came over for that race – Cheesy, Mezza, Chaz, Tommy, Jimbo, Dinita. Tim Hague for helping with the BBQ. Chris Chappell for being the first to come out. Michael Moran, the most refined Australian I'm likely to meet, for sharing a few thoughts that time. John Borrell, the most refined New Zealander I'm likely to meet, for sharing a few thoughts that other time. Friends from Poznań – Tessa, Dominic, Marcin, Magda, Max, Malwina, Maciej Kautz, Helena, Gosia, Mateusz, Natalia, Piotr, Mirek, Alina, Paulina, Walt – for making me realise that Polish people are on average far more sophisticated and charming than I am. Gabriella Cederström for changing words. Małgorzata Hordyk for the same. Ania and Czesiu for your big hearts and wise words. Joanna Suska for lending your eye for design. Andrzej for giving me a lift home in your van. Agnieszka and Przemek for letting me into your house. Jacek and Irena and Dominic and Ola and Wojciech and Grace and Danka and Szymon and Przemek and Marek for making my Christmas. Olek for drawing me a picture. The Department for Work and Pensions for its support at the end of 2018, when I quit my job as a carer in order to get the book finished. The country of Poland for returning from the moon, and the people of Poland for giving me plenty to chew on. Phillip Larkin for providing a wonderful terminus.